杉田 米行 監修

NO.10

Understanding International Relations
Second Edition
The World and Japan

竹内 俊隆 編著
TAKEUCHI Toshitaka (ed.)

大学教育出版

Preface and Introduction

This is an introductory textbook on international relations and Japan's foreign relations, written by professors who are teaching at Japanese universities. Japanese universities in general have belatedly been making much more effort to prepare their students for the globalized world, which is usually termed as "internationalization". One aspect of this effort is to teach at least some classes in English. It is now possible that a degree can be conferred with classes taught entirely in English, which makes it much easier for non-Japanese students to study in Japan, too.

Despite this effort, we believe there is one area that is lagging behind; textbooks in English that are written by Japan-based professors and published in Japan. One might think that we should use a textbook that is widely used in English-speaking countries. We can certainly do so. However, one could say that has a certain drawback, so to speak. They tend to explain international relations theories, case studies, and so forth based on mainly European-American histories and experiences; not much, if at all, on Asian experiences. We believe that we should take careful note that the students we have in mind are studying in Japan at Japanese universities, although their medium of instruction happens to be English. We consider that there had better be an international relations textbook that explains not only international relations theories, histories and current issues, but also Japan's situation in terms of foreign, economic and defense policies. Based on this kind of thinking, our textbook is born. The main focus of this introductory textbook is for international relations and Japanese foreign policy-related classes at Japanese universities. However, it is also possible to use it for an advanced English class for Japanese students. It would be easier for them to read and understand the subject that they have some knowledge of.

As might be clear from the above explanation, this textbook has mainly two groups of students in mind. One is non-Japanese students who are currently studying in Japan and who are not necessarily familiar with Japan's foreign relations. The other is Japanese students who are studying international relations in English in Japan. For the former, it should be much easier to understand Japan's foreign relations, with a

Japanese perspective for that matter, when they are in Japan. For the latter, it should be noted that the foundation for studying international relations is a firm grasp of their own country's foreign relations, without which their understanding of international relations would be shallow. It would be much less intimidating to study a subject in English where they have some familiarity, to begin with.

To briefly introduce this textbook, it has basically two parts. The first part is about international relations as such. The second part focuses on Japan. Chapter 1 is on the concept and history of the sovereign nation-state system and on other major worldviews, i.e., Islamic and Chinese. Chapter 2 is about theories of international relations such as realism, liberalism and constructivism, and has a case study on Japan about their explanatory power. Chapter 3 is on international relations history from the Cold War and after. Chapter 4 is about peace and security, which describes humans' efforts to restrain and manage nuclear weapons, missiles, and other weapons. Chapter 5 explains about the United Nations (UN) and its peace-keeping operations (PKO). Chapter 6 deals with economic aspects such as the impact of economic globalism and regionalism. This chapter also explains Japan's trade policy.

The second part that explains Japan's foreign relations as well as defense policies has four chapters. Chapter 7 explains Japan's overall foreign relations and defense policies after 1945. Chapter 8 deals with Japan's so-called "peace constitution", which prohibits her from having any "war potential" as such. This prohibition has a huge impact on her foreign as well as defense policies, if not fundamentally directing her foreign relations and defense policies. Chapter 9 is about the security alliance that Japan has with the United States, which has been the linchpin of Japan's foreign relations as well as defense policies. This chapter includes a brief discussion on the theory of alliances. The last chapter, Chapter 10, describes Japan's tense relations with her neighbors, especially with China and (South-) Korea, due to the legacy of historical issues.

Lastly, many thanks to all the contributors, who have made the job of being the editor much easier, for diligently submitting their drafts on time. And we would like to specially mention Prof. Craig Mark, one of the contributors, who did all the proof-reading singlehandedly and expeditiously. Without his wholehearted help, it would have taken much longer for this book to see the sunshine. And finally, many thanks are due also for Messrs. Satoh Mamoru and Watanabe Junichiro at UNIVERSITY EDUCATION PRESS Co., Ltd., the publisher, whose editorial work helped us, the contributors, a great deal to make our manuscripts publishable and better.

January, 2018
TAKEUCHI Toshitaka (editor)

Contents

Preface and Introduction ·· *i*

CHAPTER 1   Different World Views ·· *1*

CHAPTER 2   Different Paradigms: Realism, Liberalism, and Constructivism
·· *19*

CHAPTER 3   Recent World History: The Cold War and Beyond ················ *43*

CHAPTER 4   Peace and Security: Nuclear Deterrence and Disarmament
·· *64*

CHAPTER 5   The United Nations and Its Peacekeeping Activities ············· *83*

CHAPTER 6   Economic Globalism and New Regionalism: The WTO, FTAs and Japan's New Trade Policy ··· *102*

CHAPTER 7   Japan's Foreign Policy in the Post-War Period: A Road to Recovery and a Major Power Status ································ *122*

CHAPTER 8   Japan's Constitution and Changing Interpretations ············ *145*

CHAPTER 9   The Japan-U. S. Alliance ··· *163*

CHAPTER 10 Japan's Diplomacy and East Asia ·· *183*

Index ··· *201*

CHAPTER 1

Different World Views

In this chapter, three world views are explained. The contemporary view that is taken for granted, the nation-state (sovereign state) system, will be explained in some detail. Each sovereign state is equal in its legal rights, regardless of its geographical size and population in this system. There were quite different understandings of the world, and the most prominent of which, the Muslim and Chinese views, are briefly explained. This is to make clear that the current nation-state system is a product of history and may well be subject to change in the future.

The Origin of the Nation-State (Sovereign State) System

Nation and State

First, it should be noted that the terms nation-state and sovereign state are used somewhat interchangeably in this chapter. The former, however, is used to emphasize the citizen and popular aspects (the sense of belonging to a particular nation), the latter more about the institutional and legal aspects. A State is considered to be a legally established organization with authority. A Nation may be said to be an imagined community because it assumes that there is a group of people who share a collective memory and wants to form a unified government (or community), which is what we call a nation. The term country, by the way, is considered to be a generic term that is neutral in this nation and state distinction in this chapter.

There are basically four elements to be recognized as a legitimate state in the current international world. They are: 1) fixed territory, 2) citizens who live within the territory, 3) government which can effectively rule the territory and citizens, and 4) diplomatic recognition from other states.

The term nation-state is a combination of nation and state, which implies that nation and state had better be one and the same. That is, one's sense of belonging to a particular entity called a nation should ideally coincide with the boundary of a state. This is not necessarily the case, however. For example, a particular group of a population may have a strong sense of belonging to a particular region of a (territorial) state and hence wants to create a new state (legal entity) that would coincide with this sense of belonging. This is the reason why there have been so many ethnic conflicts and secessionist movements that sometimes get quite violent. The violent dissolution of the former Yugoslavia in the 1990s was a recent case in point.

The Thirty Years' War and Its Background

The contemporary sovereign state system is said to have come about after the signing of the Westphalia Treaty in 1648, which was the peace treaty of the Thirty Years' War. The kind of effects that the Thirty Years' War had on the creation of the system will be explored in this section. The Thirty Years' War lasted from 1618 to 1648.

In medieval Europe, the Emperor of the Holy Roman Empire had universal authority and exercised actual power in the secular sphere, whereas the Pope of the Roman Catholic Church had similar authority in the spiritual sphere. It was also the age of not only the rise of commercial capitalism, but also the Protestant movement. The former challenged the reign of the Emperor of the Holy Roman Empire, the latter that of the Pope.

In the early 17th century, there was a heightened tension between Catholics and Protestants in Germany, where the authority of the Emperor was non-existent, practically speaking. There were so many duchies and fiefdoms that were divided into two camps according to their religious beliefs. The Thirty Years' War was originally a religious conflict within Germany; however, other European countries intervened in this conflict, which eventually engulfed the entire European continent. What complicated it was that some Catholic countries such as Bourbon France supported the Protestant side, mainly because of the long-standing rivalry between the Bourbons and the Hapsburgs. Those who supported the Catholic side were all connected with the Hapsburgs such as the Holy Roman Empire and Austria.

The Westphalia Treaty and the Birth of Sovereign States

The Westphalia Peace Conference (1644-48) was the first large-scale European conference, in which 66 countries participated. There were actually two venues where it was held, one was in Münster (Catholic) and the other was in Osnabrück (mainly Protestant), both of which were in the Westphalia region of Germany.

The Conference agreed on three major points. First, all the duchies and fiefdoms in Germany were officially recognized as independent territorial states. Second, the Protestants gained an equal footing with the Catholics. Third, the Netherlands and Switzerland, both of which were under the Hapsburgs, became independent, and the borders between France and Germany as well as between Germany and Sweden were clearly delineated.

To rephrase the significance of the Treaty: first, the universal authority of the Holy Roman Empire was no longer officially recognized. This was because 300 or so German duchies and fiefdoms became independent and accordingly were regarded as sovereign entities. Second, the Pope also lost his universal authority in religious matters since Protestantism was officially recognized by the Vatican. Therefore, one can say the Treaty demolished universal religious authority as well as universal secular rule for Europe. As a consequence, the prototype of the current sovereign state system came into being.

Three Pillars of the Sovereign State System

Functions of the Three Pillars[1]

There are three fundamental elements in the sovereign state system: Sovereignty, International Law, and the Balance of Power. It consists of legally equal sovereign states, which are the basic units of the system. International law is to regulate *de jure* (legally and officially) their conduct and behavior. The balance of power is a mechanism that actually, *de facto*, kept major powers from engaging in a life-threatening kind of war among them, especially when international law was not effective to adjudicate a conflict. In this sense, the balance of power is complementary to the former two pillars. Sovereign states did have the right to wage war and it was routinely exercised from the 17th to early 20th century. Small countries' interests and wishes were most likely ignored, however. There was no final arbitrator or institution with the legitimate authority and physical force to enforce its final judgment in this international system, as opposed to an effective government that can enforce its will on the population within a state.

Sovereignty

Sovereignty is usually explained to be independence in external relations as well as the final authority and control within the state. Its precise definition is elusive, nonetheless, because it has so many connotations and is used in many contexts. Four kinds of sovereignty are identified here: namely; domestic sovereignty, interdependent sovereignty, international legal sovereignty and Westphalian sovereignty, according to Stephen Krasner. The latter two are the subjects of interest in this chapter. Nevertheless, the first two will also be explained briefly.

Domestic sovereignty is something that a citizen witnesses and experiences in everyday life. It has both authority and control as long as the Government is effective. For example, a government (the executive and the legislature) can decide to hike a sales tax and is expected to enforce it legally and legitimately on its people. Interdependent sovereignty is concerned with control only, not with authority. States have the power to regulate any trans-border flows of goods and services as well as people unless a state officially relinquishes it. The issue is how to control them.

International legal sovereignty is "concerned with establishing the status of a political entity in the international system" (Krasner, 1999: 14). This has to do with diplomatic recognition. Take, for instance, the case of Taiwan (Republic of China=ROC). Japan recognized the ROC's Kuomintang Government as the legitimate Government representing all of China in 1952, in spite of the establishment of the People's Republic of China (PRC) in 1949 that has controlled the far vaster mainland. However, Japan switched recognition to the PRC in 1972 and no official diplomatic relations have existed ever since between Japan and Taiwan. There are only 20 states, mostly small island states, which recognize the ROC as the legitimate China in 2017. Taiwan as an effective political entity has never changed since the Kuomintang seized power in Taiwan. That is, it has had a fixed territory under effective control, citizens who live there, and an effective government. What is different from the PRC is the status of official diplomatic recognition. In this sense, the ROC has been steadily losing international legal sovereignty. That is, a political entity can have all the necessary elements such as territory, population, and effective government to be recognized as a bona fide member of the international community. It may still not be included in the social circles of the community of sovereign nation-states, nonetheless, because other states do not want to have any official diplomatic dealings with it.

The flip side of the coin is that some political entities that do not necessarily conform to the "basic norm of appropriateness associated with international legal sovereignty have been recognized" (Krasner, 1999: 15). To cite only a few examples, India and the Philippines were founding members of the United Nations (UN) despite the fact they were not independent at the time of the UN's establishment. Byelorussia and the Ukraine were also founding UN members although they were part of the Soviet Union (USSR). Hong Kong was a founding member of the World Trade Organization (WTO), which was established in January 1995, when it was still a UK colony. It is still a member with the title of Hong Kong, China, even though it is now under Chinese sovereignty. China itself joined the WTO in December, 2001. One caveat is that "international legal sovereignty does not guarantee the territorial integrity of any state or even the existence of a state. Recognized states have been dismembered and even absorbed" (Krasner, 1999: 20).

Westphalian sovereignty has come into being from its namesake treaty. The gist of sovereignty that was mentioned at the outset of this chapter is based on this Westphalian sovereignty. That is to say, it is "territoriality and the exclusion of external actors from domestic authority arrangements" (Krasner, 1999: 20). Put another way, it is no meddling in internal affairs. This does not negate that political leaders take external environments into consideration in their policy decisions. Of course, they do and should in this age of globalization. The fact remains, though, they are free to choose any policy that they deem fit, given a particular external environment. No meddling into internal affairs is still a paramount principle in the code of conduct in international society. Intervention violates both international legal and Westphalian sovereignty.

However, in recent years, the 'Responsibility to Protect' (R2P) is oftentimes mentioned because there are so-called failed states, like Somalia and the Democratic Republic of the Congo. They cannot maintain law and order and, as a result, so many civilians are internally displaced and have become victims of violence. The concept of R2P in effect recognizes that the international society may intervene in internal affairs in a failed state to prevent a large-scale human tragedy from taking place. This is a sensitive and touchy issue because there is a trade-off between the idea of R2P (or fundamental human rights) and the principle of non-intervention. Some states like China and Russia, which are faced with domestic ethnic secessionist movements, tend to be wary of this concept.

In sum, the concept of sovereignty that we cherish as sacrosanct may not necessarily be iron-clad solid and there is rather large room for ambiguities. Another way to put it is that it is multi-faceted and different interpretations are possible under different contexts. As Benedict Anderson said that a "nation" may be just an "imagined community", the concept of sovereignty may also be a product of social construction that would be subject to change over time.

International Law

International law is a set of rules and customs that are considered to be binding. This is mainly to settle any international dispute without resorting to physical force among states. However, it is nowadays applied to regional or international organizations, non-state-actors, and even private citizens. Its significant shortcoming, which is totally different from domestic law, is that it does not have a bona fide final authority to judge and enforce its decisions. The closest that comes to it is the United Nations Security Council, but it does not oftentimes have the necessary means under its command to enforce its will.

There are three kinds of international law: 1) public international law, 2) private international law and 3) supra-national law. Public international law and supra-national law are of interest in international relations. The latter, supra-national law, limits the rights of the sovereign state by explicitly ceding their rights to make decisions to a regional or an international organization such as the UN. For example,

Article 25 of the UN Charter demands that its member states "accept and carry out the decisions of the Security Council".

There are three kinds of sources for public international law: 1) custom, 2) treaty, and 3) general principles, including the judgments of the International Court of Justice (ICJ). A Treaty is a binding formal agreement that is written and therefore it should be fairly clear as to what it contains, although it can be subject to interpretation. Custom and general principles are not based on written documents. Custom is the actual practices and acceptance of these practices as law by states. General principles are recognized as law by those deemed as civilized nations (explained later). The freedom of the seas was a customary international law until the UN Convention on the Law of the Sea was signed in 1982. It can be said to be codified, although some countries such as the US insist that it is still a matter of customary international law.

International law can be said to have existed since the Middle Ages. However, it was not universally applied. The expansion of the areas where international law has been applied will be explained in the context of the nation-state system in this chapter. Hugo Grotius is considered to be the father of international law. He was a Dutch jurist who wrote a tome titled "On the Law of War and Peace" (three books), that was first published in 1625. His tome was based on natural law, which itself was founded on human rationality. This is a significant departure from the traditional idea that law was dictated and given by God. In a sense, the idea of natural law has emancipated humanity, one could say, from the fetters of God.

There was a societal background that the idea of human rationality was accepted. It had mostly to do with the Industrial Revolution, which started in the latter half of the 18th Century and lasted until the first half of the 19th Century. With this revolution, there was the rise of commercial capitalism, which was also a product of the age of European voyages of discovery, from which major European powers gained many colonies. It was also the era of budding industrial capitalism, especially in the UK. The stability of markets is a "must", which requires some accepted rules and customs in order to make commercial and industrial deals safely. Then, war was the worst enemy for merchants and industrialists because it caused chaos and destruction. International law that was based on this realization and that would regulate and restrict the conduct of war was a welcome development for the budding bourgeoisie.

One might add, though, there is a view that capitalists would welcome war because it would provide a good profit opportunity if it is fought somewhere else. One could also say, from this viewpoint, that it would provide access to markets and resources through imperialist expansion.

As was mentioned before, back in the 16th to 17th centuries, war was a legitimate right of states and, accordingly, Grotius did neither push to make war illegal per se nor non-legitimate. He forcefully argued for Just War, having witnessed the atrocities committed in the Thirty Years' War, according to him, even the barbarians were ashamed of. He argued there were two kinds of war; one was a Just War that can be justified and the other kind that cannot be justified. In order to make a war a Just War, there had to be some restrictions as to the purpose, ways, and means to the conduct of a war, so he reasoned.

International law as such has its origins in the European Christian countries and, therefore, the area where it was initially applied was limited to Christian Europe only. However, it is now universally applied. This expansion happened as follows. First, it was enlarged geographically among Christian countries and then non-Christian countries were included. Finally, it was applied all over the world. For the first geographical expansion, it followed the independence of Christian countries in the Americas in the 19th century. US independence in 1776 from UK rule gave the expansion a spur. International law became applied to the US as a matter of course because it had already been implemented as a British colony. What changed was the status from a colony to a newly independent sovereign state. The same applies to Latin America, where many countries gained independence from Spain and Portugal in the 19th century. The colonial powers had converted much of the native population there to Christianity. The Americas belong to the same Christian family although North America was mainly Protestant and Latin America was overwhelmingly Catholic.

A breakthrough came about at the Treaty of Paris after the Crimean War (1853-56). The Crimean War was fought between Tsarist Russia, who wanted to expand southward, and the Ottoman Turks, who wanted to prevent Russian encroachment. The UK and France supported the Ottoman Turks out of fear that Russia might become too powerful and dominate the European continent. The Ottoman Turks were

Table 1-1 Expansion of International Law

Category	Applied Areas
Christian state (Europe)	Christian state in Europe
Christian state	+ Christian state in the Americas
Civilized state	+ Non-Christian state deemed civilized
Peace-loving state	Every state

a Muslim empire, whereas the Russians belonged to the Christian family. A peace treaty to end the war without these two main antagonists was of course impossible. Out of necessity, therefore, a Muslim empire had to be seated with a Christian empire as an equal to sign a peace treaty. Then, the fundamental criterion of Christianity had to be changed. It became whether or not a country was judged to be civilized by the European powers. A second breakthrough of sorts came about at the establishment of the UN because its membership was opened to any "peace-loving" state. It is now usually the case that any sovereign state that wishes to join the UN will be accepted without any fuss. That is to say, any sovereign state is deemed to be "peace-loving" and international law will be applied.

(Classical) Balance of Power

The balance of power that was practiced in 19th century Europe will be explained in this section. This balance of power, which is called classical balance of power here, is totally different from that of the bi-polar kind of balance of power witnessed in the Cold War era between the US and USSR. However, the idea of the balance of power itself is still believed fairly widely (See Chapter 2 for balance of power).

This classical configuration was formally approved at the Treaty of Utrecht (actually a series of agreements), signed in March and April 1713, as a peace treaty after the War of the Spanish Succession (1701-13). The war took place basically because the French House of Bourbon interfered with the Spanish House of Hapsburg's succession to the throne and founded the Bourbon dynasty in Spain in its attempt to expand its power to Spain. The UK opposed this naked aggression, and in the name of restoring the balance of power, participated in the war along with Austria, the Dutch Republic, Prussia, and Portugal, etc. against the French. The treaty recognized the Bourbon dynasty in Spain, but on the condition that France and Spain were not unified. As this succession war exemplified, it was generally the case that wars were fought between France and some other continental European countries in the 18th and the early 19th centuries.

A clear-cut configuration of the classical balance of power was established by the Treaty of Vienna (March 1815) after the Napoleonic Wars that lasted from around 1800 to 1815. This configuration is known as the Concert of Europe. The Napoleonic wars followed the French Revolution (1789-1799), which gave birth to nationalism and mass conscript armies. This intensified the severity of war, compared to the mercenary wars that were the norm before this Revolution. The Congress of Vienna was convened from 1814 to 1815 to set the political map of Europe with its boundaries. It was chaired by Prince Clement von Metternich, who was Foreign Minister of the Holy Roman Empire, which was ironically dissolved in this Congress. It was sarcastically mentioned that "the congress dances, but does not progress" because of its drawn-out nature. However, it made the Concert of Europe possible by clearly delineating boundaries and by establishing the balance of power among major states. This Concert lasted at least until the February (1848) Revolution in France. One could say that its basic framework lasted until WWI.

The objective of this arrangement was to maintain the independence of major European powers by forestalling an emergence of a dominant continental European power, usually France. The major powers were typically France, the UK, Austria, Russia and Prussia. The UK played the role of "balancer" in this arrangement because she was a naval power off the European continent. By forming an alliance against a semi-dominant power of the time so that there would be a balance of power, the system could maintain stability in the sense that no major power needed to fear that its survival would be at stake. It was assumed and somehow accepted that there could be some small-scale skirmishes and conflicts that might change their spheres of influence, and even some minor territorial adjustments. Put it another way, the interests and wishes, and for that matter the territorial integrity of small to medium countries, were essentially ignored for the sake of the major powers.

Sovereign State System in Flux?

This sovereign state system is often said to be in flux nowadays because it is seemingly under onslaught from within as well as without. The pressure from without is called globalization and from within it is localization (decentralization). Their directions are diametrically opposed, but are taking place simultaneously. Because of these totally opposed phenomena, it would be hard for the system to deal with them.

Globalization

The current trend of globalization has been apparent in the economic sphere, especially in financial markets. The post-WWII world economic system has been geared toward a freer economic system by lowering tariffs and cutting non-tariff barriers. The GATT (General Agreement on Tariffs and Trade), which is now reorganized as the WTO, became international law in January 1948 exactly for that purpose. This is because there was shared understanding that blocked economies and protectionist tendencies were partly responsible for the outbreak of WWII. Its aftermath, still on-going, is the globalized economy, sometimes referred to as economic interdependence.

The interdependent nature of our economic activities seems abundantly clear nowadays. A prominent example of late was the collapse of Lehman Brothers in September, 2008. Lehman Brothers was the 4th biggest private investment bank in the US. This shock kicked off a series of bankruptcies of big lending companies in the US and sent a shiver of a possible great economic depression in the world economy.

An incident that happens in a faraway economy would likely affect the economies of other countries. This is what globalization is. Political control and restraints on economic activities remain, of course, but to a much lesser degree than before. It can be said that globalization does not recognize any border as such any longer, at least in the economic and financial spheres.

Even in the field of political authority that has directly to do with sovereignty, the EU (European Union) can be said to be experimenting with a new bold process of partial political integration. For example, a national currency is part and parcel of fiscal and monetary sovereignty. Nonetheless, 19 out of 28 (the UK included) EU member states have a single integrated currency called the Euro in 2017. Another example is that a citizen of an EU country can freely go to a richer EU country and work there legally, partly because there is little border control among EU countries.

Localization

The pressure that the sovereign state system has been under comes from within, too. This can be termed localization. Distinct ethnic identities tend to be the driving force for localization, which sometimes takes the form of violent secessionist movements. A quintessential case was the former Yugoslavia. After the end of the Cold War and the dissolution of the USSR, East European countries came under great pressure to transform their political systems from one-party Communist rule to democratic government and from the command economy to a market economy. Distinct ethnic identities and enmities that were suppressed under Communist rule, all of a sudden, emerged as a crucial issue in maintaining a unified state. They flared up most spectacularly in the former Yugoslavia and ethnic cleansing ensued.

This kind of secessionist movement is not confined to former Communist bloc countries. It happens in quite a few places. Europe, which was the cradle of the current international system, is not spared this hard-to-deal-with problem. Belgium is an example. It is basically divided into the Dutch speaking north and the French speaking south. The language difference is the main culprit, which is causing different ethnic identities. However, it is also similar to the typical North-South problem since the North tends to be wealthier than the South. Belgium's solution was to introduce a federal system, in which they both have a regional government with much autonomous power. The language difference, by the way, is not necessarily the main culprit in ethnic tensions. Switzerland is a case in point. It has four official languages (German, French, Italian and Romansh), but this does not lead to different ethnic feelings. One can say that the Brexit, i.e., the UK trying to leave the EU in 2019, is also a more recent case in point.

Robustness of the Sovereign State Concept

Judging from the above discussion, one might conclude that the era of the sovereign (nation-) state system may be numbered. That is, sovereignty can be at bay. Despite acknowledging that it is under great pressure, however, it does not seem to be cracking under these pressures,

This concept of the sovereign nation-state is so ingrained in the thinking of the people in the world in general and, therefore, is more robust than perceived. For example, it is common to ask or to be asked when in a foreign country, "where are you from?" or "which country are you from?" This is in essence asking one's nationality or citizenship. This practice confirms that people everywhere unconsciously believe that one has a sense of belonging to a certain state or nation. The mere fact that we take this kind of question for granted means that we naturally identify an individual with a certain state or nation. This exemplifies clearly the robust nature of the sovereign (nation-) state concept per se.

Different World Views

The Muslim and Chinese Views on the world in their ideal basic forms will be briefly explained in this section. They were the dominant perspective in the Moslem world and East Asia proper centered on the Chinese Empire respectively before the nation-state concept had become the universal perspective and practice. States that are in these areas are now all member-states of the UN and, therefore, adhere to the nation-state concept. It is important, nonetheless, to understand these different views of the world that were once dominant regionally, the influence of which should not be underestimated even in contemporary international relations. They may also have some residual kind of influence in a state's domestic polity and political thought.

The Muslim View

One feature that really stands out in this Muslim view is that God is the sovereign and God and politics are one and the same. Of course, there is only one God as is the case for Christianity and Judaism. Every earthly thing is under the command of God for the Muslims, summed up as Shariah (Islamic law). The Shariah itself is based on the Koran, which God revealed to the Prophet Muhammad, and the Sunna, which described what the Prophet had said and done. The Muslims are to abide by the Shariah not only in terms of their behavior, but also their spiritual inner being. In this sense, the idea of people's sovereignty as well as the separation of church and state is fundamentally alien to them. Everything has to be within the command of God. That is, they cannot enact a law that goes beyond the limits that God set. What they can do is to decide administrative bylaws, so to speak, by interpreting and finding God's will in the areas where God's dictates are not necessarily clear-cut.

As was mentioned before, almost all Muslim countries do adhere to the nation-state concept and the separation of church and state, but the Islamic Republic of Iran can be said to have this Muslim idea of politics basically in place, as far as its domestic political system is concerned. According to their interpretation (Iran is Shi'ite), those who know the Shariah best are the clergy, who have devoted their entire lives to studying it. Since everything including politics and governance is based on Shariah, they have authority in interpreting what the Shariah says. As a consequence, they inevitably wield inordinate power. Therefore, a popularly elected President has only an administrative power under the auspices of the designated top Ayatollah, who has the final authority in interpretation. Presidential candidates themselves are vetted by a 'Guardian Council', directed by the top Ayatollah, currently Ali Khamenei in 2017.

In the view of the Muslim, everything is judged by religion, whether or not one is a pious Muslim. Theirs is a unified dyadic view that is based on religion and therefore the idea of the Ummah (Islam's religious community) is critically important. The world, for instance, is divided into the House of Peace and the House of War. In the former, it is a peaceful and stable world in which little conflict occurs because Shariah is practiced and Muslims are the majority. In the latter, it is a world of conflict and war because Shariah is not practiced and non-Muslim heretics are the majority. This is merely an ideal type of the view in its original thinking, one might add hastily, since sectarian violence has been taking place quite often in the Muslim world. It should be noted, however, that there can be many gray areas in which Muslims and non-Muslims co-exist and where there is no clear majority. Then, you cannot necessarily judge if it is in fact a House of War or Peace. In other words, there can be no clearly delineated boundary as such between them.

In their thinking, the world becomes peaceful when and if it becomes overwhelmingly Muslim. In order to make the world a better place, it is their religious duty to keep trying to proselytize non-Muslims into Muslims. This is called Jihad, the holy war. Jihad is the means to persuade and convince non-Muslims to convert to Islam. It has basically four phases. The first is in one's own soul, the second is against the devil, the third against non-Muslims, and the fourth against tyrants and hypocrites. The former two are directed toward one's own inner mind. The latter two are to guard the Muslims and their community. There are four means to Jihad. The first is by mind or spirit, the second by mouth or words, the third by financial and other material means, and the fourth is by utilizing the body or the sword. The use of force is condoned as the last resort in order to guard the Muslims and their religious community only. It is unfortunate that terrorist attacks are often carried out in the name of Jihad and its violent nature is what non-Muslim people tend to associate with the term. It should be emphasized that it is the last resort and sanctioned only to defend the religion and their religious communities, not for any other purpose such as territorial aggrandization.

Chinese World Order (Middle-Kingdom Theory)

China (The Chinese Empire) had been the dominant power in East Asia proper for a long time until the late 19th century. Its economic, political and cultural influences in East Asia and beyond were undeniably large. They had a distinct take on the world, which was formed around the time of the Tang dynasty in the 7th century and had lasted until the Ch'ing dynasty in the early 20th century. Their view of the world is of hierarchical suzerainty and a concentric circle as well. It is also all-inclusive and one-dimensional. It also functioned as a large scale trade system, which took the form of tribute. Trade and other commercial activities were safe and lucrative because traders enjoyed the protection of the Chinese Empire and some tariffs by China were exempted. The assumption was that China had everything in abundance and East Asian tributary kingdoms came to pay respect to the high virtue of the Chinese Emperor. He had given back lots of goods and services on concessionary terms for acknowledging the loyal allegiance that was expressed to him.

Figure 1-1　Center of the center: Chinese Emperor (high virtue)
(domestic=provinces, hereditary native officials, etc).

As the term Middle-Kingdom suggests, it was a Sino-centric world view in that China was always at the center of the universe and sat at the apex in the hierarchy. Its rule was considered to be a benign and benefactory reign by virtue of the Emperor, and the barbarians came to learn Chinese enlightenment so that they would become as virtuous as the Chinese. In this sense, the Emperor's virtue is the crucial factor, at least ostensibly. His reign may have been nominal only and may have had no effective rule over the so called "vassal" states. All people outside China were regarded as barbarians. The Chinese were *Hua* (splendid and cultured) and the barbarians were *Yi* (uncultured). For example, the Japanese were barbarians of the East (*Dongyi*), the Mongols were those of the North (*Beidi*), the Uighur and other Central Asians were of the West (*Xirong*), and those in the South were *Nanman*. The Chinese were to edify the *Yi* with the Emperor's virtue, and to let them learn Chinese culture and codes of conduct. The concentric hierarchy was based on the proximity to the center, which was extended to Japan, Korea, Vietnam, etc.

This hierarchy was similar to the domestic lord-vassal structure within China. It was the following: the center, provinces, and areas that were governed by hereditary native officials (*tuguan* and *tusi*: leadership of minorities by people of their own, indirect rule); territories (Mongolian, Tibetan, Uighur and other ethnic groups under the jurisdiction of the central government, but self-governance was maintained); tributes (lenient indirect rule); markets in the state of *Wu* (equal trade relationship); and outside regions (regions where edification didn't extend).

The Middle-Kingdom view might still have some influence in China even though

CHAPTER 1   Different World Views   *17*

it is now a Communist state. When China sent armed forces to fight against Vietnam in their border war in 1979, the then supreme leader Deng Xiaoping said that China wanted to teach "lessons" to the Vietnamese. The Chinese term that Deng used (懲罰 = punishment) had its origin in their Middle-Kingdom view. In this world view, Vietnam was a tributary state under China. China had the right to teach "lessons" to a wayward country. By the way, similar to the Muslim view, there is no principle of clearly delineated borders as such because it regards the world as one and unified. Then, border disputes should be much less frequent than in the sovereign nation-state system.

The Japanese view of the world will be very briefly explained. Being an East Asian island nation, Japan can be said to have incorporated the Middle-Kingdom kind of world view long ago. The hitch is that Japan, not China, was the center of the universe. Japan had never come under Chinese rule and had never accepted China's status as its assumed lord. The fact that Japan persisted in retaining the title of Emperor is the evidence. This title was possible only for the Chinese Emperor in the Chinese view. Other "vassal" countries such as Vietnam had the title of king, duke, marquis, etc. Japan had never accepted the title of King and maintained that of Emperor. Japan's view of China had been somewhat ambivalent, but had acknowledged that China was a big power to reckon with since ancient times.

Once again, only one Emperor was possible in this kind of hierarchical worldview and Kings and Lords were his underlings. Japan's Prince (regent) Shotoku sent an official letter to the Emperor Yang of Sui back in 607, which stated that "the Emperor of the land of the rising sun greets the Emperor of the land of the setting sun." This

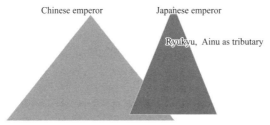

Since the Meiji period, the height of Japan and China's positions are reversed = Japan becomes the center of Asia (Was it the basis for the idea of the Greater East Asia Co-Prosperity Sphere, *hakko ichiu*--all the world under one roof?)

Figure 1-2   Japanese View

infuriated the Emperor Yang, who said that "Insolent letters from barbarians shall not be brought to me again". For the Japanese, however, it was a concession of sorts because they addressed the Chinese ruler as Emperor. For the Chinese, this was of course unacceptable since Japan's ruler was addressed as Emperor, too.

After the Meiji Restoration[2] in October 1868, Japan has fairly easily incorporated the sovereign nation-state view because Japan happens to be an island nation. That is, she has clear boundaries and a solid national identity as Japanese. It helped that they spoke one language. China had struggled to adopt the nation-state view and had been left behind Japan in the early 20th century in its economic and other developments.

To sum up very briefly, the concept of the sovereign nation-state is now taken for granted and is ingrained in our mind in spite of pressures from without and within. It is, however, a product of history and may be subject to change in the future.

Endnotes
1) The following is a description of the original, early stage of the Westphalian nation-state system.
2) Meiji Restoration is the usual translation. However, the Japanese term "ishin" (維新) does not seem to have any connotation of "restoration" to this author. The translation should more likely be "renewal", or might even be "renaissance."

References
1) Aruga Tadashi, *et al* (eds.), (1989), *Theories on International Politics*, Tokyo: University of Tokyo Press, (in Japanese)（有賀貞ほか（編）『講座国際政治① 国際政治の理論』東京：東京大学出版会）
2) Hook, Glen D, *et al* (2011), *Japan's International Relations*, London: Routledge
3) Krasner, Stephen (1999), *Sovereignty*, Princeton: Princeton University Press
4) Takeuchi Toshitaka, *et al* (1995), *Contemporary International Relations*, Tokyo: Kenpakusha, (in Japanese)（竹内俊隆ほか『現代国際関係論』東京：建帛社）
5) Takeuchi Toshitaka (ed.) (2012), *Contemporary International Relations*, Kyoto: Minerva, (in Japanese)（竹内俊隆（編）『現代国際関係入門』京都：ミネルヴァ書房）

Recommended Works
1) Brown, Daniel W. (2017), *A New Introduction to Islam*, 3rd Edition, Chichester: John Wiley & Sons
   This is an easy to read textbook on Islam per se, in which the development of Muslim beliefs and practices are discussed.
2) Fairbank, J.K. (1968), *The Chinese World Order: Traditional China's Foreign Relations*, Cambridge: Harvard University Press
   This is the classic on the Chinese world order, which argued the Sino-centric all-embracing tributary system was the key in this system.
3) Opello, Walter and Stephen Rosow (2004), *The Nation-State and Global Order: A Historical Introduction to Contemporary Politics*, Boulder: Lynne Rienner
   This book is not for a beginner, but covers similar areas that are covered in this chapter, and is somewhat detailed in historical aspects.

CHAPTER 2

Different Paradigms: Realism, Liberalism, and Constructivism

Multiple paradigms and theories have been developed to explain international relations. The emergence of different paradigms and theories has been influenced by the state of international affairs at the time of their development. They also appeared as criticisms of the paradigms and theories that were dominant at the time. This chapter will review the major paradigms and theories of international relations to clarify how they differ, why they emerged, and what they explain. This review will be followed by the application of these theories to a real-world phenomenon, the absence of wars between Japan and the United States (US) during the post-World War II period, to enhance readers' understanding of these theories.

Overview of Major Paradigms

The field of international relations emerged in Europe between the First and the Second World Wars as a criticism of the legalistic approach that had been employed prior to that time. Arguments on war and peace before World War I (WWI) centered on the importance of making wars illegal to prevent states from resorting to military means. This school of thought culminated in the argument that the League of Nations would be able to prevent inter-state wars if it possessed a collective security mechanism, through which member states could collectively punish aggressors. However, this approach failed to prevent the outbreak of World War Two (WWII). As a founding father of the contemporary field of international relations, British historian E. H. Carr referred to the legalistic approach as "utopianism", and argued that a practical, realist approach must be adopted to prevent wars. This perspective facilitated the birth of the modern field of international relations and prompted a logical focus on the causes of war and peace.

Realism

Intended to explain the causes of wars, realism has constituted the core of international relations paradigms. The origins of realism can be traced to such articulations of political thought as Thucydides' *History of the Peloponnesian War* in the 5th century BC, Machiavelli's *The Prince* in the 15th century, and Hobbes's *Leviathan* in the 17th century; however, E. H. Carr's *The Twenty Years' Crisis*, published in 1939, is considered the first modern articulation of realist arguments. Realism before and after WWII is termed "classical realism" to differentiate it from the type of realist arguments that emerged in the late Cold-War period, known as "neorealism" or "structural realism."

Several key assumptions are common across the different variants of realism: 1) international relations are anarchic; 2) the main actors in international relations are states; 3) inter-state relations are primarily determined by the relative level of power, which is principally derived from military capabilities; and 4) states are rational unitary actors seeking to preserve their national interests.

Anarchy means the absence of government. No governmental entity rules over states to regulate them in international relations; thus, realists regard international relations as anarchic and states as being in a state of "war of all against all", in the words of Thomas Hobbes. Therefore, political conflicts over power, or "power politics", become the essence of international relations. Of the various types of actors, which include international organizations, states, non-governmental organizations (NGOs), and individuals, realism assumes that states are the principal actors. Only states are legally allowed to possess military capabilities, which are the major source of power. Thus, it is the fights among states that tend to be the most devastating, and realism also considers states to be actors capable of preventing wars. Because realism analyzes how large-scale inter-state wars can be prevented, it naturally focuses on major powers, which are the states that possess strong military capabilities.

The actions of states are determined through domestic policy decision-making processes. These processes involve a number of individuals, departments, and ministries. However, realism assumes that states behave unitarily in international relations. States are sufficiently rational to make the appropriate calculations for the sake of their national interests; thus, their overall behaviors do not change drastically, irrespective of who occupies a leadership position.

What are national interests? For Hans J. Morgenthau, a prominent scholar of classical realism who is particularly known for his book *Politics Among Nations*, national interests constitute a diverse set of interests in such fields as security, economy, and culture. When states attempt to preserve their national interests in international relations, they need sufficient power to gain the influence required to achieve their goals. Thus, it is necessary for states to pursue power for the sake of national interests, and power itself eventually becomes the most important aspect of their national interests. Thus, Morgenthau defines "national interest in terms of power", and assumes that states are power maximizers.

Kenneth N. Waltz, who profoundly influenced the field with his book *Man, the State and War*, subsequently becoming the most prominent scholar of neorealism with *Theory of International Politics*, does not define national interests in terms of power. An excessive increase in a state's power could threaten other countries, even if its purpose is defensive, which could lead the threatened countries to augment their military forces. This situation could eventually threaten the original state's security. Because such a "security dilemma" (see p.69–70) is unbeneficial for states, Waltz assumes that states do not attempt to excessively increase their power. He considers the ultimate national interest of states to be not power maximization, but survival.

Given these assumptions, realists have developed multiple theories on war and peace. The sections below review three major realist theories: the balance of power, the balance of threat, and the power transition theories.

Balance of Power

The balance of power theory was originally developed to explain international relations in Europe from the 17th to the 20th centuries (see pp.9-10). According to the theory, motivations for military action tend to be restrained when power is balanced among competing countries, despite the countries existing in the context of an anarchic "war of all against all". Balance of power realists argue that states naturally tend to balance their power against that of other states to prevent the emergence of an overwhelmingly strong state. Power is primarily defined in terms of military capabilities, and the sources of military capabilities, such as economic power and population, are also frequently considered.

Two methods are generally employed to ensure the balance of power: internal balancing and external balancing. Internal balancing occurs when a country independently increases its military capabilities, whereas external balancing refers to the formation of alliances (Waltz, 1979: 118, 168). Because internal balancing requires economic development military augmentation and thus takes time, states use the external balancing method when they experience an immediate necessity of balancing. By forming alliances, states combine the military capabilities for their allies with their own abilities to decrease the relative capability of their opponents and to achieve a balance of power.

In classical realism, international relations tend to be stable when more than two great powers attain a balance of power. In this situation, alliance partners can be shifted depending on changes in states' internal strengths, but it is impossible to change alliance partners if there are only two great powers. Under such a multipolar system, a "balancer" emerges that proactively effects change in its alliance partners in a manner that achieves a balance of power among different sides. Hence, states explicitly seek to achieve a balance of power.

If developing a balance among great powers is relatively simple, why did the Napoleonic Wars occur in the early 19th century? Why did two world wars occur? From the classical realist perspective, the Napoleonic Wars occurred as a result of the collapse of the balance of power among major European countries, following the rapid increase of French power under Napoleon. The two world wars occurred because of improper management of the balance of power among European countries. Assuming occasional changes of alliance partners, Morgenthau argues that the balance of power has dynamic characteristics and thus tends to be unstable.

Why did the Cold War period not witness a great power war despite the participation of only two great powers (the US and the Soviet Union)? To explain the "long peace" during the Cold War, Waltz supplements realism with structural arguments in *Theory of International Politics*. According to his argument, the international system has a tendency to exhibit a bipolar structure, under which great powers are naturally inclined to develop a balance of power. In other words, neorealism contends that structural constraints rather than state policies lead states to balance.

Although the international system tends to be stable from a neorealist perspective, there are two cases in which the likelihood of war increases. One situation occurs when multipolarity appears for some reason. The balancing calculations are rather simple when there are only two great powers. Each great power must account only for the behaviors of the other side; hence, the calculation confers stability on the system. However, in the case of multiple great powers, balancing calculations becomes more complicated, occasionally resulting in miscalculations and wars. The second cause of war identified by Waltz occurs when one of the two great powers overreacts to the actions of the other. Because states are assumed to increase their military capabilities only to the extent that it does not cause a security dilemma, there is essentially a limited likelihood that one of the sides will overreact to the other. However, according to Waltz, such a situation can result in war (Waltz, 1979: chap.8).

Balance of Threat

Although the balance of power theory argues that states balance their power against one another, the alliances formulated by the US during the Cold War appear to have rendered the power of the Western camp greater than that of the Eastern camp. Stephen M. Walt, who developed the balance of threat argument in his book *The Origins of Alliances*, explains such state behaviors while accounting for perceptions. According to Walt, states attempt to balance their power in response to perceived threats, rather than in response to the power of another.

Why do countries perceive other countries as threats? Walt indentifies four sources of threat perception: aggregate power, offensive power, aggressive intentions, and geographical proximity (Walt, 1987: 21-26). Aggregate power can be measured by comprehensive indicators of power, which include military capabilities, economic power, and population. A country with greater aggregate power tends to pose a greater threat to other countries. Offensive power can be gauged through the military capabilities available for offensive purposes such as nuclear weapons and missiles, as opposed to defensive weapon systems such as theater missile defense (TMD), which intercepts incoming missiles before they reach their targets. Offensive power is considered a source of perceived threat, because countries with offensive weapons have a greater ability to attack others than countries with defensive weapons only.

A country would not constitute a threat if it is satisfied with the status-quo, even if it possesses significant aggregate and offensive power. Countries with aggressive intentions are the most likely to initiate wars against others, and are thus perceived as threats. With these conditions held constant, a country that is geographically closer is more threatening than one that is farther away.

Why do wars occur from the perspective of the balance of threat theory? Although this theory does not provide an explicit argument, it implies that wars occur when states fail to balance and deter perceived threats. However, it is difficult to measure when threat perception is unbalanced, because it is not objectively measurable.

Power Transition

Whereas both balance of power and balance of threat theorists argue that states tend to engage in balancing behaviors to prevent the emergence of hegemons, the power transition theory argues that hegemons tend to emerge in the international system. According to this theory, a hegemon is a country that possesses overwhelming power that exceeds the sum of the other countries' power. Hegemons tend to be benign and do not possess aggressive intentions. According to this theory, international relations are characterized by the transition of hegemonic power approximately every century. The 16th century witnessed the hegemony of Portugal and Spain, whereas the Netherlands was the hegemon during the 17th century. This role was occupied by Britain in the 18th and the 19th centuries and was later assumed by the US in the 20th century.

The power transition theory argues that states tend to bandwagon with the hegemon, which means to align with the hegemon, rather than balancing against it to protect themselves. The international system tends to be stable when a hegemon exists, because hegemons provide international public goods that stabilize the international system. Public goods are available for general use by the public and are not exhausted by the use of others. Examples of international public goods include peace, free trade, and international institutions. For instance, the US supported the international economic system by underwriting the dollar peg system in the early Cold War period, despite the negative economic repercussions for the US.

Hegemony does not endure indefinitely. As noted above, nearly every century has witnessed a transition of power. By providing international public goods, a hegemon naturally uses and loses its power, and is weakened vis-à-vis other states. Because of this "hegemon's dilemma", hegemons naturally decline, while other states accumulate power through the "advantage of backwardness". For weaker states to increase their power, they must first develop their economies. Industrialization necessary for economic development tends to occur more quickly for late comers, as they can emulate existing industrialization processes, rely on capital from advanced countries, and utilize existing advanced technologies. Challengers can thus catch up with the existing hegemon.

The likelihood of war increases when a challenger emerges. Because the hegemon sets international rules by providing international public goods, a challenger state seeks to be the next hegemon to ensure that it can establish international rules favorable to its interests. Hence, a hegemonic war between the existing hegemon and a challenger becomes inevitable, and the winner becomes the next hegemon. In the 19th century, Germany emerged as a challenger to British hegemony. Thus, war between the two countries was inevitable, manifesting as World Wars I and II. However, the ultimate winner of WWII was neither Germany nor Britain (because Britain was on the winning side of the Allies, but effectively bankrupted by the war, and lost its Empire); it was the US. As a result, the US emerged as the hegemon in the 20th century.

Liberalism

Although realism assumes that the natural state of international relations is that of competition among states, there was no great-power war during the Cold War period. Is competition among countries a natural state of affairs? According to liberalism, such competition is not necessarily natural. International relations do not always constitute a zero-sum game in which a victory for one country is offset by the losses of others; rather, it often constitutes positive-sum games in which actors can expand the size of the pie. This scenario causes countries to be concerned not only with how much they can gain relative to others, but also with how much they gain in absolute terms. From the liberal perspective, the consideration of absolute gains occasionally causes states to cooperate with one another.

Liberalism is rooted in the works of various philosophers such as John Stuart Mill and Immanuel Kant, and posits belief in the possibility of improving the nature of international relations. The legalistic approach, which E. H. Carr termed utopianism, was a forerunner of the liberal paradigm. Although a number of liberal theories have developed, currently three major liberal theories dominate the field: economic interdependence, democratic peace, and neoliberal institutionalism.

Economic Interdependence

Economic interdependence theory holds that states are rational actors that tend to avoid unilateral actions when they are interdependent of other states. Interdependence refers to the dense interaction of people, materials, money, and information among states. Under interdependence, actors have an interest in maintaining the state of interdependence because the termination of such interactions would damage their economies. This interest leads such actors to conclude that allowing relations with their partners to deteriorate is undesirable; thus, the likelihood of war between them decreases.

The current global economy is characterized by increasing interdependence. The nature of capitalism causes countries to become interdependent. According to the Heckscher-Ohlin theorem of international economics, the nature of capitalism drives countries to an international division of labor, depending on their comparative advantages in various production factors such as capital and labor. For example, in the 1990s, Japanese companies made capital investments all over the world, including China, because of their comparative advantage in capital, as China was an attractive location for investment due to low labor costs. In this case, Japan was dependent on Chinese labor, whereas China was dependent on Japanese capital. Technological evolution has further accelerated globalization, which has deepened economic interdependence among countries.

The growing interdependence among countries increases the risks of severing relations with trading partners. For example, after experiencing the two oil shocks in the 1970s, Japan has emphasized the maintenance of good relations with Arab countries. Because of its lack of natural resources, Japan depends almost entirely on imported oil, 90% of which is obtained from the Arab world. Because Japan has a vital interest in continuing to import oil from the Arab countries, it avoids unilateral behavior that could spark conflicts with oil-producing Arab countries.

Even when two countries are interdependent, one might be more dependent on its partner than the other. For example, although Saudi Arabia imports motor vehicles and computers from Japan, those goods are not vital for daily life. Even if trade relations with Japan were to be terminated for some reason, people in Saudi Arabia could survive, although they would be inconvenienced. Conversely, Saudi Arabia is a major source of oil for Japan, accounting for approximately 30% of total oil imports. In addition, oil is a crucial requirement for daily life, for industry, and thus for the entire economy. In their book *Power and Interdependence*, prominent economic interdependence theory scholars Robert Keohane and Joseph Nye argue that such an asymmetric interdependence could be exploited in the bargaining process. By leveraging the issue of oil exports, Saudi Arabia could position itself advantageously in negotiations with Japan. Thus, although economic interdependence is a liberal theory, it also incorporates the notion of power.

Democratic Peace

The balance of power theory as a major international relations theory appears to explain US-Soviet relations during the Cold War period, as the two countries had indeed achieved a balance of power. If a balance of power brings peace, then did the collapse of the Soviet Union and thus the collapse of the Cold War structure destabilize the world? Despite the prospect of instability during the post-Cold War period predicted by balance of power realists such as John J. Mearsheimer (Mearsheimer, 1990), no great-power war has occurred during the post-Cold War period so far. What can explain this fact?

The democratic peace theory, which was developed from the mid-1980s to the early 1990s in the works of such scholars as Michael Doyle and Bruce Russett, based on Immanuel Kant's 1795 work *Perpetual Peace*, argues that democratic regimes foster peace. According to Bruce Russett in *Grasping the Democratic Peace*, democracies (or countries in which more than three years has passed since the transition to democracy) rarely fight wars against one another that result in more than 1,000 deaths in battle. However, this argument does not indicate that democracies tend to adopt a peaceful stance toward any country. Only democracies, regimes in which regular elections and universal suffrage are guaranteed, are expected to not wage war on one another. In other words, democracies possess the possibility of resorting to military means only when they have conflicts with authoritarian countries.

Why do democracies tend not to wage war on one another? Bruce Russett argues that there are two principle lines of reasoning: normative and institutional explanations. The normative explanation argues that democracies tend to uphold the norm that conflicts should be solved peacefully, rather than by force, thereby encouraging peaceful relations with other democracies. Even when two democracies have conflicts, they perceive each other as peace-seeking countries, and such perceptions assist them in developing a sense of mutual trust. This mutual understanding is believed to be the cause of the peaceful relations between democracies (Russett, 1993: chap.2).

The institutional explanation argues that institutional constraints on political leaders in democracies encourage leaders to choose peaceful solutions to international conflicts. Political leaders in democracies are constrained by the legislature due to the separation of power. Political competition and pluralism in policy decision-making also inhibit the unilateral decision-making of political leaders. These leaders are also constrained by the public through elecrions, which increase the political cost for political leaders to choose military options in light of the next election results.

East and Southeast Asia has experienced a "wave of democratization" since the mid-1980s. Japan was the only democracy in the region until the mid-1980s; subsequently, countries such as the Philippines, South Korea, Taiwan, Thailand, Mongolia, and Indonesia have democratized. Thus, the East and Southeast Asian regions may be becoming increasingly peaceful through the spread of democratization.

However, according to *Electing to Fight* by Edward D. Mansfield and Jack Snyder, the likelihood of war tends to increase when countries are undergoing the democratization process. Countries transitioning to democracy are even more prone to engaging in warfare than authoritarian countries. It tends to be difficult for people in the midst of a transition to adopt long-term perspectives. This difficulty causes political leaders to implement short-term policies that may be harmful in the longer term. A relevant example is the use of nationalism. Political leaders in transitional countries are frequently tempted to create external enemies and stimulate nationalism domestically to justify the new regime and to consolidate the country. Based on their argument, if Chinese political leaders appeal to anti-Japanese nationalism when China undergoes democratization in the future, tensions between Japan and China would escalate, and the likelihood of war between the two countries might increase. Democracies tend not to wage war on one another only after the period of democratic transition.

Neoliberal Institutionalism

Although economic interdependence and democratic peace appear to explain the absence of war among, for example, Western European countries during the post-WWII period, a major feature of Western European countries is their establishment of regional institutions to promote regional integration and avoid wars. One liberal theory argues that international institutions mitigate conflicts among countries. This theory of neoliberal institutionalism argues that countries cooperate with one another through international institutions to decrease the likelihood of wars.

Generally, there are two types of institutions: formal and informal institutions. Formal institutions are organizations that are established to achieve particular purposes. For example, the World Bank is a formal institution that is intended to promote economic development by providing loans to governments in need. The United Nations was established to maintain peace, and the World Trade Organization was formed to promote free trade.

Various informal institutions also exist. Informal institutions include enduring customs and norms. In the realm of international relations, a good example is the principle of non-intervention in domestic affairs. This principle, which was a result of the Thirty Years' War of the 17th century, has been one of the guiding principles of international relations, although there is no formal organization devoted to this norm.

Why do these institutions promote peace among countries? Neoliberal institutionalism, based on the Coase theorem in economics, highlights three reasons. First, international institutions facilitate agreements on matters related to an institution's issue areas by providing rules and negotiation procedures. International conflicts result from a number of causes including matters related to security, trade, fishery, and culture. The rules and negotiation procedures that are established by institutions could align member states' expectations to ease cooperation and compromise among the conflicting parties, and to reduce conflicts. Second, by providing rules and negotiation procedures, international institutions can help states constrain various costs that are incurred throughout the negotiation process. Conflicting countries must confront transaction costs for search, bargaining, and enforcement, if they wish to solve conflicts on their own. Institutions can decrease such transaction costs by providing information, communication procedures, and decision-making mechanisms that can be used by the conflicting parties. In this manner, institutions facilitate negotiation between member states, increasing the likelihood of compromise and cooperation.

Third, the long "shadow of the future" is helpful in solving "collective action problems". These problems are also often termed "free rider problems". Even when actors are aware that the benefits of cooperation outweigh those of defection, a temptation nevertheless arises to defect when it is unclear whether the goals of cooperation can be achieved. A famous game with which to model collective action problems is known as the "stag hunt", which was initially described by Jean-Jacques Rousseau. Because a stag provides more than sufficient food to satisfy two people, two hungry people will consider it advantageous to cooperate in a stag hunt. However, they do not know when a stag will appear, and hunting a stag is difficult even in a cooperative effort. This uncertainty tempts each actor to defect and to capture a hare (which is smaller, easier to capture, and able to satisfy one person's hunger to a degree) on their own. When a situation presents a collective action problem, the shadow of the future, which is the prospect of continued long-term interaction, helps mitigate such problems. If the gains from cooperation are greater than those from cheating, then continued cheating is not beneficial for the interacting parties. Even when conflicting countries are tempted to cheat when they interact only once, they become aware of the long-term benefits of cooperation when the likelihood of continued interaction becomes apparent. Because participation in international institutions increases the prospects for continued interaction among their members, international institutions can assist in fostering cooperation among them.

Constructivism

Realist revivals tend to occur when tensions among great powers increase. Because of the heightened tension between the US and the Soviet Union, realist theories were influential in the 1950s and 1960s. Although détente in the 1970s decreased its appeal, realism gained renewed attention in the 1980s because of the heightened tensions between the two superpowers after the Soviet invasion of Afghanistan in 1979. However, the end of the Cold War and the inability of realism to explain the collapse of the bipolar structure led to increased awareness of the need to explain these changes.

This situation led to the development of constructivism. During the Cold War era, the field of international relations was strongly influenced by economics, seeking greater "scientification" of the field. As economics assumes that the individual is a rational actor, the "economic man" who seeks to maximize economic benefits, many arguments of the realist and liberal schools of international relations assumed that actors are rational. To analyze international relations objectively, scholars focused on material aspects such as military capabilities, the size of the economy, and population as measurable explanatory factors.

However, the failure of realism in predicting and explaining the end of the Cold War led to the question of whether it was reasonable to assume that actors are rational and to focus on material aspects to explain international relations. Constructivism, which is substantially influenced by sociology, argues that non-material factors such as norms, identities, and cultures determine the behavior of actors in international relations. According to constructivism, balancing prevailed during the Cold War and the superpowers accumulated arms because the dominant concept of the era emphasized the importance of military capabilities and balancing. There was no physical power to enforce balancing behaviors. The concepts shared amongst people and states led them to balance. Therefore, constructivism assumes that intersubjectively shared beliefs determine the behavior of actors and the dynamics of international relations.

Intersubjectivity indicates that one's subjective understanding is shared by others, and that all actors are aware that they share a common understanding. The normative explanation provided by the democratic peace theory, which was explained in the liberalism section, is a good example. According to the democratic peace argument, democracies have peaceful norms, and they know that other democracies share these norms. In this situation, peaceful norms are intersubjectively shared by democracies. Constructivism argues that intersubjectively shared norms and ideas determine the behaviors of actors in international relations. Alexander Wendt, a prominent constructivist scholar who is particularly known for his work *Social Theory of International Politics*, argues in his article "Anarchy is What States Make of It" that even states' self-help behavior under anarchy is not assured, but rather is a construction of intersubjective ideas in the international relations field.

Norms

Norms are behavioral principles that are intersubjectively shared among people. In other words, an actor believes that he/she "should" or "should not" engage in a given activity. This understanding of what one "should do" is believed to lead actors to behave based on "the logic of appropriateness", rather than on rationality, or "the logic or conseguence". According to the democratic peace theory, for instance, because a group of democracies share the norm that conflict "should" be solved without resorting to military means, democracies tend not to wage wars with one another even when they have conflicts.

Norms tend to be created during periods of substantial change such as devastating wars, natural disasters, and economic depressions. Norms related to human rights existed prior to the two world wars, as evident in the abolition of slavery promulgated by Abraham Lincoln's Emancipation Proclamation of 1863, and in international humanitarian laws that regulated wartime behavior such as The Hague Conventions of 1899 and 1907. However, human rights norms began disseminating rapidly worldwide after Nazi Germany's cruel genocide against Jewish people in the Holocaust. This crime against humanity led people to believe that the international community should not allow tragic events such as genocide, in which human rights are profoundly violated.

Certain individuals, known as "norm entrepreneurs," tend to be influential in creating particular norms. Consider the norm entrepreneurs who contributed to the development of the norm of sovereignty, which maintains that states possess the exclusive right to govern their subjects within their territories and are immune to intervention by external powers. Many intellectuals acted as norm entrepreneurs in the medieval period, when the notion that all of Europe constituted a single community remained strong. For instance, Jean Bodin, a political adviser to Henry III of France, argued for sovereignty as an official norm in his publication *Les Six Livres de la République* (Six Books of the Republic) in 1576. *De jure belli ac pacis libri tres* (On the Law of War and Peace) by Hugo Grotius, published in 1625 also played an important role in reconciling the concept of sovereignty with the sense of community in Europe. Given the creation and spread of the concept by such norm entrepreneurs, states came to accept sovereignty as a principle of behavior in the Peace of Westphalia concluded at the end of the Thirty Years' War in 1648.

The sovereignty norm has been a fundamental principal of international relations since the Peace of Westphalia. Since then, states have attempted to avoid interfering in the domestic affairs of other states. Despite the mass killing of the East Timorese by the Indonesian military beginning in the mid-1970s, for instance, international society refrained from political and military intervention in Indonesia until 1999. However, in general, since the end of the Cold War, the number of sovereignty violations has increased rapidly. Prior to the end of the Cold War, most violations of sovereignty had the voluntary consent of the state in which the violation occurred, but instances of involuntary sovereignty violations increased after 1990. Humanitarian interventions have been conducted in countries such as Kosovo, Rwanda, Haiti, Iraq, and Somalia, without the consent of the states in which the sovereignty violations occurred. Some of the interventions were conducted under the auspices of the United Nations, whereas others were conducted under the auspices of the North Atlantic Treaty Organization (NATO). These developments demonstrate that states are less bound by the sovereignty norm in the current era when confronting humanitarian crises. The acceptance of human rights norms by international society has been growing. Indeed, norms rise and fall, and the norms that stipulate appropriate behaviors change, albeit slowly.

Culture

Another constructivist argument that has influenced the field of international relations is the clash of civilizations argument advanced by Samuel Huntington initially in his 1993 article, "The Clash of Civilizations?", and later in his 1996 book,

The Clash of Civilizations. For Huntington, culture determines the behaviors of actors, and differences between cultures can cause conflicts. Huntington considers the civilization to be the broadest of cultural groupings, which are based on factors such as languages, history, religions, and customs. Individuals identify not only with parochial cultures but also with civilizations. According to Huntington, there are currently nine civilizations: the Western, Chinese, Japanese, Buddhist, Islamic, Hindu, Eastern Orthodox, Latin American, and African civilizations. Although the fault lines for conflicts during the Cold War were ideological, Huntington argues that wars between different civilizations could occur after the Cold War.

Why are conflicts between civilizations likely to cause wars in the post-Cold War period? Huntington provides two reasons. First, interactions among people have increased, which heightens individuals' awareness that they have irreconcilable differences with individuals from different civilizations. This awareness occasionally leads to animosity, which increases the possibility of conflict escalation. Second, the West's power is declining, which increases the likelihood that non-Western civilizations will challenge the West. Huntington argues that the West has used its power to enforce Western norms in non-Western countries. Dissatisfied with such Western behaviors, countries belonging to non-Western civilizations are motivated to challenge the international order created by the West. Huntington argues that such challenges could spur a war between "the West and the rest" (Huntington, 1993: 25-29, 39-41).

Huntington argues that the Western civilization on the one hand, and Chinese and Islamic civilizations on the other hand, may be particularly prone to future military conflicts. The Islamic civilization has the highest rate of population growth, which is causing large inflows of people from countries characterised by Islamic civilization to the countries belonging to Western civilization. In addition, countries in Chinese and Islamic civilizations have been expanding their military capabilities. Huntington argues that these movements instigate increased tensions and conflicts between people from the two sides, and could ultimately culminate in wars between them (Huntington, 1993: 45-48).

Published in the early 1990s, the clash of civilizations argument has garnered attention not only within international relations, but also outside the field, particularly because numerous conflicts have erupted between the Arab world and the West. However, we must note that this argument offers predictions without providing sufficient empirical evidence. Hypotheses must be empirically verified to be accepted as scientific theories; otherwise, arguments remain mere hypotheses.

Theory Application: Japan-US Relations during the Post-WWII Period

Although each theory represents an attempt by scholars to determine the most important causal relations underlying international relations, no theory is absolutely "correct". Because every event in a society will have numerous causes, identifying a single decisive cause for a given event is difficult or nearly impossible. Therefore, all of the theories explained above could provide different explanations for the same phenomenon. This section will apply realist, liberal, and constructivist theories to explain the absence of wars between Japan and the US during the post-WWII period.

Realist Theories

Even within the realist perspective, various theories identify different factors as the causes of war and peace. The balance of power theory of classical realism argues that wars occur when an imbalance of power exists among great powers, whereas the balance of threat theory implies that wars do not result from the imbalance of power but from the imbalance of threats. The neorealist balance of power theory of Kenneth Waltz argues that wars occur when either the international system becomes multipolar, or a great power in the bipolar system overreacts to the behavior of another power. The power transition theory argues that wars erupt when a rising power appears to challenge the hegemon.

How can we explain the absence of war between Japan and the US during the post-WWII period? The answer to this question is that the two countries have been allies and thus are not antagonistic toward each other. This answer prompts the further question of why these two countries became allies in the first place. The balance of power theory suggests that the Japan-US alliance has created a balance among great powers in the Asia Pacific region. We can assume that Japan and the US concluded a security treaty and developed an alliance in 1951 to balance against the Communist camp, which comprised the Soviet Union, China, and North Korea. Comparing the US and the Soviet Union, which were the two superpowers of the world and in the Asia Pacific, Soviet military expenditure slightly exceeded that of the US in 1950, according to Table 2-1. The People's Republic of China was established in 1949 and had substantial military spending levels, albeit the levels were much lower than those of the two superpowers. Even without considering data pertaining to North Korea's spending at that time, the Communist side had greater military expenditures in the Asia Pacific region than the US alone. Therefore, the creation of the Japan-US alliance can be explained as balancing behavior against the Communist side. The absence of war between Japan and the US may have occurred because the two countries formed an alliance to ensure an approximate balance of power between the Western and Eastern camps during the Cold War.

However, the picture is quite different when nuclear capabilities and military technologies are considered. Although there was a rough balance between the two camps in terms of military expenditures, the US far exceeded the Soviets with respect

Table 2-1 Military Expenditures of Countries in the Asia Pacific Region (1945-2010)
(Unit: millions of current-year US dollars)

year	US	Taiwan	N. Korea	S. Korea	Japan	China	Soviet/Russia
1945	90,000	–	–	–	4,002	229	8,589
1950	14,559	81	–	32	–	2,558	15,510
1955	40,518	134	–	81	378	2,575	29,542
1960	45,380	223	200	99	454	6,728	36,960
1965	51,827	319	350	112	853	13,788	46,000
1970	77,827	481	700	271	1,650	23,776	77,200
1975	90,948	1,008	879	579	4,535	28,500	128,000
1980	143,981	6,571	1,417	3,309	9,298	28,500	201,000
1985	245,154	4,100	4,196	4,550	14,189	6,350	275,000
1990	289,755	8,690	5,230	10,620	28,730	6,060	128,790
1995	277,834	13,143	5,232	14,179	50,219	32,929	82,000
2000	303,136	17,597	2,091	12,749	45,316	42,000	52,000
2005	495,326	7,978	–	21,504	43,910	29,873	18,768
2010	693,600	8,979	–	25,069	54,357	76,361	41,944

Source: "National Material Capabilities (v4.0)" in Correlates of War based on Singer, J. David. (1987). "Reconstructing the Correlates of War Dataset on Material Capabilities of States, 1816-1985" *International Interactions*, vol.14, pp.115-32.

to nuclear capabilities during the early Cold-War period. Moreover, during the mid-Cold War period, only the US had advanced missile technologies such as multiple independently targetable reentry vehicles (MIRVs). The technological gap between the US and the Communist side makes it doubtful that the conclusion of the Japan-US alliance can be explained in terms of the balance of power.

From the perspective of the balance of threat theory, we may be able to explain the absence of war between Japan and the US as follows: the two countries maintained an alliance to balance against the threat from the Communist side, and thus were not antagonistic toward each other. Although the Western camp possessed more advanced nuclear capabilities in particular and military capabilities in general, it was constantly threatened by the seemingly aggressive orientation of the Soviet Union. As the latter has experienced frequent invasions, it has historically focused excessively on security. To maximize its defensive capabilities, the Soviet Union adopted an expansionist policy, not only expanding its territory in the 20th century, but also establishing satellite states in Europe and Asia. This Soviet stance was perceived by the Western camp as aggressive and threatening. Ultimately, the Japan-US alliance served to balance against the threat presented by the Communist side and to prevent the occurrence of wars.

How would the power transition theory explain the absence of wars between Japan and the US? Although we can understand the international system during the Cold War as bipolar in terms of military expenditure, the US was the sole superpower in economic terms. Thus, it is possible to understand the international system during the Cold War as unipolar, with the US as hegemon. Despite the challenge posed by the Soviets, the US not only maintained its supremacy but also increased the economic gap with the Soviet Union. Japan, a small economy that was devastated at the end of WWII, bandwagoned with the US for security purposes. Although the subsequent increase in Japanese economic power was considered a challenge to the US in the 1980s, the collapse of the Japanese bubble economy ultimately meant that the country never challenged the US militarily.

Liberal Theories

The liberal perspective also provides explanations for the absence of war between Japan and the US during the post-WWII period. The economic relations between the two countries before and after WWII differ markedly. As shown in Table 2-2, the trade volumes between the two countries were insubstantial prior to WWII. The American embargo against Japan in 1941 further weakened the economic interdependence between the two countries. From the perspective of economic interdependence theory, this outcome increased the likelihood of war between them, eventually leading to the Pacific War. However, the post-WWII period witnessed a steady increase in the trade flows between the two countries, which deepened their economic interdependence. This outcome increased each state's dependence on the other; thus, military action became a prohibitively costly option.

The absence of war between the two countries can also be explained in terms of regime type. Although the US has been a democratic country since gaining independence in 1776, Japan was generally not a democracy prior to WWII, as shown in Table 2-3. Applying the democratic peace theory to Japan-US relations, we can argue that prior to WWII, the US was more likely to wage war against the totalitarian country of Japan than other democratic states. This explanation is consistent with the outbreak of the Pacific War between the two countries in 1941. This scenario serves as a clear contrast to the bilateral relations in the post-WWII period. After being democratized by the US in the post-WWII period, Japan came to possess not only a transparent policy-making process, but also peaceful norms. These outcomes

Table 2-2 Japan-US Trade Volume (1900-2010)

(Unit: US$ million)

year		year		year		year		year		year	
1900	38	1920	854	1940	–	1960	2,802	1980	57,540	2000	222,034
1905	106	1925	643	1945	–	1965	4,984	1985	98,479	2005	207,397
1910	106	1930	–	1952	1,023	1970	11,821	1990	145,911	2010	192,583
1915	–	1935	393	1955	1,240	1975	23,959	1995	203,075		

Source: "International Trade, 1870-2009 (v3.0)" in Correlates of War based on Singer, J. David. (1987)."Reconstructing the Correlates of War Dataset on Material Capabilities of States, 1816-1985" *International Interactions*, vol.14, pp.115-32.

Table 2-3 Regime Types in Japan and the US (1900-2010)

year	US	JPN	year	US	JPN	year	US	JPN	year	US	JPN	year	US	JPN
1900	10	1	1925	10	1	1950	10	–	1975	10	10	2000	10	10
1905	10	1	1930	10	1	1955	10	10	1980	10	10	2005	10	10
1910	10	1	1935	10	1	1960	10	10	1985	10	10	2010	10	10
1915	10	1	1940	10	1	1965	10	10	1990	10	10			
1920	10	1	1945	10	–	1970	10	10	1995	10	10			

Note 1: A score of 10 is the most democratic, and −10 is the least democratic.
Note 2: There are no scores for Japan from 1945 to 1950 because it was under the control of General Headquarters (GHQ).
Source: "Polity IV Annual Time-Series 1800-2010" in the Polity IV dataset.

facilitated the development of trust between the two countries, and this trust in turn explains the absence of war between them.

From the neoliberal institutionalist perspective, we can argue that Japan and the US may have developed mutual trust through their joint membership in international institutions over time. Japan and the US were both members of only four international organizations in 1900. The number of international organizations of which both Japan and the US were members remained small until the 1940s. The lack of trust between the two countries could have caused the decrease in the number of joint memberships: however, this decrease also diminished in areas in which the two countries could build trust. Although this result failed to prevent the two countries from commencing war in the 1940s, the increase in joint membership after WWII increased the opportunities for the two countries to build mutual confidence. Whereas this increased membership may not have been the sole reason for the absence of war between the two countries, it certainly helped foster friendly relations.

Constructivist Arguments

This final section applies constructivist normative and cultural arguments to explain the absence of war between Japan and the US during the post-WWII period. Because constructivist arguments on this topic are presented in detail in Japan's section of this book, this section only briefly discusses the application of constructivist arguments.

An important and frequently emphasized change in the post-WWII era is the rise of peaceful norms in Japan. In *Cultural Norms and National Security*, Peter Katzenstein

Table 2-4　Japan-US Dyadic Membership in International Organizations (1900-2005)

year	IOs	year	IOs	year	IOs	year	IOs	year	IOs	year	IOs	year	IOs
1900	4	1915	9	1930	15	1945	2	1965	40	1980	55	1995	69
1905	7	1920	15	1935	19	1955	30	1970	41	1985	57	2000	66
1910	11	1925	14	1940	17	1960	36	1975	48	1990	62	2005	68

Note: There are no data on 1950 because Japan was under the control of GHQ.
Source: "International Governmental Organization (IGO) Data (v2.3)" in Correlates of War based on Singer, J. David. (1987). "Reconstructing the Correlates of War Dataset on Material Capabilities of States, 1816-1985" *International Interactions*, vol.14, pp.115-32.

argues that this change represents a distinctive phenomenon, and that the rise of this norm has prevented Japan from employing force even to resolve security issues. Katzenstein highlights the American occupation and subsequent democratization of Japan as the reasons for the rise of peaceful norms. Based on the democratic peace theory, we can consider the possibility that democratization in Japan and the rise of peaceful norms prompted a mutual recognition that both Japan and the US shared such norms and helped avoid military action to resolve bilateral conflicts.

According to Huntington's clash of civilization argument, the battle lines during the Cold War were between ideologies. Given that Japan and the US have been allies in the liberal camp that share a liberal ideology, they were more likely to cooperate to fight Communist countries than each other, which explains the absence of war between Japan and the US during the Cold War.

Huntington, however, argues that the battle lines after the end of the Cold War changed to lines between civilizations, and categorizes Japan and the US as distinct civilizations (the Japanese and the Western civilizations, respectively). Based on this argument, the likelihood of war between Japan and the US might have increased after the end of the Cold War. Huntington, though, argues that war is most likely between the Western and the Islamic civilizations due to the increased cultural tensions between the two civilizations driven by the population expansion in the Islamic countries that has been pushing people from the Islamic regions to Western countries. Comparing the dyadic relations between Japan and the US to those between Islamic countries and the US, the former set has had a somewhat lower probability of war even after the end of the Cold War. This observation is consistent with the absence of war between Japan and the US.

Causations and Correlations

This chapter has explained the major international relations paradigms and theories and has applied these theories to explain real-world phenomena. This chapter also attempted to provide theoretical explanations by referring to empirical data. To determine whether the theoretical explanations provided in this chapter are accurate, they must be compared to the actual history of Japan-US relations. In the absence of such an analysis, two issues remain. First, even if the occurrence and absence of wars between the two countries appear to be correlated with the explanatory factors presented here, the correlation could be influenced by a third factor (spurious correlations). In that case, the putative explanatory factor would not actually be responsible for the occurrence and absence of war between the two countries. Second, the causal relations between the explanatory factors and the absence of wars could operate in the reverse direction (reverse causality). In other words, the proposed explanatory factor (e.g., increased interdependence) might have resulted from the absence of war. To determine which explanatory factors indeed caused the absence of war between Japan and the US during the post-WWII period, a study of the history of their relations is necessary.

References

Huntington, Samuel P. (1993), "The Clash of Civilizations?" *Foreign Affairs*, vol.72, no.3, pp.22-47.
Mearsheimer, John J. (1990), "Back to the Future: Instability in Europe after the Cold War," *International Security*, vol.15, no.1, pp.5-56.
Russett, Bruce (1993), *Grasping the Democratic Peace: Principles for a Post-Cold War World*, Princeton NJ: Princeton University Press.
Walt, Stephen M. (1987), *The Origins of Alliances*, Ithaca and London: Cornell University Press.
Waltz, Kenneth N. (1979), *Theory of International Politics*, New York: McGraw-Hill.

Recommended Works

1) Betts, Richard K. (2013), *Conflict after the Cold War: Arguments on Causes of War and Peace,* 4th ed., Boston: Pearson.
    A collection of the most prominent works on realism, liberalism, and constructivism. Only the important parts of each work are extracted, making the text readable for undergraduate students.

2) Ikenberry, G. John and Michael Mastanduno, (eds.) (2003), *International Relations Theory and the Asia-Pacific*, New York: Columbia University Press.

This edited volume attempts to understand interstate relations in the Asia Pacific region from various theoretical perspectives.

3) Russett, Bruce M. and John R. O'Neal (2001), *Triangulating Peace: Democracy, Interdependence, and International Organizations*, New York: Norton.

Using statistical analysis, this book explains international relations in terms of the three liberal theories that are explained in this chapter.

CHAPTER 3

Recent World History: The Cold War and Beyond

The Cold War dominated global politics from the end of the Second World War in 1945, until the disintegration of the Soviet Union in 1991. The strategic and ideological rivalry between the two superpowers, the US and USSR, played out in the division of Europe, proxy wars in the developing world, and the nuclear arms race which could potentially end human civilization. After the end of the Cold War, international relations remained complex, with the "War on Terror" from 2001, and the Global Financial Crisis (GFC) since 2008. Shifts in geostrategic relations between the traditional "great powers" and the rapidly developing emerging economies are continuing amidst the ongoing economic and technological processes of globalization.

Beginnings of the Cold War

1940's Europe

Relations between the former Allies of the Second World War quickly deteriorated into the geostrategic rivalry of the Cold War, which dominated international relations from 1945 to 1991. The Cold War had its origins in the Russian Revolution. From 1917, the Soviet Union (officially the Union of Soviet Socialist Republics–the USSR), was led initially by Lenin, eventually succeeded by Stalin after 1924. There was an immediate ideological divide between the new Communist regime in the Soviet Union, and the capitalist Western democracies. The First World War Allies, including the United Kingdom (UK), France, the United States (US) and Japan, carried out failed interventions against the USSR in 1918-22, during the Russian Civil War.

Fear of Communism increased in the West, as it endured the Great Depression of the 1930s, which also saw the rise of fascism in Central Europe. Western suspicion towards the Soviet Union increased over its temporary alliance with Nazi Germany

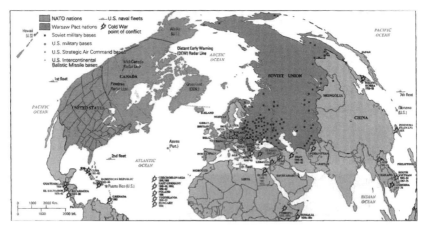

Map 1 Cold War Confrontation
(*Source: University of Michigan*)

in September 1939, when both countries invaded and divided Poland, beginning the Second World War. After the USSR was invaded by Nazi Germany in June 1941, a wartime alliance between the UK, US, the USSR and the other "United Nations", saw the eventual defeat by 1945 of their mutual enemies: Fascist Italy, Nazi Germany, and finally Imperial Japan. However, hegemonic competition between the two dominant postwar military superpowers, the US and USSR was inevitable, given their inherent ideological opposition.

Following the Yalta and Potsdam Conferences in 1945, Germany was divided into Occupied Zones between the wartime Allies: the US, UK and France in the West; the USSR in the East. This soon became an enduring militarized division of Europe between East and West, along the "Iron Curtain", as termed by wartime British Prime Minister Winston Churchill. Determined to ensure their western frontiers would remain secure from invasion, the USSR used its occupation by the Red Army to impose Communist regimes throughout Eastern Europe; Soviet leader Joseph Stalin was determined to secure them as satellite states, subject to control from Moscow. An exception was Yugoslavia, where the Communist regime under Marshal Tito remained outside Soviet dominion. The US and its British and French allies used their liberation of Western Europe to support pro-Western governments, suppressing the influence of local Communist Parties, particularly in France and Italy (Beevor, 2012:

764-767,781-782).

By 1947, a permanent "National Security State" had been established by the US. The wartime Office of Strategic Services (OSS), responsible for espionage and covert action, was upgraded into the Central Intelligence Agency (CIA). The US policy of containment directed against the USSR sought to oppose and reverse Communist influence anywhere in the world. Postwar demobilization was reversed, and a new arms buildup, particularly in nuclear weapons was implemented. A massive foreign aid program, the Marshall Plan, delivered over $13 billion from the US to reconstruct Western European economies, rebuilding them as capitalist democracies capable of resisting Communist encroachment.

The Greek Civil War had already broken out in 1944, demonstrating the ideological contest for control of Europe and global politics was already under way as proxy warfare. By 1948, the Greek Communist guerrillas were suppressed by the Greek National Army, backed by the US and the UK, securing Greece as an anti-Communist outpost in the Balkans. The fascist dictatorships of General Franco in Spain, and of Portugal, were also drawn into the Western sphere of influence. The US and its democratic allies were willing to support authoritarian regimes such as these if they aligned against Communism. This *realpolitik* (the pursuit of power politics, at the expense of morality) would be exercised throughout the Cold War, often at drastic cost to principles of universal human rights and international law.

These principles had been established in 1945 in the United Nations (UN) Charter, aimed at avoiding any repeat of the horrors of world war. Despite its aims of securing international peace and security, the UN was already severely impeded in its operations by the geopolitics of the Cold War. The other main task of the UN was overseeing the transformation towards new independent sovereign states, as the former European colonial powers, the UK, France, the Netherlands and Portugal, relinquished their former Empires. Decolonization took place over the next few decades in the Middle East, Africa and Asia; there were varying levels of success and conflict, as the newly independent states took their place in the international system.

Two of the most important, and flawed postcolonial transitions took place from 1947. The partition of India and Pakistan upon independence from the UK saw over a million killed in communal violence, with the resulting border dispute over divided

Kashmir. The still unresolved rivalry between India and Pakistan would regularly erupt into large-scale armed conflict throughout and beyond the Cold War, in 1965, 1971, and 1999. The formation of the state of Israel followed a failed UN plan to divide the former British Palestinian mandate into two separate Arab and Jewish states. Backed by the US, Israel secured its independence in the first Arab-Israeli war in 1947-49. The USSR would later support Israel's rival Arab neighbors, especially Egypt and Syria.

In the winter of 1948-49, Stalin attempted to drive the Western allies out of their occupied zone in West Berlin, now isolated in Soviet-occupied East Germany, through a land blockade of all economic provisions. The US and UK responded with the Berlin Airlift, a huge deployment of air transport to keep the civilian population fed and supplied. Stalin eventually backed down and ended the blockade. This confrontation openly demonstrated that the US and its allies in Western Europe were now in stark opposition to the USSR and Soviet-controlled Eastern Europe. In response to the blockade, the North Atlantic Treaty Organization (NATO) was formed in 1949.

NATO was established as a military alliance among most states of Western Europe and the US, with Canada and Turkey included, originally aimed at deterring the USSR from any military attack against the West. The division of Germany was confirmed by the formation of two separate states: the Federal Republic of Germany in the West, and the Communist-controlled Democratic Republic of Germany in the East. The USSR set up the Warsaw Pact in 1955, an anti-Western military alliance among its satellite states of Eastern Europe.

The US monopoly on possession of nuclear weapons was broken in 1949 by the first Soviet atomic weapons test, using technical knowledge largely obtained from the West through espionage. The awareness that any international crisis now had the possibility of escalating into nuclear war between the US and USSR would haunt policymakers and the world. The presence of nuclear weapons bestowed a fearful sense of underlying tension in global politics throughout the period of the Cold War, the dire potential of which still endures today (Gaddis, 1986: 23-24).

Cold War Origins in Asia

The Cold War spread to Asia following the defeat of Japan, and its military occupation by the US from 1945 to 1952. The Chinese Civil War recommenced after the Second World War; the Communist Party resumed its war against the Kuomintang (KMT) Nationalist Government, which was backed by the US. Similar to Germany, Korea was divided into occupation zones. Soviet troops initially occupied the North, establishing a Communist regime, the Democratic People's Republic of Korea (DPRK), under Kim Il Sung. US forces occupied the South, backing the anti-Communist Republic of Korea (ROK), under the increasingly autocratic rule of Rhee Syngman. To facilitate its new postwar role, Japan had Article 9 renouncing war enshrined into its new US-designed constitution. This nevertheless allowed the maintenance of Japan's Self Defense Forces (SDF) from 1954. Japan has also hosted US military bases on Okinawa and its mainland to the present day; these would provide important logistic support for the US in the Korean and Vietnam Wars. Under US protection, Japan embarked on its remarkable postwar economic reconstruction.

In Indo-China, from 1946 the Communist *Viet Minh*, led by Ho Chi Minh, fought a rebellion to prevent France from restoring colonial rule (interrupted by Japanese occupation from 1940 to 1945). The *Viet Minh* had been covertly supported by the American OSS as guerrilla forces against Japan during the Second World War, but the roles were quickly reversed after the war. Surrendered Japanese troops in Indochina were temporarily used to secure cities such as Saigon against the *Viet Minh*, pending the return of French military forces. The US was not enthusiastic to see former European colonial powers resume control, but still provided arms to the French, battling the *Viet Minh*'s intensifying guerrilla campaign. Elsewhere in Southeast Asia, from 1945 to 1949, Indonesia fought its war of independence against the Dutch, whose forces were initially supported by the British, again employing surrendered Japanese troops.

In China, the Civil War reached its climax in 1949, when the Communist People's Liberation Army (PLA) drove the KMT from the mainland into perpetual exile on Taiwan. This ensured the separation of Taiwan from direct control by Beijing ever since. The PLA also secured its domination over the western frontier areas of

China, occupying Tibet from 1950; suppression of a Tibetan uprising in 1959 saw the Tibetan Dalai Lama flee into exile. Led by Mao Zedong, the newly victorious People's Republic of China (PRC) was initially supported by the USSR as a fellow Communist ally. However, this alliance would not last into the latter period of the Cold War, as ideological and strategic rivalries would later divide the two Communist powers. The US certainly regarded the Communist takeover of China as confirmation of the threat of international Communism, fearing its growing global power and influence at the expense of the US and its allies.

The Cold War in Asia intensified with the Korean War in 1950. Encouraged and armed by Stalin, North Korea invaded the South, which was almost overrun until US reinforcements based from Japan held back the North's army, in a perimeter around the southeastern city of Pusan. The United Nations authorized a multinational "police action" led by the US to defend South Korea. This unique action by the UN was enabled due to the USSR's boycott of UN Security Council (UNSC) meetings at the time, in protest at Taiwan still holding China's Permanent Five (P5) member seat on the UNSC. Because of this abstention, the Soviet Union forfeited its right to exercise a veto against the US-sponsored defense of South Korea (Stueck, 2010: 266-267).

The US led a counteroffensive against the North Korean forces, liberating Seoul after a dramatic amphibious landing at Inchon. The US/UN commander General Douglas MacArthur then exceeded his authority (resulting in his eventual dismissal by President Harry S. Truman) by advancing into North Korea up to the Chinese border. This was enough provocation for China to intervene; the Soviet-armed Chinese PLA drove US forces back past Seoul by January 1951. A final UN counteroffensive recaptured Seoul; the frontline stabilized roughly along the original dividing 38th parallel from June 1951. Inconclusive bloody fighting dragged on alongside intermittent peace talks, until an armistice was finally agreed in July 1953, after the death of Stalin in March. Despite being a "limited" conventional war, it was fought intensely; around 3 million Koreans died, as well as over 150,000 Chinese forces and around 50,000 US and allied UN forces killed. The division of the Korean peninsula between North and South is entrenched along the highly militarized "demilitarized zone" (DMZ).

In Indochina, France was forced to concede colonial rule in 1954, after its defeat by the *Viet Minh* at the siege of Dien Bien Phu. The UN-brokered Geneva Accords were meant to oversee elections for the whole of Vietnam, but were ignored by the US. As with Korea, Vietnam was divided into North and South: the US backed an anti-Communist regime in the south, the Republic of Vietnam (RVN); the Communists entrenched monopoly control in the north, as the People's Republic of Vietnam (PVN). Neighboring Laos and Cambodia attempted precarious neutrality in their newly-independent kingdoms. Elsewhere in Southeast Asia, in Malaya (later Malaysia) the UK fought an anti-Communist insurgency from 1948 to 1960, as part of the gradual postcolonial disengagement from its former colonies.

The Cold War into the 1950s and 1960s

Early *Détente*

Following the end of the Korean War, in the latter half of the 1950s, tensions temporarily eased between the two superpowers in a period termed *détente* (relaxation) under US President Dwight Eisenhower and Soviet Premier Nikita Khrushchev. The risk of direct armed conflict scaled back, although the nuclear and conventional arms race would continue throughout the Cold War. Part of this effort was diverted into the "space race", initially led by the USSR: the Soviets launched the first satellite into orbit in 1957, and conducted the first manned space flight in 1961. This was a more peaceful means of competition between the US and USSR, as each attempted to portray their economic models as superior; the USSR through its rocket program, the US with its booming postwar mass consumer society.

A "secret war" of espionage was also waged, as the intelligence agencies of the US and USSR and their respective allies conducted covert operations. An overall feeling of paranoia disseminated among both superpowers during the Cold War, as they sought to identify and expose suspected subversive elements within their societies. In the USSR, this meant the suppression of dissidents by its authoritarian secret police (the KGB), and through an extensive "gulag" system of prison camps. China also endured vast suffering due to Mao's disastrous "Great Leap Forward", an economic collectivization program from 1958 to 1962 that led to extreme famine, killing up to

36 million (Jisheng, 2012: 12-17).

In the US, the FBI led by J. Edgar Hoover was concerned with "Communist subversion", neglecting action against the organized crime of the "Mafia". Politicians such as Senator Joseph McCarthy and Republican Vice-President Richard M. Nixon pursued an agenda of hunting out Communist sympathizers within American society. The 1950s also saw the rise of the civil rights movement in the US, aiming for equal treatment of African-Americans. This often saw violent resistance from state and local authorities, especially in the Southern states of the US, with vigilante violence inflicted by the racist Ku Klux Klan movement.

The US and USSR continued to compete for influence in the newly decolonizing states of the developing world, in Asia, Africa and the Middle East. Founded in 1961, the Non-Aligned Movement (NAM) group of states (which still continues, with 125 members) declared a position of relative neutrality, most prominently led by India, Indonesia, and Yugoslavia. Ultimately though, the international relations of countries throughout the world were affected to some extent by the Cold War. In Iran, after attempting to nationalize Western oil companies in 1953, the democratic Mossadeq government was overthrown in a military coup backed by the US and the UK. It was replaced by the pro-Western monarchy of the Shah of Iran, repressing political opposition with an oppressive US-trained secret police force. In Kenya, the UK put down the anticolonial Mau-Mau rebellion from 1952 to 1956, employing a system of internment camps.

In Guatemala, the democratically-elected reformist Arbenz government was overthrown in a US-sponsored military coup in 1954, which installed a repressive military-dominated regime that endured into the 1990s. The US also attempted to replicate the NATO alliance in other regions, with the Southeast Asia Treaty Organization (SEATO) pact from 1954, and in the Middle East with the Central Treaty Organization (CENTO) from 1955. However, these pacts remained weak and ineffectual; they would both unravel by the end of the 1970s.

The USSR violently repressed any dissent in Eastern Europe, invading Hungary in 1956 when an anti-Communist rebellion briefly seized power. Another crisis also arose in 1956 when the Suez Canal in Egypt was nationalized by President Abdel Nasser, who had overthrown the monarchy in a coup in 1952 (a fate which also befell the Iraqi monarchy in 1958). In response, the UK and France coordinated an amphibious assault on the Canal Zone with an Israeli offensive in the Sinai. However, this military action was not supported by the US, and the British and French forces withdrew, under a UN-supervised peace plan. In Algeria, France engaged in a counterinsurgency from 1954, resorting to torture against the rebel anticolonial guerrilla movement. The French were forced to concede independence in 1962, after losing over 25,000 troops; around a million Algerians died.

Crises and Proxy Wars

The period of *détente* continued to unravel following the Cuban Revolution in 1959, when Fidel Castro's rebel movement overthrew the US-backed Batista dictatorship. Castro soon aligned his revolutionary regime with the USSR; after a failed CIA-organized amphibious invasion in the "Bay of Pigs" by Cuban exiles in 1961, the Soviet Union began to covertly set up missile bases in Cuba. Tensions between the superpowers also increased in Europe, after the USSR suddenly erected the Berlin Wall in 1961, to try to stem a flood of asylum seekers fleeing from East Germany to the West.

The deployment of Soviet missiles to Cuba was discovered by US surveillance flights in October 1962. US President John F. Kennedy immediately imposed a naval blockade of Cuba, demanding the USSR withdraw its missiles. In a tense standoff, both sides initially refused to back down, and the world was the closest it has ever come to nuclear war. If the Soviets had forced the blockade, the US would have launched air strikes against Soviet positions in Cuba, possibly followed up by an amphibious invasion. War between the superpowers would have then broken out in Europe, with escalation to full-scale nuclear war sure to have followed.

Fortunately, Soviet Premier Khrushchev backed down, realizing the USSR's numerical disadvantage in nuclear forces was nearly 10 to 1. In return, Kennedy secretly agreed to withdraw US nuclear weapons based in Turkey; balancing against these weapons had been the original motivation for the Soviet missile deployment to Cuba. The Cuban Missile Crisis prompted the USSR into a major expansion of its nuclear arsenal, continuing the vastly expensive arms race with the US. The US also sought to maintain strategic dominance in the Caribbean through a military intervention in the

Dominican Republic's brief civil war in 1965 (Allison, 2012: 256-272).

Proxy Cold War tensions also violently escalated through growing US involvement in Vietnam. From 1957, the *Viet Cong* Communist guerilla insurgency in South Vietnam was backed by the North Vietnamese Army (NVA), with weapons and logistic support from China and the USSR. The US increased the number of its military advisers, from 1961 to bolster a series of corrupt and unstable South Vietnamese regimes. The NVA infiltrated into South Vietnam via the Ho Chi Minh Trail, a logistics route through neutral Laos and Cambodia. The US began an intensive bombing campaign against North Vietnamese targets in 1964, and deployed combat troops from 1965. This escalated both the war, and domestic opposition to it from a growing anti-war movement in the US. US allies also sent troops to support South Vietnam, from Australia, New Zealand, and South Korea, with Thailand hosting US air bases.

The US also backed anti-Communist dictatorships in the Congo, in the Philippines under Ferdinand Marcos, and in Indonesia under General Suharto. A purge by the Indonesian military in 1965-66 led to over 500,000 suspected Communist sympathizers being killed, with the founding President Sukarno ousted by Suharto in 1967. The Arab-Israeli Six-Day War in June 1967 also had proxy Cold War ramifications; Israel was armed and backed by the US, and Egypt, Jordan and Syria were supported by the USSR. The war resulted in Israeli occupation of the Palestinian territories of the West Bank and Gaza, the Sinai Peninsula taken from Egypt, and the Golan Heights from Syria. This defeat radicalized the Palestinian resistance movement, the Palestinian Liberation Organization (PLO). Under its leader Yasser Arafat, the PLO engaged in guerrilla operations against Israel and other radical Islamist groups embarked on terrorist attacks.

In 1968, widespread social and political unrest peaked in many Western countries. Numerous protests and riots such as the May general strike in Paris, were partly driven by the escalation of the Vietnam War. The *Viet Cong* and North Vietnamese Tet Offensive in February 1968 was a tactical defeat, as it was eventually halted by the superior conventional military power of US forces. However, it was a strategic defeat for the US, as it demonstrated America did not have the political endurance needed to win the war. In August 1968, the USSR and other Warsaw Pact forces occupied Czechoslovakia, to suppress the dissident Communist Dubcek regime from attempting liberal reforms. From 1967, China underwent immense political and social turmoil in the Cultural Revolution, as Mao purged ideological opponents by encouraging revolutionary extremism. Ideological divisions and geostrategic rivalry also saw relations between the USSR and China deteriorate, and armed clashes along their border broke out in 1969.

The Cold War in the 1970s and 1980s

More Crises and *"Second Détente"*

The US sought to exploit the Sino-Soviet split in 1972, when US President Richard Nixon visited China. This was partly an attempt to offset the deteriorating situation for the US in Vietnam; the US temporarily invaded Cambodia in 1970 to try to interdict the Ho Chi Minh Trail. The aftermath of this invasion saw a military junta overthrow the Sihanouk monarchy. The disruption caused by massive secret and illegal US bombing of Cambodia allowed the extreme Maoist Khmer Rouge guerrillas to eventually seize power by April 1975. The Khmer Rouge regime under Pol Pot, backed by China, caused the deaths of over 2 million people, due to starvation from enforced collectivization, and mass torture and execution of those considered political opponents.

The US continued to withdraw troops from South Vietnam, amid growing US casualties and domestic anti-war dissent. The final US intervention was a huge bombing campaign in 1972 to stop a North Vietnamese offensive against the South, and to pressure for an armistice. This was achieved with the Paris Peace Accords, signed in January 1973. After US forces withdrew following the armistice, the North was free to complete its final offensive into the South, leading to the fall of South Vietnam in April 1975. Over 58,000 US troops, and over three million Vietnamese were killed in the Vietnam War, the worst military defeat for the US in its history, so far.

Vietnam invaded Cambodia in December 1978, overthrowing the Khmer Rouge, which would continue an insurgency based from Thailand, along with other political factions. In response to the overthrow of its Khmer Rouge ally, in February 1979 China instigated a month-long border war with Vietnam. China was undergoing its great economic transformation by this stage; after the death of Mao in 1976, the new Chinese leader Deng Xiaoping ended the Cultural Revolution, and embarked on a series of free-market reforms. This began to liberalize the economy, and opened China to foreign trade and investment.

In Latin America, the US again proved willing to compromise democratic ideals in the name of anti-Communism. In Chile in September 1973, the CIA sponsored a military coup led by General Pinochet, which overthrew the democratically elected socialist government of Salvador Allende, who died in the takeover. The US also backed military-dominated authoritarian regimes in the region, including Brazil, Argentina and Nicaragua.

During the October 1973 Arab-Israeli War, superpower tensions, were raised as the US again supplied weapons to Israel, and the USSR armed the Arab states, principally Egypt and Syria. However, diplomatic intervention led by US Secretary of State Henry Kissinger helped to implement a ceasefire.

The diplomatic resolution of the 1973 Arab-Israeli War indicated another attempt at relative *détente* to stabilize superpower relations. The war had wider global economic implications; the increasingly wealthy oil-producing Arab countries restricted oil supplies in response to the war. This led to global inflation, which caused recessions in most developed economies. Elsewhere in the Middle East, in 1975 civil war broke out in Lebanon between various religious and political factions; it escalated further with Israeli incursions from 1978 against PLO guerrillas based in southern Lebanon.

The US was by then consumed by political scandal, when President Nixon was forced to resign in 1974 over the Watergate scandal. His administration came under investigation by the US Congress, after it was found to have engaged in a criminal conspiracy to cover up an illegal break-in of the opposition Democratic Party's headquarters. After 1976, Democratic President Jimmy Carter pursued the Strategic Arms Limitation Talks (SALT) between the US and USSR, which agreed to cap levels of strategic nuclear weapons. However, this period of *détente* came to an end after the Soviet invasion of Afghanistan in December 1979, to prop up a client Communist regime which faced an Islamist rebellion. Also by this time, the Iranian Revolution led by Ayatollah Khomeini deposed the Shah in 1979. This established an authoritarian Islamic Republic, and staff of the US embassy were held hostage for over a year afterwards by Iranian militants.

The *"Second"* Cold War

From 1980, superpower tensions continued to rise, as Republican President Ronald Reagan pursued an aggressively anti-Communist foreign policy. Reagan abandonad the SALT arms control process, and commenced a renewed nuclear arms race. New weapons systems were developed, including research for a Ballistic Missile Defense (BMD) system, called the Strategic Defense Initiative, or "Star Wars". The Soviet Union responded with its own nuclear weapons buildup. Intermediate Range Ballistic Missiles (IRBMs) were deployed in Europe by both the US and USSR, generating large protests from the disarmament movement in Western Europe, particularly in West Germany and the UK.

The superpowers again came close to nuclear confrontation. In November 1983, during a simulated nuclear attack drill held by NATO, named "Able Archer", Soviet forces went on high alert, suspecting the US was preparing a real surprise nuclear attack. NATO reacted by increasing its own alert levels. Both sides backed down once the exercise ended. While it received far less public attention than the Cuban Missile Crisis of 1962, the "Able Archer" crisis showed the world remained in danger from potential nuclear war (Gray, 2012: 241-242).

Proxy conflicts continued in developing countries, with opposing rebels or government forces respectively supported by the US and USSR. In Central America, after 1979 the revolutionary *Sandinista* Government of Nicaragua was backed by the USSR; the Reagan Administration covertly supported the far-right *Contra* rebels. This clandestine US military aid was partially funded by illegal secret arms sales to Iran, in defiance of Congress; the "Iran-Contra" scandal was exposed in 1986. In El Salvador from 1979, the US backed an authoritarian military-dominated regime fighting a civil war against Marxist rebels.

In April 1982, the military junta controlling Argentina invaded the British held territory of the Falkland Islands. Prime Minister Margaret Thatcher countered by sending a naval task force, which retook the islands by June, after a short but intense military campaign, leading to the junta's downfall. In October 1983, the US also invaded the tiny Caribbean island nation of Grenada, to overthrow a Cuban-backed military junta which had seized power. In Africa, numerous postcolonial struggles for independence morphed into Cold War proxy wars, including conflicts in Angola, Ethiopia, Mozambique, Somalia, Sudan and Zimbabwe. Nationalist resistance against Soviet domination also rose in Eastern Europe; dissident movements were active in Czechoslovakia, and in East Germany, struggling against the extensive *Stasi* secret police network. In Poland, from 1981 the Solidarity trade union movement, supported by the Catholic Church, led non-violent resistance against a Communist-led military regime.

Conflict continued in the Middle East; Saddam Hussein's *Baath* party regime invaded Iran in 1980, starting a large-scale conventional war which lasted until 1988, with over a million killed. Iraq was armed and supplied by both the US and the USSR, in order to weaken revolutionary Iran, which was hostile to both superpowers. Following an escalation of involvement in Lebanon's civil war by Israel and Syria from 1982, a multinational peacekeeping force intervened in 1983.

It was withdrawn after US Marines suffered severe casualties from a suicide bombing inflicted by *Hezbollah*, a Shi'ite Lebanese militia backed by Iran. The war would drag on until 1990, killing around 150,000. Israel occupied southern Lebanon until 2000; Syria occupied much of the rest of Lebanon until 2005.

The Ending of the Cold War

The Soviet Unraveling

In 1985, the ascension of Mikhail Gorbachev to leadership of the Soviet Union would prove to be a key development towards ending the Cold War. He began a series of reforms aimed at reversing the economic stagnation of the USSR, and to calm rising dissent against the Communist Party. In 1986, Gorbachev instigated the *glasnost* (openness) reforms, allowing greater media freedoms and criticism of the government. In 1987, the *perestroika* (restructuring) reforms were attempted, allowing more private markets to operate in the extremely inefficient and bureaucratic centrally planned economy; improved provision of consumer goods was a major incentive. Gorbachev also sought improved diplomatic relations with the West, and cooperated with Reagan in nuclear arms control; the Intermediate Nuclear Forces Treaty of 1987 led to the removal of US and Soviet IRBMs from Europe. In February 1989, the USSR withdrew its last troops from Afghanistan, having suffered over 15,000 killed by the *mujahadeen* Afghan rebels, which had been backed by Saudi Arabia and the US, via Pakistan. Civil war has continued in Afghanistan long after the Soviet withdrawal though.

However, Gorbachev's attempts at political and economic reform came too late. Throughout Eastern Europe and the various Republics of the USSR, economic decline and rising nationalistic tensions saw widespread protests against Communist rulers. Gorbachev backed away from using force to suppress this dissent, as he admitted the USSR would no longer prop up its client Communist states with the Soviet military. By 1989, unstoppable momentum against Communist rule led to its downfall in East Germany, Hungary, Czechoslovakia, Albania, and Bulgaria.

The Ceausescu dictatorship in Romania did attempt to violently suppress a popular uprising in December 1989, but the army turned against the regime. In November 1989, the Berlin Wall "fell"; Germany unified the next year, and democratic elections were held throughout Eastern Europe. The USSR was dissolved on December 26, 1991, after the former Soviet Republics declared independence, led by the Baltic countries. With these dramatic events, the Cold War was suddenly and unexpectedly over.

Post-Cold War Crises

This brief period of optimism in global affairs was soon challenged. In China, on June 4th 1989, pro-democracy demonstrators in Beijing were violently driven from Tiananmen Square by the People's Liberation Army, with around a thousand killed. Unlike the USSR, the Chinese Communist Party was determined to use military force to maintain its authoritarian monopoly on political power. In December 1989, the US invaded Panama to overthrow the Noriega regime, which the US had backed in the Cold War, to secure control of the Panama Canal Zone. In August 1990, Iraq invaded neighboring Kuwait. Mobilizing over half a million US and allied troops, US

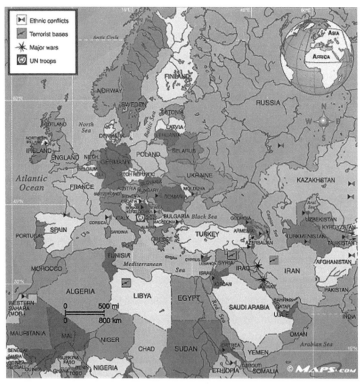

Map 2 Post-Cold War Europe, Middle East, and North Africa, 1990-1995
(Source: maps.com)

President George H.W. Bush ordered the liberation of Kuwait, authorized by the UN Security Council; most of the expenses for this operation were funded by Japan and Germany. In a six-week air and ground campaign from February 1991, US-led forces routed the Iraqi army, but left Saddam Hussein's regime intact, allowing a bloody suppression of uprisings by Iraqi Shi'ites and Kurds.

Nationalism also violently reasserted itself in wars following the break-up of Yugoslavia from 1991 to 1995, and also in former Soviet republics in the Caucasus and Central Asia. An intense war was fought by Russia against a separatist rebellion in Chechnya from 1994 to 1996, and again from 1999 until 2009. Cold War proxy conflicts morphed again into "weak state" civil wars, such as in Afghanistan, Algeria, Angola, and Somalia. The UN greatly increased the number and scale of its peacekeeping operations, but some were drastic failures, in Bosnia, Somalia, and in Rwanda, which suffered a horrific genocide in 1994. This conflict spilled over into a wider war in the neighboring Congo, which has led to the deaths of around 5 million people. Newly independent Eritrea engaged in a border war with Ethiopia from 1998 to 2000, proving interstate wars were still possible in the post-Cold War era.

After the Cold War

Post-Cold War Era Progress

More positively, peace and democracy seemed to advance in many countries and regions with end of the Cold War. Central and South America became largely peaceful and democratic, except for Communist Cuba, and Peru and Colombia, where Marxist insurgencies were fuelled by narcotics smuggling. East Asia saw more democratic governments emerge, beginning with a "people power" revolution, which overthrew the Marcos dictatorship in the Philippines in 1986.

Democracy was gained soon after in South Korea and Taiwan. In 1998, the Suharto dictatorship was deposed in Indonesia after a popular uprising, sparked by the regional "Asian Financial Crisis".

A UN peacekeeping force in Cambodia from 1991 to 1993 led to its first democratic election, and the end of the Khmer Rouge rebel movement. Some of the long-running wars in Africa finally came to an end, such as in Ethiopia and Mozambique. In South Africa, the racist *apartheid* system of white minority rule was finally replaced by democratic government in 1994, after African National Congress leader Nelson Mandela was released from prison, and elected President (Ackerman and Duvall, 2000: 364-368, 381-395).

In 1992 the European Union (EU) was formed, developing out of the European Economic Community (EEC) free trade zone. Along with the expansion of NATO membership into Eastern Europe, this seemed to confirm the Cold War was fading into history. After NATO conducted an air campaign against Serbia in 1999, to resolve the Kosovo War in former Yugoslavia, this final eruption of nationalistic violence in Europe appeared to reach its climax. Optimists hoped the 21st century would see further progress in peace, international law and prosperity. The forces of economic globalization, driven by the communications technologies of satellites and the internet, and through cheaper air travel and commercial shipping, saw more open markets, foreign investment and trade overcoming constraints imposed against them throughout the Cold War.

The "War on Terror" and the Global Financial Crisis: a new multipolar order?

The terrorist attacks on September 11, 2001 against the US by the extremist Islamist group *al-Qaeda*, brought an end to the perceived peace and optimism of the post-Cold War era. *Al-Qaeda's* leader Osama Bin Laden had been a Saudi organizer of the *mujahedeen* against the Soviet occupation of Afghanistan; he returned to base his organization there after the extremist *Taliban* movement took control of most of the country in 1997. Bin Laden aimed to drive Western influence out of the Middle East, and so ordered the 9/11 terrorists to infiltrate the US via Germany, to hijack airliners. They struck the Twin Towers of the World Trade Center in New York City, and the Pentagon in Washington; and another airliner was brought down in Pennsylvania. US President George W. Bush vowed a "War on Terror", in revenge for the nearly 3,000 killed in the attacks. This resulted in the US-led invasions of Afghanistan in October 2001, and more controversially, of Iraq in March 2003 (Bergen, 2011: 60-67, 155-172).

The Bush Administration claimed Iraq had frequently violated UN sanctions and weapons inspections following the 1991 Gulf War, and was developing Weapons of Mass Destruction and links with *al-Qaeda*. These claims proved to be false, based on manipulated intelligence reports. Both the *Taliban* in Afghanistan and Saddam Hussein's regime in Iraq were quickly overthrown. However, long-running insurgencies against US-led forces and the post-invasion governments established by the US have persisted to the present day. US combat forces were withdrawn from Iraq after 2011, and NATO's combat forces withdrawn from Afghanistan after 2014. However, American and allied military advisers and air power, including drone strikes, have still remained involved in these countries, particularly after the Islamic State terrorist group seized control of swathes of territory in Iraq and Syria in 2014.

Terrorist attacks claimed by Islamic State have since regularly occurred in Europe and the US, as well as the Middle East.

While wars are no longer occurring at the same rate of intensity or lethality as during much of the Cold War, as of 2017, armed conflicts were ongoing in over 30 countries, displacing over 65 million people, including over 22 million refugees. Russia invaded Georgia in a brief interstate war in 2008, and has supported separatist rebels in eastern Ukraine since 2014. A luridly violent conflict between drug cartels and the government has raged in Mexico. Other civil wars and insurgencies persist in South Asia and Africa, particularly in Nigeria, Somalia, South Sudan and the Central African Republic. Israel waged armed incursions against the militant Islamist group *Hezbollah* in Lebanon in 2006; and against the Palestinian militant group *Hamas* in the Gaza Strip, in 2008-09, and again in 2012. Previewed by the Green Revolution protests in Iran, violently suppressed in 2009, the Arab Spring popular uprisings against authoritarian regimes began in Tunisia in December 2010, and spread through the Middle East. Dictatorships were temporarily overthrown in Egypt and Yemen, and in Libya in 2011, supported by a NATO air campaign against the Gaddafi regime. However, the uprising against the Assad regime in Syria since March 2011 degenerated into an intractable civil war, which also occurred in Yemen and Libya (IISS, 2012: 9-30).

From 2008, a property bubble in the US lurched the global economy into its greatest financial crisis since the Great Depression of the 1930s. This caused recession and high unemployment in the US and Europe, from which there has only been a tepid recovery. In the wake of this crisis, there has been a rise of nationalist populism in many democracies around the world. This was notably seen in 2016, when the UK voted to leave the EU, and Republican candidate Donald Trump was elected US President. Multipolar 'great power' rivalry has returned to global politics, where Russia and China are asserting growing geostrategic influence to varying degrees. This is challenging the previous dominance of the US, Western Europe and Japan, particularly the competition for international influence stemming from China's long-running high economic growth (Kaplan, 2012: 100-102).

The end of the Cold War brought great hopes for international peace, prosperity and freedom, as the world drew back from the prospect of nuclear conflict between the superpowers. However, numerous serious challenges remain in global politics. These include: climate change and environmental damage, sustainable development, persistent poverty, terrorism, proliferation of weapons of mass destruction, refugees and protection of human rights, and ongoing instability in the global economy. It is unclear whether current institutions of international law and global governance, such as the UN, the G20, and regional groupings such as the EU, the African Union, ASEAN, APEC, and the East Asia Summit are able to successfully handle contemporary international relations, which remain incredibly complex.

References

1) Ackerman, Peter, and Jack Duvall, (2000), *A Force More Powerful: A Century of Nonviolent Conflict*, New York: Palgrave
2) Allison, Graham, "The Cuban Missile Crisis", in Steve, Smith, *et al,* (2012), *Foreign Policy: Theory, Actors, Cases*, Oxford: Oxford University Press
3) Beevor, Antony (2012), *The Second World War*, London: Weidenfeld & Nicolson
4) Bergen, Peter (2011), *The Longest War: The Enduring Conflict Between America and Al-Qaeda*, London: Simon & Schuster
5) Gaddis, John Lewis (1986), "The Long Peace: Elements of Stability in the Postwar International System", *International Security,* Vol.10, No.4, pp.23-24.
6) Gray, Colin S. (2012), *War, Peace and International Relations: An Introduction to Strategic History,* Abingdon: Routledge
7) International Institute for Strategic Studies (IISS) (2012), *The Military Balance*, Vol.112, Issue 1
8) Jisheng, Yang (2012), *Tombstone: The Great Chinese Famine 1958-1962*, New York: Farrer, Straus and Giroux
9) Kaplan, Robert D. (2012), *The Revenge of Geography: What the Map Tells Us About Coming Conflicts and the Battle Against Fate*, New York: Random House
10) Stueck, William, "The United Nations, the Security Council, and the Korean War", in Lowe Vaughan, Adam Roberts, Jennifer Welsh, and Dominik Zaum (eds.) (2010), *The United Nations Security Council and War: The Evolution of Thought and Practice Since 1945*, Oxford: Oxford University Press

Recommended Works

1) Gaddis, John Lewis (2005), *The Cold War: A New History*, London: Penguin

   A highly regarded, eloquent and dramatically written general history of the Cold War by a distinguished Yale history professor.

2) McMahon, Robert (2003), *The Cold War: A Very Short Introduction*, Oxford: Oxford University Press

   Part of Oxford University Press's *Very Short Introduction* series, this is a concise, easily read and basic outline of the major events and developments of the Cold War.

3) Yergin, Daniel (1990), *Shattered Peace: The Origins of the Cold War*, Harmondworth: Penguin

   Considered a now-classic work on how and why the growing ideological and strategic rivalry between the victorious Allies of the Second World War slipped into the dangerous confrontation of the Cold War.

CHAPTER 4

Peace and Security: Nuclear Deterrence and Disarmament

In this chapter, basic terms and concepts such as defense, deterrence, disarmament, arms control and MAD will be explained at the outset. Then, basic concepts of Prisoner's Dilemma and Chicken Game will be explained in order to understand why it is hard to achieve complete disarmament. Following it, efforts that humankind has made in trying to rein in the nuclear arms race will be described somewhat in detail. The focus is on non-proliferation of nuclear weapons, but chemical and biological weapons will be also mentioned.

Basic Terms

Terms such as defense and disarmament are used somewhat interchangeably because we may not have a clear-cut understanding as to the difference between these terms. Defense and disarmament are similar in philosophy since they focus more on physical capabilities than the human mind. Deterrence and arms control are similar in their focus on the human mind.

Defense and Deterrence

What is the difference between defense and deterrence? Defense is to protect, for instance, one's territorial integrity by using physical means when being attacked. That is, the assumption behind it is that a physical attack has happened and one is compelled to use one's own physical means to repel it. The focus is on the physical capabilities. Deterrence, on the other hand, is more focused on the human mind so that an aggression itself would not happen, even if an adversary is contemplating doing so. It is an effort by means of persuasion, threat, rewards and so on, to prevent an action that might harm one's interests from taking place. Deterrence is to make one's adversary(s) realize that it is not in her (their) interest(s) to initiate an aggression by influencing her (their) estimated cost and benefit calculation(s). That is, an attack would cause her

Table 4-1 Two Major Concepts of Deterrence

Concept	Goal	Means
Deterrence by punishment	Unbearable damage	MAD
Deterrence by denial	Damage limitation	Missile defense

(them) more losses than gains.

There are basically two kinds of nuclear deterrence: deterrence by punishment and deterrence by denial. The former refers to a situation where the estimated gains by the initiator would be (preferably by far) outweighed by the estimated losses from her (i.e., the initiator's) opponent's retaliatory actions. The latter refers to a situation where the initiator can expect little gain in the first place, thereby negating any incentive to attack first.

The quintessential example of the former type is Mutual Assured Destruction (MAD), which is based on the "triad" of ICBMs (Inter-Continental Ballistic Missile), SLBMs (Submarine-Launched Ballistic Missile) and long-range strategic bombers. MAD was formulated in the early 1960s around the time of the John F. Kennedy administration in the US. This is the doctrine that both antagonists (the US and USSR in the Cold War era) know for sure (assured) that they would suffer unbearable destruction by a nuclear exchange. The scenario is as follows: a first strike targets an opponent's military capabilities such as missile silos and communications facilities in order to cut down her retaliatory second strike capabilities significantly. A retaliatory second strike aims at population centers and economic bases of the initiator country. If this second strike is successful as to make the destruction unbearable, then the initiator country has no incentive to wage a first strike. Therefore, a nuclear war would be avoided.

The Anti-Ballistic Missile (ABM) Treaty that was signed in May 1972, along with SALT I (explained later) between the US and USSR, was interpreted to mean that the MAD system was institutionalized. The treaty limited the number of ABMs that could be deployed to 100 each at initially two sites, then at only one site. It was to make sure that neither side had effective intercept capability against retaliatory second strike missiles, thereby assuring unacceptable damage to both of them.

Deterrence by denial seems akin to defense, but there is a crucial difference. It is to persuade the opponent not to wage a war in the first place. This is best exemplified by ballistic missile defense (BMD), or simply missile defense (MD). BMD is designed to shoot down any incoming missiles so that a first strike would not have any intended effect. This was what US President Ronald Reagan had in mind when he gave the Strategic Defense Initiative (SDI) speech in March 1983. Its ultimate goal was to have a perfect space-based shield against any incoming Soviet missiles by intercepting every one of them in several stages. Thus, the US would suffer no damage from a Soviet attack.

The SDI in its ideal form was more than alarming from the Soviet perspective because it meant that the US would have little disincentive to initiate aggression against the USSR. Then, the USSR would have no choice but to increase its nuclear capabilities in order to penetrate this shield. This is a classic case of the security dilemma (explained later).

Arms control and Disarmament

Arms control and disarmament are terms that tend to be used interchangeably in everyday conversation because they both aim to achieve a world of no wars and little damage from conflicts. The difference is the means or path to achieve it. The idea behind disarmament is simple and straight forward. The world would be safer and war may be hard to fight if we can get rid of any arms as such. As long as there are no weapons, there must be little damage from any conflict. How to implement disarmament, however, is not at all easy. For example, what about a knife? A knife is necessary to prepare food. A knife, however, can be used for ulterior purposes as well as for legitimate self-defense. This argument goes for what are called dual-purpose technologies. It may not be the tools per se that should be blamed, but the intent of the humans who utilize them. Out of these realizations, the idea of arms control was born.

Arms control is more focused on the human mind, that is, on incentives and cost-benefit calculations of decision-makers. There are basically three objectives in arms control: the first and foremost is to lessen the possibility of war. It is people who decide whether or not to initiate a war in order to achieve some purpose. A way to avoid a war is by deterrence. Arms control aims to reduce incentives or increase disincentives for physical conflicts. Therefore, in an extreme case, according to the arms control school, an arms build-up may be condoned if it is deemed to be contributing to lessen the possibility of a conflict. This is where disarmament and arms control are starkly different. The second objective is to reduce the damage from a war once it starts. The third is to cut down the social and economic costs associated with armaments such as defense expenditure.

Prisoner's Dilemma and the Chicken Game

Prisoner's Dilemma

Why can't humanity get rid of arms altogether despite persistent calls for disarmament? Why is it so hard to achieve? This difficulty is explained by using a game theoretic concept called Prisoner's Dilemma (PD). The basic scenario of the PD is as follows: there are two criminals who were caught red-handed committing petty theft, thus a guilty verdict is certain. They are also suspected of having committed a major bank robbery, which they indeed did. There is plenty of circumstantial evidence, but not enough to convict them. A confession of guilt by one of them will suffice. Since it assumed that plea bargaining is legal, the law enforcement side offers that the one who confesses will be let go without any criminal charge, if only one of them confesses. If both of them confess, then the offer is cancelled. The one who refuses is lying, and thus will get a longer sentence than usual. They are in solitary confinement and cannot communicate. Namely, no collusion is possible.

The lengths of imprisonment are as follows: first, let us assume one gets 3 years' incarceration for the theft and also 3 years for the bank robbery. If both confess, they each get 6 years. However, if only one confesses, the one who does is set free. The other one who does not gets punished, which will add 3 more years' incarceration. This will be 3+3+3=9 years. Then, we get the following in a matrix form called a payoff matrix.

First, one needs to know how to read the matrix below. Both players (prisoners)

		Prisoner B	
		not confess	confess
Prisoner A	not confess	3, 3	9, 0
	confess	0, 9	6, 6

have 2 choices, "confess" or "not confess". The left side of each cell is the payoff (the length of incarceration in years) for prisoner A, the right side for B. When both players choose to "not confess", then the outcome is represented in the upper-left cell. The payoff is 3 years for each. When A does "confess" and B does "not confess", it gets to the lower-left cell. A is released and B gets 9 years in this case. How would these players make a choice?

Let us first think of A. A does not know how B would choose because there is no communication between them. So, A will decide which to select based on B's choice. For example, when B chooses "not confess", A gets 3 years for "not confess" and is set free for "confess". The shorter the sentence, the better. Then, A chooses "confess". When B chooses "confess", A gets 9 years for "not confess" and 6 years for "confess". Then, A chooses to "confess". After all, it is the case that A should always select "confess" whichever B chooses. Likewise, from B's perspective. That is, B should always choose "confess" whichever A chooses. The outcome is that both A and B should select "confess" all the time. Then, the answer for this game is the lower-right cell of (6, 6). This is called the Nash Equilibrium (NE). One should bear in mind, though, that this is from the perspective of prisoner A and B as an individual.

A totally different picture emerges, however, if taken from the viewpoint of the collective (society or community). A state might form an alliance (collective) such as the Japan-US alliance. Then, instead of one's own "national interest", one needs to think about the interest of the alliance as such. Let us suppose that prisoners A and B form a community or collective and can be regarded as one single player. To illustrate the point, let's suppose that you are a member of your university's varsity basketball team, which has 20 members. Let's suppose that you represent your basketball team when there is a meeting of various varsity teams. Then, you yourself are representing the whole basketball team at the meeting. Your basketball team can be considered to be a single player in this kind of setting.

Let's assume that it would be possible to add up the years in each cell, which becomes the payoff for the single collective (player). Then, it is easy to see that the above NE is the worst this collective player can get since it is 6+6=12. The best is the upper-left cell of only 6 years (3+3). It means that both players should select "not confess", the exact opposite of the conclusion above. The upper-left cell is much better than the lower-right cell for even A and B as an individual because A as well as B gets only 3 years, compared to NE's 6 years. This is an irony because the upper-left cell that will never be achieved from an individual perspective[1] is much better even for A and B as an individual.

These players are assumed to be in solitary confinement and cannot work out any agreement. Would this dilemma be solved by making communication possible? It is not so simple, unfortunately. Let us assume that they agreed or promised to each other to "not confess". If you have 100% confidence that the other player keeps the promise, then you should keep it as well. However, if you have even a miniscule amount of doubt about the other player, you should not keep your promise of "not confess" in order to protect yourself. The motive is to protect yourself, not to deceive and betray the other player. Playing it safe is called being risk-averse.

Let us suppose you are A. You did promise that you would choose "not confess". If you are 100% confident that B also keeps his promise, then the outcome is (3, 3). However, when you are not so sure, then you have to think of the possibility, no matter how slim it may be, that B would not keep his promise and dupe you. In that case, you get 9 years, the worst possible sentence. If you want to play it safe and do not want to be fooled, you should select "confess". If this is a matter of life and death, as is often the case of war, it is more than prudent to be risk-averse. You do not want to risk your country's catastrophic loss because of your false optimism that the other country is trustworthy. In this sense, communication may not be a panacea as is hoped. It does no doubt help, nevertheless, in confidence building and mutual understanding. So, we are back to square one. It is the level of confidence and trust in the other player that is crucial, not communication as such. It is easy to say that trust is crucial, but hard to build it. It is trust of the 100% kind that is needed, for that matter. It would be almost impossible, especially among those that are contemplating armed conflicts.

Security Dilemma.

The same risk-averse behavior explained above can be applied to the concept of the Security Dilemma. The Security Dilemma refers to a situation in which actions by a state to secure its own safety are interpreted by another state (other states) as aggressive actions that would threaten the latter. This leads to heightened tensions that might increase the chances of armed conflict. Say, for example, you feel insecure because your neighboring country is increasing its defense budget rapidly. The neighbor merely wants to have better capabilities to defend itself and has no intention whatsoever to utilize them for offensive purposes. However, this beefed-up capability might possibly be utilized against you. Then, you want to play it safe (risk-averse) and you yourself should also increase defense capabilities. So, the security dilemma situation ensues.

This outcome of the security dilemma (arms race) is equivalent to the NE in the PD above. No wonder no nuclear weapon states[2] have gotten rid of their nuclear weapons despite their lip service for a world without nuclear weapons. Keep in mind that it is a matter of precaution and prudence so that one will not be put into a dangerous corner by optimistically believing a promise made. What the argument so far suggests is that the idea of unilateral arms reduction that might induce a virtuous cycle of mutual arms reduction would have little chance to commence. The problem is who should start first, especially because the starter of unilateral arms reduction knows that there is a chance that it might be cheated.

The Chicken Game and Brinksmanship

The Chicken Game describes a dangerous brinksmanship kind of situation. North Korea's harsh diplomatic behavior and bellicose statements such as "Putting Seoul in a sea of fire" come to mind. The game's scenario usually goes as follows: There are two bosses of two rival youth gangs. Their bosses want to brag about their daredevil nature. It is of critical importance for them and for their groups who will come out on top. So, it is decided to see who is more daring by driving cars at full throttle on a straight road towards each other, which will ultimately lead to a head-on collision. They both fear death, no matter how plucky they pretend to be. They also know that they will die when collided. They have two choices, either go straight ahead or swerve. When you go ahead anyway, you risk a certain death that you fear the most. Nonetheless, you despise being disparaged as a chicken by swerving. Of course, you want to become a hero by not swerving. If both chickened out and swerve, it is a draw. Then, you would get the following kind of matrix. What is important is the order of preferences, not the exact figures.

The upper-left cell of $(-1, -1)$ is when they both swerved. Hence, they have lost bragging rights and their group mates would say, "Hey, he is just a chicken boy!" So, they get a slight minus. The lower-right cell is a minus infinity because it means death. For the upper-right and lower-left cells, $(-20, 50)$ and $(50, -20)$ respectively, it is a shame to swerve for a boss because swerving shows he is really a chicken. This is especially so because the other guy did stick to his word in spite of possible death. He became a hero. Thus, the guy who chickened out gets a lot of minus, -20, and the guy who did not blink gets a lot of plus, 50.

		B	
		swerve	not swerve
A	swerve	$-1, -1$	$-20, 50$
	not swerve	$50, -20$	$-\infty, -\infty$

Let us see how this game would be played out. It is assumed that there is communication between A and B in this game. Your choice is contingent upon the other player's choice. For example, from A's perspective, you have no choice but to choose "swerve" when B chooses "not swerve", and vice versa from B's viewpoint. This game is of a menacing nature because you have to make the other guy "swerve". A gentle persuasion would not suffice because it is against the other guy's interest. The only way to make him "swerve" is to tell him that you are determined to go straight ahead no matter what, a kind of ultimatum. However, this ultimatum carries little credibility since it is common knowledge for both of them that they are afraid of death. As long as you fear death, your interest is to "swerve" to avoid colliding at the end of the day. Then, it will be an endless game of brinkmanship and bluffing, in which both threaten to "not swerve" no matter what. Then, the game becomes a matter of who blinks first.

There is no clear way out of this quagmire. One can imagine an unconventional way to get one's wish realized, though. It is to constrain your choices so that you will have no possibility but to go straight ahead even though you want to "swerve". For example, you cut off the steering wheel so that you cannot swerve. The other guy realizes this immediately and has no choice but to "swerve" in order not to die. To act first is crucial. Once it becomes clear that your rival can do nothing about handling the car, this situation becomes a given to the other guy, who is forced to act accordingly. Namely, he has to swerve.

Cuban Missile Crisis

Let us analyze the Cuban missile crisis of 1962 by utilizing the concept of the chicken game. Humankind came razor-thin close to a nuclear war in this crisis. It started when the US found out that the USSR installed medium range missiles in Cuba that could hit the US heartland. It was also found that a Soviet fleet with missiles on board was heading towards Cuba. The US President John F. Kennedy decided to impose a naval quarantine (blockade) against the incoming fleet and announced its imposition to the world so that it would appear that he was dead-set determined to make the quarantine a red line. He also ordered the US military to be on the highest alert. He wanted to show his determination to the Soviets that he would never, ever flinch. There was of course a possibility that he might blink at the end of the day, so he made it deliberately difficult to do a flip-flop. It appeared as if the die were cast and it was in the Soviet hand. The USSR faced a really difficult decision. If they decided to cross the declared red line, it might well provoke a nuclear horror. Their nuclear might in this region was far outnumbered by the US, too. On the other hand, if they did not, they would most likely be regarded as a chicken that could not stand up to a US challenge. The USSR's final decision was to turn back the fleet, which is what the US desired. The US also made it easier for the USSR to accept it by withdrawing missiles from Turkey, for example.

To recap, the US took the first action and declared that the red-line decision was final and a given. But, it was of course reversible at the last minute. The USSR had to make a final judgment as to the credibility of the US announcement. The USSR eventually took a cautious, risk-averse kind of action, as the above discussion suggested, because to do otherwise may as well mean the end of human civilization.

Halting the Spread of Weapons of Mass Destruction

Weapons of Mass Destruction (WMD) refers to nuclear, chemical, and biological weapons. In this section, we will mainly talk about nuclear weapons in the order of, first, the fear of fallout because of atmospheric nuclear tests, which gave birth to the nuclear test ban movement. Next, efforts to halt the spread of nuclear weapons in the section on the Non-Proliferation Treaty (NPT) and also regional and legal efforts to ban nuclear weapons will be described. Then, some brief discussion on chemical and biological weapons will also be made at the end.

Dawn of the Nuclear Age and Fear of Nuclear Fall-out

The 20th century can be said to be the age of nuclear weapons. During WWII, the US (with some UK cooperation) had conducted the secret Manhattan project to develop atomic bombs (A-bomb). This was a really big and costly (more than US$ 2 billion) project, in which nearly a hundred thousand scientists and engineers were involved. The first ever detonation of an A-bomb, which was of a yield of about 20Kt (kilotons), was conducted in Alamogordo, New Mexico, on July 16th, 1945. The US dropped an A-bomb on Hiroshima on August 6th and on Nagasaki on the 9th successively, estimated to have killed more than 140 and 70 thousand respectively by the end of 1945. This became a trauma in Japanese minds and they developed a so-called nuclear allergy.

The US had conducted a series of A-bomb tests in rapid fashion. The first hydrogen bomb (H-bomb) test was done at the Eniwetok Atoll in the Marshall Islands in November 1952. The USSR tested its first A-bomb at Semipalatinsk, Kazakhstan (formerly part of the USSR), in August 1949. So far, besides the US and USSR, the UK, France, China, India, Pakistan and North Korea are known to have tested nuclear devices. The H-bomb test called Castle Bravo in March 1954 was the largest by the US, which contaminated a Japanese tuna fishing trawler called the Lucky Dragon No.5 (Daigo Fukuryu Maru). Her 23 crew members suffered from radioactive fallout, one of whom died directly from it.

Banning Nuclear Tests

The vast majority of early nuclear tests were conducted in the open atmosphere and this caused a great deal of fear about radioactive contamination. This fear inspired nuclear test-ban movements all over the world, particularly in Japan. The Partial (Limited) Test Ban Treaty (PTBT or LTBT) was born out of this fear as well as the Cuban missile crisis. It prohibited any nuclear test detonation, except underground. It had gradually lessened the fear of nuclear fallout. This prohibition would have in effect hindered the nuclear development of late-comers such as France and China, who had not yet been able to conduct an underground test. Therefore, they refused to sign the PTBT. France tested her first A-bomb in February, 1960, in Algeria, a French colony back then. China conducted her first A-bomb test in October, 1964, in Lop Nor in the Xinjiang Uyghur Autonomous Region.

Table 4-2 Nuclear Test Ban and Non-Proliferation Treaties

Name	Open for Signature	Entry into Force	Number of Member States
PTBT	August, 1963	August, 1963	3=US, UK, USSR (Russia)
CTBT	September, 1996	Not Yet	166 (ratified)
NPT	June, 1968	March, 1970	191

as of December 2017

The next step from "partial" must be "comprehensive". However, it took more than 30 years after the PTBT to agree on the Comprehensive (Nuclear) Test Ban Treaty (CTBT). It is because the US and USSR had aggressively built up their nuclear capabilities and nuclear tests were necessary to improve their weapons, so they reasoned. The end of the Cold War changed it all. One "peace dividend" was a nuclear test moratorium by the 5 nuclear weapon states, except China. With this benign atmosphere, Presidents Clinton (US) and Yeltsin (Russia) agreed in April 1993 to commence negotiations for a CTBT.

The CTBT's Article 1 says in part: "not to carry out any nuclear weapon test explosion or any other nuclear explosion". No explosion means no chain reactions that would result in a nuclear yield. Put another way, any test that would result in no yield, which is called a sub-critical test, would not be prohibited. The prospect for its entry into force (EIF) is dim indeed because of Article 14, which requires ratification of 44 specific states, of which India, Pakistan and North Korea have not signed. Furthermore, the US, China, Iran, and Israel have signed it, but have not ratified yet. All 5 nuclear weapon states, however, have abstained from nuclear explosive tests since China and France last tested in 1996. One significant feature of the CTBT is that a robust on-site inspection (OSI), which is in effect a "challenge OSI"[3], can be conducted.

One further step will be the Fissile Material Cut-off Treaty (FMCT). Nuclear weapons would be neither produced nor maintained without fissile materials, practically speaking. The FMCT is to achieve this goal. However, its negotiation has not yet started.

NPT

The concern for horizontal nuclear proliferation led to the Treaty on the Non-Proliferation of Nuclear Weapons (NPT). The NPT is to prevent any more countries from possessing nuclear weapons. US President John Kennedy expressed a fear in 1963 that, "I am haunted by the feeling that by 1970, unless we are successful, there may be 10 nuclear powers instead of 4, and by 1975, 15 to 20." (Williams, et el, 2012: 24). We know that we have more nuclear weapon possessing countries than in the time of Kennedy, but not as bad as he was afraid of. This arguable success can be at least partly attributable to the NPT.

The NPT is a two-tier treaty which can be said to be discriminatory because those that are designated to be nuclear weapon states can possess nuclear weapons legally and legitimately, whereas the other non-nuclear weapon states cannot. The US, USSR (Russia), UK, France and China are the declared nuclear weapon states. The NPT was extended indefinitely in May 1995.

The NPT has three key elements: The first and foremost is to prevent the spread of nuclear weapons and technologies. There are only a few stubborn hold-out states; namely, India, Pakistan, and Israel. North Korea joined the NPT in December 1985, but declared withdrawal from it in January 2003. India and Pakistan conducted nuclear tests in May 1998; North Korea 6 times starting October 2006 as of December 2017. India also conducted a so-called "peaceful" nuclear test in May 1974. Israel is assumed to have nuclear weapons.

The second is to strive for the cessation of the arms race and to achieve general and complete disarmament. The NPT merely requires to "pursue negotiations in good faith" toward disarmament, however. This phrase is obviously a matter of contention because the term "in good faith" is opaque indeed.

The third pillar is an active promotion of peaceful nuclear technology such as nuclear energy. It is deemed as the "inalienable right" of member states, especially non-nuclear weapon states. It may seem somewhat ironic after the Fukushima nuclear accident in March 2011 in Japan, but nuclear energy was a great hoped-for source of energy before. This emphasis on nuclear energy was a quid pro quo requested by the non-nuclear weapon states for not possessing nuclear weapons.

One problem in the NPT is that its member states might cheat. Iraq under the Saddam Hussein regime was a case in point. The IAEA (International Atomic Energy Agency) confirmed after the first Gulf War of 1991 that Iraq did conceal its nuclear weapons program, which did not go well, despite the fact that the IAEA had been issuing clean bills for Iraq. This was because the IAEA had no authority to inspect non-declared nuclear facilities. Iraq did not declare her secret facilities on purpose. This deficiency was rectified by the adoption of the so-called Additional Protocol of May 1997, which gave the IAEA the authority to inspect non-declared facilities.

Efforts towards Banning Nuclear Weapons

There are other measures to reduce the utility of nuclear weapons. A Nuclear Weapons Free Zone (NWFZ), which is to establish zones of no nuclear weapons, is an example. There are five NWFZs currently. They are: the Treaties of Tlatelolco (Latin America) in 1967, of Rarotonga (South Pacific) in 1985, of Bangkok (Southeast Asia) in 1995, of Pelindaba (Africa) in 1996 and of Semipalatinsk (Central Asia) in 2006. The point is, however, whether or not the 5 nuclear weapon states would adhere to the treaties' provisions because NWFZ countries neither have nor intend to have any nuclear weapons in the first place. The US, for example, is not about to accept these provisions because they would conflict with the freedom of navigation of her nuclear-armed ships on the high seas.

Another attempt against nuclear weapons is to make their possession and/or use

NUCLEAR-WEAPON-FREE AREAS
Demarcation of nuclear-weapon-free zones, nuclear-weapon-free status and nuclear-weapon-free geographical regions

TREATIES ESTABLISHING NUCLEAR-WEAPON-FREE AREAS

(*Source: United Nations Office for Disarmament Affairs*)

illegal. An advisory opinion by the International Court of Justice (ICJ) in July 1996 said that "the threat or use of nuclear weapons would generally be contrary to the rules of international law applicable in armed conflict". The judgment is ambiguous and non-committal, but it was generally hailed because it mentioned for the first time "contrary to the rules of international law". In July 2017, the United Nations General Assembly adopted the Treaty on the Prohibition of Nuclear Weapons with 122 countries' support. It aims to ban the acquisition, development, production, manufacture, possession, transfer, receipt, testing, extraterritorial stationing, use and threat of use of nuclear weapons. This would be epoch making. Japan along with Australia, Canada, Norway and others, however, did not participate because most of these countries are dependent on the US nuclear umbrella (extended nuclear deterrence). They could not afford losing this umbrella, so they regard, given the prevailing circumstances.

Chemical and Biological Weapons

It is known that toxic chemical agents have been used in war and conflict since ancient times and chemical weapons such as mustard gas were used in WWI. A more recent case was a sarin gas attack on the Tokyo subway in March 1995 by a religious cult called Aum Shinrikyo. There is no confirmed use of biological weapons in recent history. However, something akin to it, such as plague infected bodies, was used in ancient conflicts. These weapons were considered to be inhumane and abhorrent, which culminated in the 1925 Geneva Protocol after WWI.

The nettlesome problem is that chemical and biological weapons can be made from common industrial and household goods. For example, agricultural pesticides, ammonia and even chlorine can be used for making a chemical weapon. However, chlorine is needed for treating drinking water. Likewise, biological weapons can be easily made from common infectious diseases such as smallpox and cholera. These natural pathogens are needed for medical science to deal with sickness. It is this dual-use nature that is nettlesome.

Humankind has devoted considerable effort, however, to prevent or curtail the spread of these weapons. The Chemical Weapons Convention (CWC) and Biological Weapons Convention (BWC) are the fruits of this effort. The CWC is a success story, but the BWC cannot be said to be successful.

The CWC aims to "eliminate an entire category of weapons of mass destruction by prohibiting the development, production, acquisition, stockpiling, retention, transfer or use of chemical weapons" (OPCW website). Member states are obligated to destroy and eliminate all chemical weapons. It is administered by the Organisation for the Prohibition of Chemical Weapons (OPCW) in The Hague in the Netherlands. The CWC adopted a so-called "challenge inspection", with no right of refusal. This is a really powerful weapon against would-be cheaters.

The BWC banned all microbial and other biological agents or toxins, as well as their means of delivery. Although biological weapons may not be practical to use for a responsible state, they may as well be for a terrorist group to wage a psychological onslaught. Therefore, one can point out that the BWC's weakness is that it has neither

Table 4-3 CWC and BWC

Name	Open for Signature	Entry into Force	Number of Member States
CWC	January, 1993	April, 1997	192
BWC	April, 1972	March, 1975	179

as of December 2017

a formal organization to monitor compliance, like the OPCW mentioned above, nor effective inspection and verification systems per se.

Restricting Delivery Vehicles and Warheads

Another way to reduce the threat of nuclear weapons is to limit or reduce the number of delivery vehicles such as missile launchers and warheads themselves. This was attempted even in the age of Cold War. The steps that the US and USSR (Russia) have taken in this regard will be briefly sketched.

SALT

Having had an unrestrained arms race since the end of WWII, the US and USSR had feared that things might just get out of hand. The impetus for starting a negotiation was the signing of the NPT as well as the announced deployment of ABMs (Anti-Ballistic Missile) by the US. This negotiation culminated as SALT (Strategic Arms Limitation Talks) 1, which was the first major agreement between the US and USSR that limited or put caps on strategic weapons (launchers) at the then-existing levels. The number is based on launchers, not warheads, which was a major deficiency. This is because a major development of MIRVs (Multiple Independently targetable Re-entry Vehicles) was taking place, which enables a single launcher (missile) to carry multiple warheads. SALT 1 limited the number of ICBMs at 1618 for the USSR, and 1054 for the US, and of SLBMs at 740 for both countries.

It took seven long years from 1972 to 1979 to conclude SALT II, which never entered into force (EIF). Nonetheless, both superpowers honored its terms in practice.

Table 4-4 Treaties on Delivery Vehicles between the US and USSR (Russia)

Name	Signed	Major Features
SALT I	May, 1972	Limited ICBMs and SLBMs
SALT II	June, 1979	No EIF. Limited MIRVed missiles
START 1	July, 1991	Cap of 1600 on warheads on all delivery vehicles
START II	January, 1993	No EIF. strategic nuke warheads to 3000−3500
SORT	May, 2002	No provisions on verification
New START	April, 2010	Strategic nuke warheads to 1550

It achieved a real reduction of all strategic delivery vehicles (ICBMs, SLBMs, Heavy Bombers and Air-to Surface Ballistic Missiles=ASBMs) to 2400 each initially, then up to 2250 from January 1981. By placing an upper limit of 1320 on MIRVed missiles, it rectified the drawbacks of SALT I. It was also significant that the so-called National Technical Means (NTM) of verification was permitted to be utilized. The NTM in essence meant various monitoring technologies such as spy satellites.

START

Then, once again there was a long hiatus until the Strategic Arms Reduction Treaty (START) I was signed. Note here that it says reduction, not limitation. It put a cap of 1,600 deployed strategic nuclear delivery vehicles (ICBMs, SLBMs and heavy bombers) and also for warheads (6000). It is of note that on-site-inspection (OSI), which the USSR had resisted so strenuously before, was accepted.

One complicating factor was that there were 4 nuclear capable states: namely, the Russian Federation, Belarus, Ukraine, and Kazakhstan since the USSR was dissolved in December 1991. They all needed to ratify the treaty in order to make it effective, which they did by December 1994. All three break-out states returned all of their nuclear weapons to Russia.

Following the doomed START II and ineffective Strategic Offensive Reductions Treaty (SORT), a new Strategic Arms Reduction Treaty (New START) was concluded. It limited "deployed" strategic nuclear warheads to 1550 and the "deployed as well as non-deployed" ICBMs, SLBM launchers and heavy bombers to 800. This is the current situation on delivery vehicles.

INF and CFE

INF and CFE should also be mentioned. The INF (Intermediate-Range Nuclear Forces) Treaty was signed in December 1987 between the US and USSR. It eliminated all intermediate range (500-5500Km) ground-launched nuclear ballistic and cruise missiles. Its verification system also permitted for the first time to send inspectors to sensitive US and USSR missile facilities. This was a big breakthrough.

Japan had much to do with it. Japan had worried that the USSR would simply relocate its SS-20s to Asia if the US and USSR agreed to ban them only in Europe.

This would put Japan within their easy range. So, Prime Minister Nakasone Yasuhiro advocated eliminating all INFs wherever they were located, which was eventually accepted by the US and USSR.

The CFE (Conventional Armed Forces in Europe) Treaty was signed in November 1990 by 22 states grouped into NATO and the Warsaw Pact. It put an equal ceiling for the two groups and mandated the destruction of excessive conventional weapons. The reduction in conventional arms is its significance.

Bottle Half Full and Half Empty

In concluding this chapter, one can say that humankind has made a great stride in constraining the spread of nuclear weapons and banning nuclear tests, contrary to some doomsayers. For example, former US President Barack Obama expressed America's commitment in his Prague speech in April 2009 "to seek the peace and security of a world without nuclear weapons". However, the fact of the matter is that it is humankind that invented nuclear weapons in the first place and there is much to be done. As Obama said, "a world without nuclear weapons" would take patience and persistence to achieve.

Endnotes

1) This is never achieved since this game is supposed to be played only once, a one-shot game. However, there is a possibility that it may be achieved if it can be repeated indefinitely.
2) Nuclear weapon states is a term that is used in the NPT. It means the US, USSR, UK, France and China, in essence. There have been some countries that did abandon their nuclear weapons such as South Africa.
3) Inspections triggered by a suspected violation of a treaty or agreement. On-site inspections under the CTBT are challenge inspections as the State Party subjected to an on-site inspection cannot refuse to allow it to take place.
http://www.ctbto.org/index.php?id=280&no_cache=1&letter=c#challenge-inspections

References

1) Takeuchi Toshitaka (ed.) (2008), *Guidebook, International Relations*, Osaka: Osaka University Press (in Japanese). (竹内俊隆（編）『ガイドブック国際関係論』大阪：大阪大学出版会)
2) Williams, Robert and Paul Viotti (eds.) (2012), *Arms Control: History, Theory, and Policy*, Volume 2, Santa Barbara: Praeger

3) OPCW website: http://www.opcw.org/chemical-weapons-convention/
4) UNODA website: http://www.un.org/disarmament/WMD/Bio/

Recommended Works

1) Blacker, Coit D. and Gloria Duffy (eds.) (1984), *International Arms Control: Issues and Agreements*, (2nd Edition), Stanford: Stanford University Press

   This is an old textbook intended mainly for upper-level students. But, it is also comprehensive and very informative.

2) Burns, Richard (2009), *The evolution of Arms Control: From Antiquity to the Nuclear Age*, Santa Barbara: Praeger

   This is a good short guide for arms control, spanning from ancient times to the present nuclear age. It explains about negotiation, verification, and compliance, among others.

3) Nye, Joseph S. and David A. Welch (2017), *Understanding Global Conflict and Cooperation: An Introduction to Theory and History*, (10th Edition), Boston: Pearson

   This is a widely used textbook on international politics, which describes and explains the theory and history of conflicts.

CHAPTER 5

The United Nations and Its Peacekeeping Activities

One of the aims of the United Nations (UN) when it was founded in 1945 was to make it more resilient than its failed predecessor, the League of Nations. Its various bodies include: the Security Council, the General Assembly, the Secretariat, and the Economic and Social Council, among many other diverse bodies with varying powers and responsibilities. Since the founding of the UN, its Peacekeeping Operations (PKOs) have evolved from relatively small-scale monitoring of ceasefires in armed conflicts during the Cold War, to more forceful, large-scale humanitarian interventions in the post-Cold War period. These have increasingly been justified under the emerging doctrine of the 'Responsibility to Protect' (R2P).

Origins of the United Nations

The Founding Purpose of the UN

The overall role and purpose of the United Nations is to attempt to provide global governance-*not* global government. The UN is the largest of the world's IGOs, (International Governmental Organization). A grouping of 193 sovereign states, its purpose is cooperation towards states' collective self-interests in international relations. But, the UN can only accomplish as much as the consensus of its member states allows it to do. As such, it is often difficult for the UN to achieve results whenever its more powerful member states engage in "power politics" over controversial issues. The UN has nevertheless been able to achieve a great deal of its intended aims, promoting international peace and security, social and economic development, and environmental protection.

The predecessor of the UN, the League of Nations, was established following World War One (WWI), with the Treaty of Versailles in 1919, promoted by US President

Woodrow Wilson. Its major aim was to prevent another global war, as WWI had suffered the greatest loss of life of any conflict in history. However, the League of Nations was weakened from the start, as the US Congress blocked America from joining. Aggressive territorial expansion conducted by the revisionist powers of Nazi Germany, Fascist Italy and Imperial Japan in the 1930s further exposed the League's impotence. After protests against the inasion of Manchuria by its Kwantung Army in 1931, Japan left the League in 1933. The League attempted to impose economic sanctions against Italy, when it invaded Abyssinia (now Ethiopia) in 1935-36, but this proved ineffective. The USSR also distrusted the League, viewing it as a hostile "capitalist-dominated" institution. (Taylor, 1963: 27-128)

The League of Nation's ultimate failure was the outbreak of the Second World War in 1939. In August 1941, Britain and the US drafted the Atlantic Charter, which outlined hopes for a postwar world without territorial aggression, defending the right of self-determination for all peoples. On January 1st 1942, the 26 countries comprising the World War II Allies signed the Atlantic Charter, issuing the "Declarations by United Nations", the first time the name of the UN was officially used. The eventually victorious Allied powers were determined that the United Nations would have greater collective powers to preserve global peace and security from the international crime of aggression. Following its founding conference at San Francisco in June 1945, the UN formally came into being on October 24th 1945, when the United Nations Charter was ratified by its 51 founding members.

The UN Charter and the Use of Force

The UN was granted a more elaborate structure than that of the League of Nations, aiming to be more internationally representative and bureaucratically effective. The main branches of the UN established were: The General Assembly; the Economic and Social Council; the Trusteeship Council; the Security Council; and the Secretariat. The principles of non-aggression were laid out in Article 2 (4) of the UN Charter:

> "All members shall refrain in their international relations from the threat or use of force against the territorial integrity or political independence of any state or in any other manner inconsistent with the purposes of the United Nations"

The UN, primarily through the Security Council, was to have a key role in encouraging settlement of international disputes, as outlined in Article 33:

> "Para 1: The parties to any dispute, the continuance of which is likely to endanger the maintenance of international peace and security, shall, first of all, seek a solution by negotiation, enquiry, mediation, conciliation, arbitration, judicial settlement, resort to regional agencies or arrangements, or other peaceful means of their own choice.
> Para 2: The Security Council shall, when it deems necessary, call upon the parties to settle their dispute by such means."

The use of force was not outlawed by the UN Charter; while aggression was criminalized under international law, states still maintained the right of self-defense; this included collective action authorized under the authority of the Security Council, as stated in Article 51:

> "Nothing in the present Charter shall impair the inherent right of individual or collective self-defence if an armed attack occurs against a Member of the United Nations, until the Security Council has taken the measures necessary to maintain international peace and security"

Structure of the UN

The General Assembly

The United Nations General Assembly (UNGA) acts as the "parliament" of the UN, although it does not have the range of legislative powers of normal parliaments. All 193 full member states are represented, with full two-week sessions held annually at UN Headquarters in New York. The UNGA is the UN's main deliberative body, with each member state having a single vote of equal value for UNGA resolutions; these must be carried by a two-thirds majority. The UNGA can debate and pass motions on any matter covered by the Charter. Its specific responsibilities are: to examine and approve the UN budget and determine the level of financial contributions its members should make; and to elect the UN Secretary-General, in conjunction with the UN Security Council, and the International Court of Justice (ICJ).

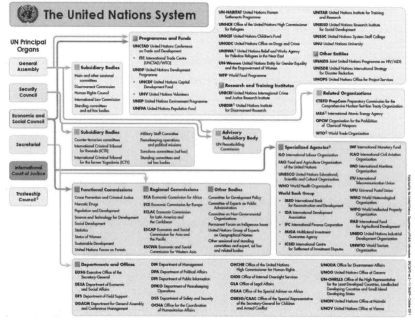

Chart 1 The United Nations System
(Source: United Nations)

Apart from these activities, the UNGA does not pursue any actual legislative function, and it does not have the power to directly oversee or scrutinize the Security Council, or the Secretariat. Unlike the resolutions of the Security Council, those of the UNGA are not binding under international law. They are only recommendations for the international community to follow, providing a consensus of global opinion on various issues which may be of international concern. The UNGA can make rulings which affect international security, including approving membership of the UN itself, as seen in the 2012 vote to grant Palestine observer status at the UN. The UNGA also supervises and coordinates with various specialized agencies and bodies of the UN related to security such as the UN Human Rights Council (UNHRC).

One of the more influential functions of the UNGA is when it votes to determine the ten non-permanent members of the Security Council, electing half of the rotating seats each year. It can also overrule a deadlock in the Security Council and approve PKOs itself; this requires an Emergency Special Session to be held, with at least a two-thirds majority vote needed. However this provision, known as the "Uniting for Peace" Resolution (A/RES/377 A) (passed in 1950 at the instigation of the US, to overcome potential vetoes by the USSR), has only been rarely exercised.

The Economic and Social Council (ECOSOC)

ECOSOC supervises and coordinates many of the UN bodies which carry out much of the UN's work in attempting global governance and welfare, in the fields of the environment, health, economic and social policy. ECOSOC has 54 member states, elected by the UNGA from regionally based blocs for three-year terms, and meets annually for a month-long session each July. It oversees the activities of 10 functional Commissions, including the Human Rights Council in conjunction with the UNGA; five Regional Commissions; and some 20 specialized agencies. These include: the World Bank, which provides loans for development; the International Monetary Fund (IMF), which provides emergency funding for states' financial systems; and the World Trade Organization (WTO), which promotes free trade.

In other areas, the World Health Organization (WHO) is concerned with improving global public health; the UN Educational, Scientific and Cultural Organization (UNESCO) promotes education, science and culture, including the protection of World Heritage Sites. The UN High Commissioner for Refugees (UNHCR) supervises the provision of aid and resettlement of refugees; the UN International Children' Fund (UNICEF) operates various aid programs for the protection and welfare of vulnerable children. The World Food Program (WFP) coordinates emergency famine relief aid; the Food and Agriculture Organization (FAO) promotes development of sustainable agriculture and food security. The UN Environment Program (UNEP) coordinates research and global cooperation on environmental protection; and the UN Development Program (UNDP) aims to coordinate cooperation on development and poverty reduction.

The Trusteeship Council

To avoid repeating the mistakes of the League of Nations, the UN pursued the principle of universal membership, given its purpose as the association of the world's sovereign states. Imperialism was discredited after the aggressive invasions and occupations by the

Axis powers in the Second World War. The US in particular felt driven to support principles of independence and self-determination; this opposed the desires of its main wartime allies, Britain and France, and other European colonial powers, such as the Netherlands, Portugal and Belgium, to retain their imperial possessions.

An important postwar role for the UN was therefore to assist decolonization, with former colonies joining the UN as full members, supervised by the UN Trusteeship Council. As it would turn out, a number of postcolonial states would find themselves subject to instability and armed conflict, necessitating a potential role for UN intervention and PKOs. Since the process of postwar decolonization is effectively complete, the Trusteeship Council has been inoperative since 1994.

The Security Council

The United Nations Security Council (UNSC) was established as the most powerful body of the UN. Tasked to maintain international peace and security, it is meant to resolve armed conflicts and deal with other international security threats. As part of the negotiations for establishing the UN, the victorious main allies granted themselves permanent membership of the UNSC, known as the P5: the US, the USSR (succeeded by Russia), the UK, France, and China. The remainder of the Security Council is made up of a rotating membership of ten seats, elected for non-consecutive 2-year terms each; five members are replaced each year, voted for in the General Assembly, based on regional representation.

The UNSC's resolutions are binding under international law, with diplomatic and economic sanctions, and ultimately military force among the potential range of options to have its resolutions enforced. The UNSC also has the power to suspend or even expel member states from the UN. Specialized agencies of the UN concerned with security issues, such as the International Atomic Energy Agency (IAEA) and the International Criminal Court (ICC) often coordinate activities with the UNSC.

The Secretariat

The UN Secretary-General is the chief diplomat and administrator for the UN, leading the UN Secretariat which administers the programs of the UN's various institutions. The Secretary-General (since 2017, former Prime Minister of Portugal

Antonio Guterres) plays a major role in trying to coordinate international cooperation and applying the moral suasion of the office to attempt resolution of international disputes. Secretary-Generals are appointed by the General Assembly on the recommendation of the Security Council, for a renewable 5-year term. The Secretariat contains nine separate Offices such as those of the UN High Commissioners for Human Rights (OHCHR) and Refugees (UNHCR); and eight Departments, including the Department of Peacekeeping Operations (DPKO).

The main headquarters of the UN is in New York City, but other regional offices and bodies are also located around the world. The Secretariat has a complex bureaucracy, staffed by public servants from different countries, with a staff level of around 44,000. The operating budget for the UN (apart from the cost of PKOs) was US$5.4 billion for 2016-2017, funded by proportional contributions from member states, The Secretary-General often has the challenge of promoting the status and policy direction of the UN in the face of competing agendas among member states, especially those of the P5 "great powers". The bureaucracy of the UN has also often been accused by critics of past scandals, inefficiency and mismanagement, which Secretary-Generals have battled to resolve.

The International Court of Justice and the International Criminal Court

The International Court of Justice (ICJ) is the main judicial body of the UN, based in The Hague in the Netherlands. It consists of 15 judges, elected jointly by the UNGA and UNSC. The ICJ can hear disputes between UN member states on a range of issues, most commonly regarding territorial disputes, and on other contested issues. For example, Australia successfully won its case heard by the ICJ in 2014 against Japan's whaling program. However, a significant limitation of the ICJ is that participation in its cases is voluntary. If a state participates, it is obliged to comply with the ICJ's decisions, but its rulings are nevertheless not enforceable under international law. If a state does not agree to appear, it is still required to issue a statement to the ICJ justifying its position.

The ICJ's major influence is therefore to provide a level of diplomatic "moral pressure" to encourage compliance with its judgments. The ICJ can also provide advisory opinions on issues in international law to the UNSC, UNGA and other UN agencies. For example, in 1996 it provided a controversial opinion on the legality of nuclear weapons; their use would be illegal under the international rules of war, but their possession for the purpose of deterrence may not necessarily be so.

After a long campaign by human rights NGOs, the International Criminal Court (ICC) was established in 1998 by the Rome Statute, and went into operation from July 2002. It is the first permanent international tribunal to try indicted war criminals, including heads of state. The ICC therefore overturns the longstanding principle of "sovereign immunity". As well as trying government officials and members of military forces accused of war crimes, the ICC also indicts non-state actors such as rebels, warlords and militia leaders. The ICC has jurisdiction over four criminal areas: grave and serious breaches of the laws of war; crimes against humanity; genocide; and aggression. Cases are tried by the ICC if domestic courts are unable or unwilling to do so, when crimes are committed in the territory of a party to the Rome Statute, or when the accused is a national of a party to the Statute. As of 2017, there are 124 parties to the Rome Statute; non-parties include the US, China, Japan, Indonesia, and North and South Korea. These states claim their armed forces and nationals are not under ICC jurisdiction, fearing they will be potentially subject to politically motivated prosecutions.

The ICC consists of 18 judges, elected for 9-year terms, from states that are parties to the Rome Statute. Prosecutions are only initiated by the ICC Office of the Prosecutor, after authorization is obtained from a separate pretrial chamber, comprised of seven other judges. The UN Security Council can delay investigations for up to 12 months, if it passes a resolution; it has done so twice, in 2002, to prevent investigations against UN peacekeepers. So far, there have been 39 indictments by the ICC, covering eight African countries; prominent among these include the late Colonel Gaddafi of Libya and his son Saif, President al-Bashir of Sudan, and Ugandan rebel leader Joseph Kony. There have been three convictions for war crimes upheld so far; two Congolese rebel leaders, and an Islamist militia leader from Mali. Burundi announced in 2016 it planned to withdraw from the ICC, with other African Union states also threatening to leave, citing the ICC's disproportionate concentration on African cases.

UN Peacekeeping

The Role and Purpose of Peacekeeping Operations

UN Peacekeeping Operations (PKOs) are the deployment of military forces acting on behalf of the UN to supervise and support the preservation of ceasefires to armed conflicts, where all parties have consented to a cessation of hostilities. Mandated by the UN Security Council, and organized through the UN Secretariat, it is up to the member states of the UN to volunteer and fund the services of their military forces as peacekeepers. Civilian staff such as police, medical and aid workers and administrators also comprise personnel involved in PKOs. In 2017, the cost of the UN's 15 PKOs was around US$6.8 billion (which is less them 0.5% of total global military expenditure), funding over 110,000 personnel, including nearly 94,000 peacekeeping troops, contributed by 126 member states of the UN (United Nations Peacekeeping, "Peacekeeping Fact Sheet", 2017).

The Security Council's powers to authorize PKOs are derived from Chapters 6 and 7 of the UN Charter. Interestingly, there is no direct reference to peacekeeping itself in the Charter. Chapter 6, "Pacific Settlement of Disputes", directs conflicting parties to use peaceful negotiation and mediation to resolve disputes, with the Security Council authorized to provide advisory, but not binding recommendations if requested. Chapter 7, "Action with Respect to Threats to the Peace, Breaches of the Peace, and Acts of Aggression", grants the Security Council powers of intervention against sovereign states which have aggressively violated international law; from severance of diplomatic relations and imposition of economic sanctions, up to the use of armed force "necessary to maintain or restore international peace and security". Chapter 7 has only been invoked on a couple of occasions; the Korean War in 1950-53, and the Gulf War in 1990-91.

Once the UNSC approves the mandate for a PKO, after negotiated requests from the parties in dispute, the Secretariats' Department of Peacekeeping Operations (DPKO) establishes a command structure. A Special Representative of the Secretary-General heads the PKO, responsible for diplomatic coordination between the disputing parties, the UN and its contributing member states. The Force Commander is the military commander of the PKO's forces, typically the senior commander of the country providing the majority of forces.

The DPKO requests contributions of troops and funding from member states, forming the size and structure of the PKO, depending on its mandate granted by the authorizing UNSC resolution. Once the PKO forces are assembled, they can be deployed in the field, facilitated by ongoing diplomatic negotiations conducted by the Secretariat. ECOSOC's various organs often cooperate with PKOs. They assist in the provision of emergency aid relief and long-term post-conflict reconstruction, particularly directed towards civilians and non-combatants requiring protection and assistance in conflict zones.

As the UN has attempted to meet its aims of promoting peaceful resolution of armed conflicts, PKOs have become an integral feature of international security. Nevertheless, they have often met with controversy and criticism, despite often overlooked and unacknowledged positive achievements. The use of force by peacekeepers has been one of the more contentious aspects of PKOs. Peacekeeping troops have generally only been granted Rules of Engagement (RoE) allowing use of weapons only for personal self-defense. In more recent PKOs, a doctrine of more robust RoE appears to be emerging; peacekeepers are increasingly authorized to use force more proactively, to protect vulnerable civilians under threat from a resumption of armed conflict by one of the involved parties (Berdal, 2010: 176-186).

The First Peacekeeping Operations

Early PKOs of the Cold War period were small-scale observer missions, monitoring ceasefires in armed conflicts in the Middle East and South Asia. This reflected the Cold War stagnation within the Security Council; PKOs could only be established and operate with mutual consent of all parties, if they were not blocked or vetoed by either of the Cold War superpowers or their P5 allies. The US and USSR rarely contributed to PKOs, which were instead commonly made up of a mix of Western and "neutral" non-aligned states' military forces. PKOs during the Cold War generally comprised of small numbers of military observers, usually only lightly armed, and quite often unarmed.

The earliest PKOs have the remarkable distinction of being the oldest ongoing missions, tragically reflecting the intransigence of the conflicts involved: UNTSO, to monitor the ceasefire after the first Arab-Israeli War; and UNMOGIP, in the wake of the first India-Pakistan War of 1947. Both UNTSO and UNMOGIP have comprised small teams of unarmed observers. As the Cold War intensified, there was an ongoing lack of consensus among the members of the Security Council, particularly between the divided superpower rivals of the P5, in allowing PKOs to be established. Only two more missions were instigated in the 1950s, both in the Middle East: following the Suez Crisis of 1956; and in Lebanon in 1958. More PKOs were launched in the 1960s, beginning with an ambitious and controversial mission in the Congo. Following its independence from Belgium in 1960, the vast and desperately poor Congo was wracked by political instability and violence. ONUC was established to prevent the break-up of the Congo, threatened by infiltration of foreign mercenaries assisting separatist rebels in Katanga province. ONUC was the first PKO in sub-Saharan Africa, and also the largest-scale and most expensive up to that time, costing over $400 million. It peaked at nearly 20,000 relatively well-armed troops (with large contingents from Ireland, Canada and Sweden), including air support being used for the first time for a PKO.

A large civilian staff component was also involved, another pioneering development for UN PKOs. ONUC suffered 250 casualties, mainly in clashes with Katangan forces, reflecting the dangerous and chaotic nature of the conflict, which wound down by 1964. UN Secretary-General Dag Hammarskjold was even killed in a plane crash in 1961, while on the way to the Congo to facilitate peace talks. The first PKOs in other regions were also established: UNSF in West Papua in 1962-63; UNFICYP in Cyprus, in 1964; and DOMREP in the Dominican Republic, in 1965. More PKOs resulted from the Arab-Israeli conflicts of the 1970s: UNEF II and UNDOF after the 1973 October War; and UNFIL after the Israeli invasion of southern Lebanon in 1978, intervening in Lebanon's civil war.

The Post-Cold War Expansion of PKOs

Throughout most of the 1980s, no new PKOs were instigated, again reflecting another period of increased tensions between the Cold War superpowers, which blocked effective cooperation in the Security Council. The first missions from 1988 supervised the ceasefire of the Iran-Iraq War, and an unsuccessful mission between Afghanistan and Pakistan. As the influence of the Cold War wound down, PKOs returned to Africa, in Angola and Namibia; and to Latin America, in Nicaragua.

The end of the Cold War saw a great expansion in the scope of PKOs, freed from the constraints of the superpower deadlock in the Security Council, which had commonly been in place throughout the Cold War. There were far higher numbers of PKOs approved and implemented since 1991: 53, compared to 18 during the entire Cold War period, a nearly four-fold increase. Post-Cold War PKOs expanded not just in numbers, but in the size and scope of their mandates and operations; from small groups of lightly armed observers, to large multinational forces of peacekeeping troops and their support services. These have required much greater resources, funding, and of course more personnel to be provided by member states of the UN.

The larger post-Cold War PKOs were set a multidimensional range of tasks, including: providing security for civilian populations, humanitarian and developmental aid delivery, demobilization of combatants, demining operations, supervising elections, and rebuilding state institutions and structures of governance. This often required a greater degree of cooperation between other humanitarian and developmental agencies of the UN, including the UNHCR, UNICEF and the WFP, as well as human rights and development aid NGOs such as the Red Cross and Doctors Without Borders. There were high ambitions and expectations of this more activist role for UN PKOs; they faced great challenges and suffered several dire failures, however.

As well as assisting the end of Cold War-era conflicts in El Salvador and Guatemala, one of the first large-scale "nation building" post-Cold War PKOs was UNAMIC/UNTAC in Cambodia. A largely Australian-led diplomatic initiative, UNTAC supervised a ceasefire in the civil war following the withdrawal of Vietnamese forces in 1989, and supported the first democratic elections in Cambodia. UNTAC had a maximum strength of up to 16,000 troops and 3,500 civilian police, at a cost of $1.6 billion. It was also significant in that it involved the first participation of Japan's Self Defense Forces (SDF) in UN peacekeeping (Howard, 2008: 131-177).

Controversial PKOs occurred in the wake of the wars following the dissolution of Yugoslavia from 1991. To attempt to protect noncombatants and separate the warring parties, UNPROFOR was established in Bosnia, Croatia and Macedonia in 1992.

Reaching its peak strength of over 38,000 troops, with the UK, France and other European countries providing the largest contingents, UNPROFOR's main task was to monitor local ceasefires and protect humanitarian aid relief convoys. However, it soon became widely criticized for its weak mandate, regularly failing to protect civilians from war crimes, even in UN-declared "safe havens". The worst atrocity was the Srebrenica massacre of over 8,000 Bosnian civilians by Serbian forces in 1995, which Dutch UN peacekeepers were unable to prevent.

After diplomatic vacillation by the Clinton Administration in the US, the EU, and the UN Secretariat, an air campaign by NATO in 1995 ultimately drove Serbia to end the war, with a number of PKOs set up to monitor the various ceasefires following the Dayton Peace Accords. The renewal of war in the Balkans over Kosovo led to another intervention by NATO in 1999, in another bombing campaign against Serbia, in support of the Kosovo Liberation Army (KLA) rebels. This led to another ceasefire, supervised by UNMIK, which remains ongoing

More PKOs were established in the post-Cold War period in Africa, with varying degrees of effectiveness. The failed state of Somalia had suffered civil war since the 1970s, and had deteriorated into famine. UNOSOM I was established in 1992 to protect the delivery of famine aid relief, being upgraded to UNSOM II in 1993, with a strengthened mandate. With its peak strength of up to 28,000 troops, UNOSOM II saw the first major participation by the US in a UN PKO, although American forces remained under their own direct military command. However, the direct engagement of US forces in the war against the militia of one of the Somali warlords culminated in the chaotic Battle of Mogadishu in 1993. American forces withdrew after they incurred casualties; UNOSOM II was withdrawn in 1995, while the war continued.

An even more controversial failure was the PKO in Rwanda. UNAMIR was already in place from 1993, attempting to resolve a civil war which had broken out in 1990, between the Tutsi-based Rwandan People's Army (RPA) rebels, based in Uganda, and the Hutu-led Rwandan government. The war deteriorated into the Rwandan Genocide in July 1994, as Rwandan government forces and Hutu militias committed mass killings against Tutsis and other government opponents. The poorly-armed UNAMIR peacekeepers did not have the mandate to protect civilians from genocide. The UN Secretariat and the influential states which could have potentially intervened, particularly France and the US, refrained from taking swift action. The killing of over 800,000 people only ended after the RPA drove the Hutu Government forces and militias into the Congo, by September 1994. A belatedly reinforced UNAMIR only then resumed providing protection for international aid relief efforts, before it ended in 1996.

Another large and controversial PKO intervened in another civil war in Africa, in Sierra Leone. UNOMSIL was meant to monitor the demobilization of various armed factions following a ceasefire from 1998, but its peacekeepers found themselves under attack by the vicious Revolutionary United Front (RUF) rebels, violating the ceasefire. It was upgraded to UNAMSIL in 1999, rising to peak strength of 17,500 troops; however, it came under increasing RUF attack, with peacekeepers taken hostage. After the RUF was finally defeated, largely due to British military intervention in 2000, UNAMSIL did manage to supervise postwar stabilization and disarmament, ending in 2005.

UN PKOs returned to the Congo in 1999, confronting the world's deadliest post-Cold War conflict, which caused up to 5 million deaths. MONUC aimed to monitor ceasefires between the Congolese government forces and various rebel and militia groups backed by different African countries intervening in the war. MONUC was upgraded to MONUSCO in 2010, with over 22,000 military personnel. Despite a strengthened mandate, including the use of helicopter gunships, MONUSCO has been criticized for failing to adequately protect civilians, especially women, from war crimes committed by both government and rebel forces.

In the Caribbean, a coup in Haiti led to UNMIH, supported by substantial US military intervention in 1994, which aimed to stabilize the country and restore democracy after decades of dictatorship. Following another coup and more widespread political violence in 2004, the UN returned with MINUSTAH, which became a humanitarian aid relief operation after an earthquake in 2010 devastated much of Haiti.

A series of PKOs were unexpectedly required in the Asia-Pacific, with the emergency of East Timor in 1999. Indonesia had invaded East Timor in 1975, following its independence from Portugal, despite UNSC resolutions against its harsh occupation. After the fall of the Suharto dictatorship in 1998, East Timor was granted and passed a referendum on its independence in 1999, despite intense violence from military-backed militias. With US diplomatic backing and a UNSC mandate, Australia insisted on deployment of the INTERFET (International Forces East Timor) peacekeeping force, led by the Australian Defence Force (ADF). This became UNAMET, transferring again from 1999 to UNTAET, assisting East Timor in its security and development, succeeded by UNMISET from 2002 to 2005. After a mutiny within the new East Timorese defense forces in 2006, UNMIT resumed peacekeeping duties, again largely with ADF forces. The mission was completed following a return to stability and a peaceful election in 2012.

Ongoing Challenges for PKOs

The failures of the missions of the 1990s, especially in Bosnia, Somalia and Rwanda, led to extensive reconsideration of PKOs. There were also arguments within the UN about the level of burden sharing among states contributing to PKOs. Developing states, particularly those of South Asia: Pakistan, India, Bangladesh and Nepal; and African states such as Ethiopia, Nigeria and Ghana, have contributed the majority of personnel to recent PKOs, although countries such as Australia, Canada, and Ireland also have a long tradition of participation. Developed states, particularly the US, Japan, the UK, Germany and France have taken on more of the financial burden, while China has also increased its funding and involvement in PKOs, as it has gained greater economic and military prominence. Since the 1990s, China's People's Liberation Army (PLA) has deployed over 3,500 troops, in 10 operations.

The Global Financial Crisis of 2008 increased pressure on foreign aid budgets, and subsequently the funding states were willing to make available for PKOs. To partially offset this, there has been a greater level of cooperation with Regional Governmental Organizations (RGOs) in peacekeeping, especially with the African Union (AU). One example is UNAMID in the Darfur region in Sudan, set up in 2007 with 16,000 troops, and over 5,000 police, in cooperation with the AU and the European Union. Another is MINUSCA, which in 2014 upgraded an AU force attempting to stabilize the civil war in the Central African Republic. Economic Community of West African States (ECOWAS) troops have also been involved in the UNSC-authorized intervention in Mali since 2013, to retake its northern region from al-Qaeda-linked militias, assisted by US intelligence, UK logistics and French air and ground support. The UN PKO

MINUSMA, which replaced the French/ECOWAS forces, has included over 500 Chinese troops, China's largest single contribution to a PKO so far. Following the independence of South Sudan in 2011, the UNMISS PKO was established, with a strength of up to 12,500 personnel, to which Japan also contributed deployments of SDF troops, until mid-2017. UNMISS has also been controversial, being unable to prevent outbreaks of violence between government forces and rebel factions.

The major limitation of PKOs is that ultimately, they can only achieve what their assigned mandates and rules of engagement allow. They are not a "UN Legion", which can perform as an independent military actor. This is because PKOs can only operate as they are collectively directed to by the UN, acting as the association of the world's sovereign states. There is debate about whether the growing number of corporate private security contractors could be more widely employed as peacekeepers, when states are unwilling or unable to do so. However, this is a controversial proposal, given the dubious record of these private security companies, particularly their roles in the US-led wars in Iraq and Afghanistan. Such a move would be strongly opposed by most UN member states (Patterson, 2009: 60-74).

Map 1   Ongoing UN Peacekeeping Missions, Sepdember 2017
(Source: United Nations)

The Future of PKOs

The Responsibility to Protect

Following the various failures of PKOs in the 1990s, critiques and proposals were debated within the UN and among the international community. The Canadian government sponsored the International Commission on Intervention and State Sovereignty (ICISS) in 2000-2001, releasing its report, *The Responsibility to Protect* (R2P). It argued that when states commit or are unable to prevent mass atrocities and crimes against humanity, the international community then has a duty to intervene to protect noncombatants, overriding traditional norms of state sovereignty.

The UN's Report of the Panel on United Nations Peace Operations (also known as the Brahimi Report) was also released in 2000, critiquing failures in funding, resources and intelligence support given to PKOs by UN member states. The Brahimi Report also addressed the shameful issue of peacekeeping troops abusing human rights of civilians meant to be under their protection in conflict zones, principally sexual abuse against women and children (Benner, *et al*, 2011: 24-41).

Following these reports, the UN delivered another finding in 2004, the UN High-level Panel Report on Threats, Challenges and Change; this was a wide-ranging review of global security issues, not just restricted to PKOs. Based on this report, the R2P principle was formally adopted at the UN World Summit in 2005. The R2P would be applicable to the international crimes of genocide, war crimes, ethnic cleansing, and crimes against humanity, confirmed by UN Security Council Resolution 1674. It was reinforced by Secretary-General Ban Ki Moon's report, *Implementing the Responsibility to Protect*, supported by the UN General Assembly in UNGA Resolution A/RES/63/308.

The R2P is controversial; it can conceivably be applied without UNSC approval, as claimed by NATO for its intervention in Kosovo against Serbia in 1999. It was also invoked for the NATO intervention in Libya in 2011, which was approved with UNSC Resolution 1973 (although Russia and China abstained). Citing the R2P, future PKOs may seek more aggressive rules of engagement, which could enable greater protection of civilians. However, if they are conducted without UNSC authorization, such R2P interventions could lack international legitimacy, if they are primarily serving the geopolitical interests of the intervening states. The ongoing humanitarian crises in civil wars such as Syria and Yemen have shown the hazards of R2P doctrine, as intervention by external powers such as Russia, the US, Turkey, Iran and Saudi Arabia has exacerbated these conflicts.

Conclusion–Assessing PKOs

Despite their past failings, PKOs have nevertheless delivered a greater degree of international security overall, where they have protected civilian populations at risk in armed conflicts, saving countless lives. At least two-thirds of all PKOs have successfully prevented, reduced or resolved the armed conflicts they intervened in, with deaths from political violence and war almost always reduced by the presence of UN peacekeeping troops. By preventing armed conflicts from resuming and helping to rebuild societies shattered by war, PKOs are a highly valuable mechanism of global governance, at a relatively low cost (of around $69 billion between 1948 and 2010), compared to most wasteful military spending (Human Security Centre, 2005: 153-155.).

Reflecting these efforts, UN Peacekeepers were collectively awarded the Nobel Peace Prize in 1988, in honor of their service and sacrifice, with over 3,000 peacekeepers having lost their lives. The UN also issues medals to peacekeeping troops to recognize their contribution, for attempting to secure peace and protect the most vulnerable victims of war and armed conflict. For all the faults of PKOs, the UN Flag and the blue helmets and berets of UN peacekeepers remain symbols of safety, protection, and hope for peace in the world.

References
1) Benner, Thorsten, Mergenthaler, Stephan, and Rotmann, Philipp (2011), *The New World of UN Peace Operations: Learning to Build Peace?*, Oxford: Oxford University Press
2) Berdal, Mats, 'The Security Council and Peacekeeping', in Lowe, Vaughan, Adam Roberts, Jennifer Welsh, and Dominik Zaum (eds.) (2010), *The United Nations Security Council and War: The Evolution of Thought and Practice Since 1945*, Oxford: Oxford University Press
3) Howard, Lise Morje (2008), *UN Peacekeeping in Civil Wars*, Cambridge: Cambridge University Press

4) Human Security Centre (2005). *Human Security Report 2005: War and Peace in the 21st Century*, New York: Oxford University Press
5) Patterson, Malcolm Hugh (2009), *Privatising Peace: A Corporate Adjunct to United Nations Peacekeeping and Humanitarian Operations*, Basinstoke: Palgrave Macmillan
6) Taylor, A.J.P. (1963), *The Origins of the Second World War*, Harmondsworth: Penguin
7) United Nations Peacekeeping (2017), 'Peacekeeping Fact Sheet', New York: UN Publications
http://www.un.org/en/peacekeeping/resources/statistics/factsheet.shtml

Recommended Books

1) Bosco, David L. (2009), *Five to Rule Them All: The UN Security Council and the Making of the Modern World,* New York: Oxford University Press

   A history and analysis of the role the UN Security Council has played in the overall direction of the UN and in global politics in general since its formation.

2) Dobson, Hugo (2003), *Japan and United Nations Peacekeeping: New Pressures, New Responses*, London: Routledge Curzon

   This book examines how Japan has come to play an increasing role in UN peacekeeping, and the domestic and international political implications this has generated.

3) Weiss, Thomas G., and Sam Daws (eds.) (2008), *The Oxford Handbook on the United Nations*, Oxford: Oxford University Press

   A very comprehensive reference work, encompassing a large range of subjects and debates concerning the UN, written by an extensive list of distinguished scholars.

CHAPTER 6
Economic Globalism and New Regionalism: The WTO, FTAs and Japan's New Trade Policy

The new wave of regionalism has become an important feature of global political economy today. Since the 1990s, free trade agreements (FTAs) have become a global trend due to the stagnation of the GATT Uruguay Round. The number of bilateral and regional FTAs that have been signed has increased dramatically. In international political economy, whether the recent surge of the "third wave" of FTAs promotes or hinders multilateral liberalization has been a topic of heated debate. There are sharply competing views on bilateral agreements, whether they are possible "stepping stones" or "stumbling blocks" to broader accords. Among East Asian countries, Japan pursued a single-track approach for almost fifty years, focusing its trade negotiation efforts exclusively on the multilateral forum while shunning regionalism as harmful to the GATT/WTO system. However, the Japanese government today is actively and strategically pursuing bilateral FTAs and the Trans-Pacific Partnership Agreement (TPP), which would weave a web of bilateral trade agreements among Asia-Pacific countries.

This chapter is composed of two parts: a theoretical review and the Japanese FTA/TPP case study. Firstly, I examine the theoretical reviews on both economic globalism and regionalism. How will bilateralism affect other types of trade arrangements? Will it play a complementary or substitutive role? I also review the competing views on bilateral agreements, whether they are possible "stepping stones" or "stumbling blocks" to broader accords. In the next section, I give an overview of the trends and characteristics of Japan's FTA/TPP, focusing on the domestic factors of how Japan's foreign economic policy has evolved from multilateralism to regionalism and bilateralism. I also analyze the motivation behind Japan's FTA/TPP strategy and highlight the obstacles, such as the agriculture issue, and conclude with the need for strong Japanese political leadership in East Asia.

Theoretical review: Economic globalization and regionalism

Economic globalization and new regionalism

IPE and economic globalization

In today's world, politics and economics are merging. Study of the two is merged in the field of international political economy (IPE). This field attempts to answer questions such as how changes in the international distribution of power among states affected the degree of openness in the international trading system, and how to explain the relative poverty of the Global South. These issues are of increasing importance because of globalization.

A preliminary definition of globalization is: "an unprecedented compression of time and space reflected in the tremendous intensification of social, political, economic, and cultural interconnections and interdependencies on a global scale". The word globalization refers to a process of de-territorialization or supra-territoriality. Conceptually, globalization is often elided with notions of liberalization, internationalization, universalization, Westernization, or modernization.

There are many aspects to globalization. Economic globalization is generally specified in reasonably precise terms as the emergence and operation of a single, worldwide economy. It is the integration of markets, finance, and technology in a way that shrinks the world. It refers to various quantitative and qualitative developments, ranging from: a dramatic increase in international transactions, especially in trade and finance; to the international and spatial reorganization of production, the global harmonization of tastes and standards, liberalization, deregulation, the global diffusion of information, the spread of a worldwide preference for democracy, and the erosion of the nation state.

Economic globalization can be understood as either a positive or a negative phenomenon. Economic globalization has occurred over the last thirty years under the General Agreement on Tariffs and Trade (GATT) and the World Trade Organization (WTO), successor to the GATT from 1995, which encouraged countries gradually to decrease trade barriers. This recent phenomenon has been explained by developed economies integrating with less developed economies, by foreign direct investment and the reduction of trade barriers. It can be said that economic globalization is an irreversible trend. There is statistical evidence for positive financial effects, but there is a power imbalance between developing and developed countries in the global economy.

Regionalism and regionalization

As a response to economic globalization, regionalism has emerged. The new wave of regionalism has become an important feature of global political economy today. First, the definitions of "regionalism" and "regionalization" should be distinguished. It is often argued that regionalism and regionalization have the same meaning, but they are clearly different concepts and must be differentiated as such. Regionalization is an energetic "bottom-up" process based on the economic connections between social actors. This means that it is a phenomenon in which economic exchange is regionally concentrated and, conceptually, it is similar to regional economic interdependence. In contrast, regionalism (e.g., APEC, EU, NAFTA, ASEAN+3) is a political "top-down" process that involves institutionalization. It can be understood as a political process in which measures such as economic policy cooperation and regulation are taken as standard.

History of economic globalization

The Bretton Woods System

Closed economic blocs and economic instability were thought to have contributed to the Great Depression and the Second World War. US policy makers wanted to find a way to prevent further depressions and wars, and created the Bretton Woods system as an international economic structure in 1944. It included institutions and rules intended to prevent national trade barriers, because the lack of free trade was considered to have been a main cause of war. Based upon the experience of the inter-war years, US policymakers developed an economic security concept that a liberal international economic system would enhance the possibilities of peace. For instance, Cordell Hull, the United States Secretary of State from 1933 to 1944, argued that the fundamental causes of the two world wars were economic discrimination and trade warfare, and also believed that the trade and exchange controls of Nazi Germany and the preference system practiced by Britain were provoked by French and American protectionist policies.

The Bretton Woods system established two international institutions to play a role in international lending that had previously been left to private markets: the International Monetary Fund (IMF) and the International Bank for Reconstruction and Development (IBRD, also known as the World Bank). The IMF was to provide short-term loans to help countries finance their temporary balance of payments deficits. The IBRD was created to aid recovery from the war, providing long-term loans for reconstruction and development. The U.S. supported this system by maintaining the dollar at a fixed rate of $35 per ounce of gold, and committed to dollar convertibility.

The developed countries also agreed that the liberal international economic system required government intervention. After the Great Depression, public management of the economy had emerged as a main purpose of governments in the developed states. To ensure economic stability and political peace, states agreed to cooperate to regulate the production of their individual currencies, to maintain fixed exchange rates between countries to facilitate international trade. This was the foundation of the US idea of postwar world free trade, which also involved lowering tariffs and maintaining a balance of trade through fixed exchange rates. In a sense, the new international monetary system was a return to a system similar to the pre-war gold standard, only using US dollars as the world's new reserve currency until the world's gold supply could be reallocated by international trade.

The End of the Bretton Woods system

As early as 1960, strains in the system began to make it difficult for the US to continue to support it. The need for a reformed system stemmed from the failure of the US to adjust its policies, so it could continue to serve as a hegemonic power in international finance. In 1971, President Richard Nixon ended dollar convertibility, and the system of fixed exchange rates gave way to a system of floating exchange rates. Market forces determined currency values, correcting the value of a state's exchange rate, and got rid of the need for official devaluation.

As a result, many countries have experienced financial crises since the 1970s. Financial crises have become increasingly frequent throughout the world due to the inability of states to manage their debt and interest rates. In reaction, there was recognition of the need for the big powers to coordinate their financial policies to stabilize international exchange rates. In sum, from the late 1950s until 1971, the IMF and World Bank became more active lenders, but they had a less central role in the system.

WTO and FTAs

The GATT and the WTO

In 1947, 23 countries agreed to the General Agreement on Tariffs and Trade (GATT), to institute bilateral tariff concessions as a way to promote world trade and prevent another depression. In 1995, the GATT was superseded by the World Trade Organization (WTO), which is an intergovernmental organization with a formal decision-making structure and a dispute settlement process. The purpose of the WTO is to ensure that trade flows smoothly; how to lower trade barriers in order to raise standards of living. Some charge that the WTO undermines state sovereignty by interfering in states' domestic affairs. Others argue that the yielding of sovereignty is voluntary, and leads to greater gains for all members.

Definition of FTA/EPA

A Free Trade Agreement refers to a bilateral or regional agreement that eliminates import duties on goods or liberalizes trade in services within the region. It represents a policy of preferential trade agreements between specific countries aimed at eliminating tariff and non-tariff barriers, and as such run contrary to the most favored nation treatment that is the basic principle of the WTO. In addition to the thorough elimination of tariff and non-tariff barriers between signatory countries that is included in traditional FTAs, most of Japan's FTAs also incorporate economic cooperation in a variety of fields, such as the liberalization of direct investment, the facilitation of trade and direct investment, and the promotion of human resource training and small-to-medium enterprises (see Figure 6-1). Since these agreements form such a comprehensive framework, the Japanese government refers to them as Economic Partnership Agreements (EPAs) rather than FTAs.

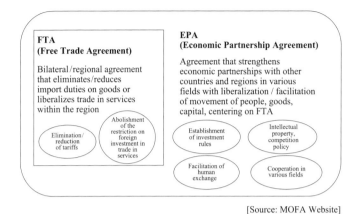

[Source: MOFA Website]

Figure 6-1 Definition of EPA/FTA

Economic integration and FTAs

An FTA is a lower level of economic integration than a customs union – which applies joint tariffs to other countries – and results in a lesser degree of institutionalization. However, with regard to the trading of goods, an FTA abolishes tariffs and further deepens economic integration. Balassa (1961) categorized the degree of economic integration into six stages; ranging from free trade areas to customs unions, common markets, economic and monetary unions, and finally to complete economic union (See Figure 6-2). Economic integration also tends to precede political integration. In fact, Balassa believed that supra-national common markets, with their free movement of economic factors across national borders, naturally generate demand for further integration, not only economically (via monetary unions) but also politically. And thus, economic communities naturally evolve into political unions over time.

FTAs as an exception to the WTO

FTAs (i.e. regional trade agreements) are one example of regionalism, which is a formal process of intergovernmental collaboration between two or more states. It should be distinguished from regionalization, which refers to the growth of economic interdependence within a geographical area. FTAs are the most important exception that the WTO permits to the principle that countries should not discriminate in their

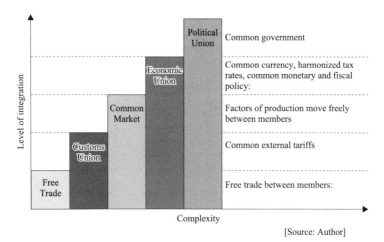

Figure 6-2 Economic Integration stage (Balassa)

treatment of other members.

In the GATT/WTO, FTAs, which violate one of its basic principles of non-discrimination, are permitted under GATT Article XXIV, with several conditions. They include liberalization of substantially all the trade of its members, not increasing trade barriers on non-members, and completing the FTA process within ten years. For developing members, more lenient conditions are applied under the enabling clause.

Three sets of rules in the WTO permit the creation of FTAs (See Figure 6-3) :

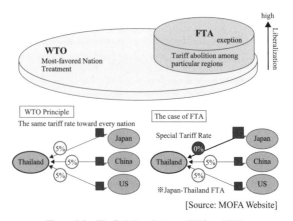

[Source: MOFA Website]

Figure 6-3 The Relations between WTO and FTA

- Article XXIV of the GATT/WTO lays down conditions for the establishment and operation of free trade agreements and customs unions covering trade in goods.
- The Enabling Clause, formally the 1979 Decision on Differential and More Favourable Treatment, Reciprocity and Fuller Participation of Developing Countries, permits regional agreements among developing countries on trade in goods.
- Article V of the General Agreement on Trade in Services (GATS) establishes conditions that permit liberalization of trade in services among regional partners.

Impacts of FTAs

Merits and Demerits of FTAs for the Multilateral System

The development consequences of FTAs are not limited to their effects on members; they also extend to the multilateral system. In one sense, FTAs are a step toward greater openness in the global trade system, in that they promote trade and generate new domestic constituencies with an interest in openness. Moreover, some regional trade policies—such as measures to improve customs, speed transactions at ports or border crossings, and open services markets—can be beneficial in a non-discriminatory way. Such measures can complement unilateral and multilateral policies.

However, this view overlooks the effects that FTAs can have on excluded countries. The fact is that preferences for some countries means discrimination against others, whereas the GATT, born out of the sad experience of discrimination in the prewar years, was based on the principle of non-discrimination. Inevitably some countries get left out of trade agreements, because they are not favored politically, because they cannot afford the costs of many separate negotiations, or because their region is less open.

The economic impacts of FTAs can be classified into static effects and dynamic effects. Static effects are mainly "trade creation effects" and "trade diversion effects", while the dynamic effects include "market expansion effects". Trade creation effects result from the elimination of trade barriers among FTA members. Therefore, it might lead to new trade creation, resulting in an improvement in resource allocation. Trade diversion effects address the ways that FTAs replace highly efficient products of nonmember countries, by imports from less efficient FTA members. As for the dynamic effects of FTAs, market expansion effects contribute to economic growth of FTA members. It involves the expanded market size needed to achieve efficient production and economies of scale. For non-FTA members, effects are likely to have positive impacts, as economic growth of FTA members tends to promote the exports of non-members to the members.

The "spaghetti bowl effect"

As a result of the proliferation of FTAs, the "spaghetti bowl effect" became a hot issue. It refers to a situation where numerous and crisscrossing FTAs with different Rules of Origin (ROOs) increases transaction costs and facilitates protectionism, thereby reducing the welfare of both FTA members and non-members. ROOs play a key role in determining the impacts of FTAs on foreign trade, since FTAs give preference to the products produced in FTA partner members, and the nationality of the products are determined by ROOs. In East Asia, some researchers call it the "noodle bowl" effect, and it attracted a lot of concern. However, its negative impacts may be exaggerated, because the spaghetti bowl effect may not increase trade costs from the pre-FTA level, and thus it does not affect trade.

Why this rush of recent FTAs?

External factors

Since the 1990s, the number of bilateral or regional FTAs that have been signed has increased dramatically. In the Asia-Pacific region, for instance, countries such as the United States, Canada, Mexico, and Chile have pursued FTAs as one of their trade policy options since the early 1990s. The sudden proliferation of regional bilateral FTAs has been regarded as one of the most important recent developments in the Asia-Pacific regional political economy. While the number of FTA agreements has also surged on a global level since the early 1990s, the rapid increase in FTAs in the Asia-Pacific is particularly noteworthy, given the relative dearth of such arrangements in the region before the 1990s.

Interest in FTAs increased even after the establishment of the WTO in 1995, which succeeded the GATT with a broader coverage and stronger legal foundation, especially after the new multilateral trade negotiations, the Doha Development Agenda under the WTO entered into deadlock. The failure of Asia Pacific Economic Cooperation (APEC) and global regimes such as the WTO to make substantial progress with trade liberalization at the multilateral level after the late 1990s, led several states in the region to consider bilateral trade agreements as a second best choice.

WTO data reflects the explosion in the number of regional arrangements that has occurred since the early 1990s. Throughout its entire existence from 1948 to 1994, the GATT received 142 notifications of regional trade agreements (RTAs), of which only 65 were still in force when it was replaced by the WTO. As of October 2017, some 659 notifications of RTAs had been received by the WTO. Of these, 445 were in force (see Figure 6-4).

Internal factors

Firstly, countries may develop FTAs in order to obtain bargaining leverage within the multilateral regime. On the fear of being "left out", for example, for South Korea at the initial stage of FTA policy development, the main drive was to prevent isolation from falling behind the tide. Also, the new FTA trends can be understood in terms of FTA catch-up. The Japanese case also shows that one of the main reasons for pursuing FTAs has been that "everyone else is doing it". Japan has been particularly

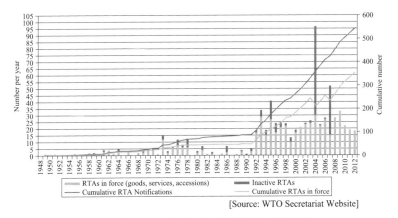

[Source: WTO Secretariat Website]

Figure 6-4   RTAs notified to the GATT/WTO (1948-2012)

motivated to seek FTAs when major economic powers such as the United States and China are involved in FTA arrangements. Facing the world market with many discriminatory FTAs in Europe and North America, Japan felt the need to secure markets for Japanese firms by setting up FTAs. At the ASEAN Plus Three (APT) meeting in Brunei in 2001, China dramatically proposed an ASEAN-China FTA to be put into place within ten years. Challenged to demonstrate Japanese leadership within East Asia, the best choice that Japan could grasp was promoting FTAs with Southeast Asian countries.

Secondly, domestic political incentives can heavily influence policymakers' decision to pursue FTAs. They considered FTAs as an effective way to force domestic economic structural reform, and to revitalize the stagnant economy. An FTA exposes companies in both participating countries to direct foreign competition, the result of which is likely to be either structural reform through peer pressure, or ongoing loss of market share and eventual industrial restructuring. Japanese leaders became increasingly interested in the ways in which the European Union (EU) and North American Free Trade Agreement (NAFTA) had used FTAs to promote domestic structural reform. In addition, policymakers may be motivated by domestic political considerations when entering into an FTA, motivated by a belief that the FTA will be beneficial to a specific group with political clout, though not necessarily to the economy as a whole. Similarly, there is an argument that democratic leaders may have a strong domestic political reason to promote FTAs, since they are pursuing economic policies geared toward the welfare of the voter, rather than toward special interests.

Thirdly, pressures from economic interest groups; for instance, in the case of the Japan-Mexico FTA, Japanese business groups such as Keidanren (the Japan Federation of Economic Organizations) pushed the Japanese government to have an FTA with Mexico to overcome the disadvantage resulting from their non-FTA member status. Because of NAFTA and the EU-Mexico FTA, EU and US firms can export their products to Mexico without tariffs, and Japanese firms had to pay high tariffs (16.2% in 2001) to export their products to Mexico. Faced with this problem, Keidanren organized an intensive series of meetings, and issued a report which detailed the anticipated negative effects, stating that the removal of tariffs on EU steel products was predicted to result in losses of $300 million annually for Japanese firms exporting steel products to Mexico. In addition to demands laid out in formal position papers, Keidanren also directly lobbied senior government officials in both countries for an expeditious accord.

Case study: Japanese FTA/TPP policy

Current Japanese FTAs/TPP

Japanese FTA Policy

Regarding East Asia, despite the diffusion of FTAs, the region was for the most part characterized by a near absence of formal FTAs and regional institutions. However, currently East Asian countries are pursuing greater formal economic institutionalization, linking existing bilateral and multilateral FTAs, and creating new ones as well. The APT has held regular meetings, and the East Asia Summit (EAS) brings together an additional three countries; India, Australia and New Zealand, with the United States and Russia joining the summit in 2011.

Among East Asian countries, Japan pursued a single-track approach for almost fifty years, focusing their trade negotiation efforts exclusively on the WTO, which emphasized multilateral trade liberalization based on the most favored nation principle, and shunning regionalism as harmful to the GATT/WTO system. However, the Japanese government today is also aggressively promoting FTAs with its trade partners. Currently, Japan has put a total of 13 FTAs into effect, 12 bilateral FTAs with partner countries, and one regional FTA with ASEAN, and is carrying out negotiations for FTAs with five further countries. Tokyo signed the Japan-Singapore EPA in January 2002, followed by bilateral FTA negotiations with Mexico, Malaysia, the Philippines, Thailand, and others (see Table 6-1).

As such, FTAs represent a policy of preferential trade agreements between specific countries aimed at eliminating tariff and non-tariff barriers, contrary to the most favored nation treatment that is the basic principle of the WTO. With this in mind, Japan's active and sustained engagement in FTAs in recent years can be interpreted as a significant shift in its trade policy.

The Japan-Singapore EPA (JSEPA) was the first FTA for Japan. A main reason

Table 6-1 Japanese Current FTA

(FAt with Australia implemented January 2015)

Implemented		Under negotiation	Under study
Singapore	November 2002	Korea	ASEAN+3
Mexico	April 2005	GCC	China, Japan, Korea
Malaysia	July 2006	Australia	RCEP
Chile	September 2007	Mougolia	TPP
Thailand	November 2007	Canada	EU
Indonesia	July 2008		Turkey
Brunei	July 2008		Colombia
Philippines	December 2008		
ASEAN	December 2008		
Switzerland	September 2009		
Vietnam	October 2009		
India	August 2011		
Peru	March 2012		

[Source: Author]

Japan chose Singapore as the first partner was that the country exported minimal agricultural products. Dairy products and cut flowers made up only 3% of Japan's imports from Singapore. Nonetheless, the treatment of the agricultural sector became a controversial issue during the negotiations. For example, in an article regarding JSEPA in August 2001, the Ministry of Agriculture, Forestry and Fisheries (MAFF) stated that Japanese agriculture, tariffs on agriculture, forestry and fisheries should be discussed at the WTO negotiations, and that further tariff reductions should not be made at negotiations over individual FTAs. It also showed its stance that further cuts of tariffs on agriculture-related products would not be achieved through bilateral negotiations.

The second FTA was with Mexico, and the negotiations were hard. Unlike the case of Singapore, agricultural products constituted 20.6% of the Japan's total imports from Mexico. In particular, the Mexican government strongly demanded the reduction of tariffs on major export items, such as pork, which made up 10.2% of Japan's imports from Mexico, and orange juice. The MAFF made considerable concessions, showing a flexible stance on the FTA with Mexico.

The new FTA shift towards the TPP

Recently, the Japanese government also announced its participation in the TPP negotiations. Since the agreement requires complete elimination of tariffs, including those applicable to agricultural products which are highly protected in the country, the Japanese government had been "not ready yet" to enter the grouping. However, Prime Minister Noda Yoshihiko publicly announced Japan's interest in joining TPP negotiations at the APEC Summit in Honolulu in 2011.

Given the circumstances, several questions arise. Why had Japan been pursuing regional trade strategies centered on the FTA/TPP, instead of relying solely on bilateral FTAs? What are the factors that promoted or hindered Japanese participation in the TPP? In what follows, this chapter addresses these questions, and makes suggestions regarding the Japanese government's trade policy to cope with the economic downturn after the tsunami disaster of March 2011.

The TPP and Japan

The TPP as a high-standard FTA

What then is the TPP? From a historical perspective, it is also perceived as taking the Asia-Pacific region beyond the end of the Cold War. It is a comprehensive agreement known as a high-standard 21st-century trade agreement, which attempts to promote trade liberalization, including the elimination of tariffs and expansion of trade in services beyond the existing framework of the WTO. TPP member states are aiming to establish new rules for service trade, investment, competition, government procurement, intellectual property and labor. Regarding trade, it sets principles of immediate or gradual abolition of tariffs on all items, including agricultural products, within 10 years. Thus it aims to advance the process of multilateralizing the "noodle bowl" of bilateral RTAs in the Asia-Pacific region, and it will be open to future accessions.

The TPP was originally established as the Trans-Pacific Strategic Economic Partnership agreement: the P4 amongst four relatively small countries in the Asia-Pacific —Singapore, New Zealand, Chile, and Brunei—and came into effect in May 2006. In March 2010, the US, Australia, Peru, and Vietnam became involved in negotiations among a total of eight countries. Malaysia entered the negotiations in October of the same year, followed by Mexico and Canada in October 2012, and Japan in July 2013.

Until recently, the Japanese government had not paid much attention to the TPP, and focused instead on bilateral FTA activities in parallel with its policy for Asian economic integration. According to the Trade White Paper 2001, the Japanese government noted clearly they would adopt an FTA strategy instead of the WTO's multilateral trade liberalization, and mentioned FTAs/EPAs as one form of regional integration. The Japanese government has long been an advocate of regionalism. In 2006, Japan proposed and strongly promoted a Comprehensive Economic Partnership in East Asia (CEPEA: ASEAN+6FTA). CEPEA is an economic integration proposal that considers trade liberalization and economic cooperation as the two pillars, and also ASEAN as the center of the hub. Even though TPP issues currently dominate the Japanese government, it regards the CEPEA as not contradictory to the TPP, and as being organically connected with the TPP as a building block of the FTAAP.

The Background of Japan's TPP Proposal

The significance of the TPP

For the Japanese government, the significance of the TPP is to participate in building the economic order of the Asia-Pacific under the new international environment, such as the economic and military emergence of China, the U.S.'s return to Asia, and Japan's lowered presence. This means that it will create an opening toward an FTA with the U.S., for the purpose of responding to the request of Japan's export industries to catch up with South Korea's "simultaneous FTA strategy". In other words, to solve the Japanese economy's problems, which have been referred to as the "lost 20 years", the TPP was regarded as an opportunity for new demand and job creation, and as a growth-stimulating policy. Therefore, participation in the TPP means an active FTA strategy to develop the Japanese economy, by incorporating the high growth of the Asia-Pacific and maintaining Japanese industry's global competitiveness.

Internationally, the impact of the Japanese government's statement of participation in the TPP was enormous. Specifically, it affected the East Asian regional integration movement which had been centered on ASEAN. In addition to Canada and Mexico, two countries that had shown their interest in participation in the TPP, China, which had been focused on the ASEAN+3 framework, softened its attitude flexibly toward

Japan's ASEAN+6 proposal (Okabe, 2012: 100). For instance, in the informal ASEAN+6 Conference in 2011, China and Japan declared to establish a workshop for the liberalization of trade, investment and services, regardless of their favored integration framework. Since it is difficult for China to participate in the TPP under the current situation, it finally decided to proceed with the East Asian integration negotiation process, despite its competitive strategies thus far.

Three main reasons

The Japanese government's "TPP consideration" was driven by three main reasons. The first is the Japan-US relations factor. The U.S. has consistently demanded that Japan open its agricultural market. At the same time, both sides attempted to strengthen the Japan-US alliance by fixing the earlier discord between Japan and the U.S. The Hatoyama administration had put an emphasis on Japan-China relations, and asserted the desirability of an East Asian Community. Moreover, the harshly contested Okinawa Futenma issue between Japan and the U.S. led to the worsening of the bilateral relationship. Since the U.S. could potentially decide that they don't have to keep the Japan-US bilateral alliance anymore, Japan should make an effort to keep it. The TPP was understood as one policy option to promote U.S. engagement in the Japan-US alliance relationship, through Japan-U.S. market integration. For example, some Japanese media reported that the conclusion of the TPP would strengthen Japan-U.S. relations and reduce Chinese power in Asia.

Secondly, there was a business group request trying to expand their export markets as a response to the U.S. request. Since many countries in the Asia-Pacific, including the U.S., who had not participated in the FTA proposal, were participating in the TPP, and aiming for high-level trade liberalization, the TPP rule has been considered as a possible de facto regulatory institution in the Asia-Pacific. Keidanren has pointed out the significance of rule-making, and urged early on for Japan to join the TPP. Given the recognition that Japanese participation was inevitable, Keidanren asserted the need of Japan's early participation saying, even if Japan finally participated in the TPP in the future, the rule would have been already set up, and urged Japan to passively accept it without its consent. Japan should lead rule-making of the Asia-Pacific region, and make a contribution to regional economic growth and job creation.

The third factor is South Korea. The South Korean government concluded its FTA negotiations with the U.S. in 2007, signed an FTA with the EU in 2010, and declared the start of its FTA negotiations with China. Given this situation, it is apparent that South Korea is actively promoting its FTAs with the U.S., EU and China, the three main export markets for Japan. To the Japanese government, already fearful of being left out of the FTA competition in East Asia, South Korea's push toward FTAs heightened the sense of crisis about Japan's economic and diplomatic disadvantage.

Hindering factors

On the other hand, strong domestic opposition existed against TPP participation, especially from the agriculture sector. The first indicator of strong interest group mobilization was the existence of informal political meetings, called the "Meeting for Careful Consideration of TPP". This group was initiated by about 140 members, one-third of Democratic Party of Japan (DPJ) politicians and supported by the Central Union of Agricultural Cooperatives (Zenkoku Nōgyō-kyōdō-kumiai Chuōkai), in short JA-Zenchu. It held meetings with agriculture groups opposing the FTA, and hosted lectures by anti-FTA scholars. The TPP was touted as a big problem which might entirely change the nation's architecture, by going to zero in terms of not only tariffs, but also finance, insurance, medical and services. The MAFF strongly opposed the TPP and regarded it as the "black ship (kurofune)" which would propel the complete collapse of Japanese agriculture.

Secondly, there was also the existence of JA-Zenchu, which was opposed to the strengthening of "individual income support allowance for farmers (side-payments)". JA-Zenchu's major activities include its role as a comprehensive advisory organization of agricultural administration, but also lobbying and appealing to government and parliament officials. For instance, JA-Zenchu submitted a request to the parliament opposing participation in TPP negotiations. A strong agricultural policy subgovernment led by JA-Zenchu, agricultural factions (farmer-supporting politicians in the ruling Liberal Democratic Party (LDP)) and MAFF bureaucrats, who shared strong common interests in promoting and protecting domestic agriculture, have played a primary role in establishing agricultural trade policy, and hindered agricultural liberalization. There had been close relationships between this agricultural policy triangle. The LDP made it possible to conduct pro-agricultural policy through party policy councils such as the LDP's Agricultural Committee, before the Parliamentary negotiation process. It is significant that 80% of LDP politicians agreed to the anti-TPP parliamentary appeal. In other words, Japan's trade policymaking process was influenced by informal institutions involving various agricultural groups, including JA-Zenchu and politicians.

Towards the promotion of FTA/TPP

In January 2017, President Trump signed an executive order formally ending U.S. participation in the TPP, thus casting a shadow on the future of the TPP. However, while the main purpose of the TPP is free trade, it is based on the idea of political stability to improve governance in the region through economic partnership, and its significance should not be underestimated. That is, with the stagnation of the Doha round, the TPP has become a major driving force, with regional liberalization as the central stage for trade talks, and, at the same time, carrying the strategic value of strengthening the relations between the member countries. In the future, the TPP can become the cornerstone for a WTO consensus. Be it through the Regional Comprehensive Economic Partnership (RCEP) or TPP, the concept of a framework established by Japan and other Asian countries imposing global trade rules presents a state of affairs different from the trends dictated by the West. Furthermore, Japan, which has a mature market economy and is proficient in creating an elaborate system, is expected to play a key role in establishing international regulations. The TPP is expected to play a major role in the development of regional order in the Asia-Pacific.

In promoting FTAs, it is necessary to consider the liberalization of agriculture by examining the role of agriculture in building a competitive Japanese economy, and implementing policies to strengthen the agriculture sector and improving the skills of agricultural workers. One conceivable solution to this problem is support for the acquisition of technical skills, to encourage job transfers to more productive occupations. Considering the fact that many agricultural workers are senior in age and have difficulty in switching careers, income benefits are likely to be the most realistic measure.

Similarly, to overcome the FTA obstacles, it is essential to have strong political leadership in East Asian countries with a strong determination. Particularly important are leaderships in Japan, China, Korea and ASEAN, which have decisive positions in determining the course of regional development. As the country with the highest level of economic development in East Asia, Japan needs to contribute in a variety of ways to the construction of an FTA that incorporates East Asia. Discussions have begun on an FTA with the countries of East Asia as signatories, and Japan needs to play a leading role in making an intellectual contribution to the debate on planning an East Asian FTA and the realization of it.

To carry out those roles, it is essential that Japan should build cooperative relations with the countries of East Asia. For an East Asia-wide FTA, not only economic factors but also political factors have to be dealt with. Accordingly, maintaining good political relationships is very important for the formation of a region-wide FTA. Having noted the crucial role of political leadership in formulating and implementing desirable policies for the region, one cannot overemphasize not only domestic reform and positive structural adjustment measures, but also the important role that the public plays for supporting political leaders.

References

1) Balassa, B.A. (1961), *The Theory of Economic Integration*, Homewood, Illinois: R.D. Irwin.
2) Grieco, J.M. and G.H. Ikenberry (2003), *State Power and World Markets: The International Political Economy*, New York: W.W. Norton.
3) Mattli, W. (1999), *The Logic of Regional Integration: Europe and Beyond*, New York: Cambridge University Press.
4) Okabe, N. (2012), "TPP to Higashi Ajia no ketsugo mezase." [Aim for the TPP and East Asian regional integration] *Kaigai Jijou*, 60 (4), 93-103.
5) Scholte, J. A. (2000), *Globalization: A Critical Introduction*, London: Macmillan.

Recommended Works

1) Aggarwal, V.K. and S. Urata (2006) *Bilateral Trade Agreements in the Asia-Pacific: Origins, Evolution, and Implications*, New York and London: Routledge.
   This edited volume attempts to highlight the underlying political and economic factors driving the Asia-Pacific region's bilateral preferential trade agreements. It provides detailed analysis of the trade strategies of Asian countries and the United States.
2) Mansfield, E.D. and H.V. Milner (eds.) (1997), *The Political Economy of Regionalism*, New York: Columbia University Press.

The purpose of this volume is to address a wide variety of issues pertaining to the political economy of regionalism. It also bears on longstanding debates in the field of international relations concerning the relative importance of domestic and international factors in explaining international outcomes.

3) Stiglitz, J. E. (2006), *Making Globalization Work*, New York: W.W. Norton.

Attempting to address how to make globalization work for the world, especially for the developing countries, this volume examines an obstacle to equitable globalization and provides a set of possible solutions.

CHAPTER 7

Japan's Foreign Policy in the Post-War Period: A Road to Recovery and Major Power Status[1]

After its disastrous defeat in the Second World War, Japan embarked on a nation building process again, which exclusively focused on reconstructing and strengthening its economy. Fortunately, the so-called Yoshida line — depend on the U.S. for national security and put first priority on economic growth — functioned successfully, enabling Japan to achieve the desired goal. While Japan's approach toward the world was entirely economic-orientated during the Cold War era, the changing security environment and the protracted ailing economy in the post-Cold War period compelled Japan to modify its one-dimensional economic approach, by expanding its reach to the security field. This chapter surveys Japan's foreign and security policy after the Second World War.

Japan's Foreign and Security Policy during the Cold War Period

Change of U.S. occupation policy

Japan's defeat in the Second World War resulted in an American occupation, which continued until 1952. The occupation itself can best be divided into two distinct periods. In the early days, the Americans were intent on disarming and weakening Japan, so that it would never pose a future threat to the world. The Japanese must be humbled by the occupation forces, with living standards forced to match those of neighboring countries (Borden, 1984: 62-67). Reflecting this conception, America's first investigating mission urged that Japan be kept weak through a series of reparation payments that would forcibly relocate Japan's remaining industrial facilities to other countries. An impoverished Japan would not pose a threat.

However, the Communist uprisings in Asia made the Americans quickly realize that they needed an economically strong Japan to stabilize the region and contain

Communism. By 1945, anti-colonial, independent governments had sprouted in Indonesia and Vietnam. These consequences did not only alarm their former European colonial masters, but the Americans as well. Vietnam became an instant trouble spot, exemplified by the Indochina War against France (1946-54), as the Vietnamese leader, Ho Chi Minh, was labeled a Communist. In 1948, Kim Il Sung established a Communist North Korea. But more importantly, American-supported Chiang Kai-shek seemed incapable of winning the battle against Communist Mao Zedong in China. Circumstances thus had fortuitously changed Japan's status.

These geopolitical changes soon made the Cold War the top agenda. By 1948, the punitive focus on reparations had been discarded in favor of reconstructing the Japanese economy as a strong ally. Marking the turnaround in 1948, the U.S. National Security Council (NSC 13/2) not only stopped the financial drain of imposed repayments, but also insisted on making "economic rehabilitation" a priority. This significant shift in American occupation policy became irreversible by developments in China and Korea.

In October 1949, the Chinese Communists achieved victory over their Kuomintang foes, and almost immediately concluded a Sino-Soviet Treaty of Friendship and Alliance. Moreover, the outbreak of the Korean War in June 1950 unexpectedly made Asia, not Europe, the center of Cold War confrontations. America, backed by a United Nations (UN) resolution, plunged into the war on the Korean Peninsula, which made a confrontation between the U.S. and China unavoidable. Responding to these current threats, American strategy now regarded Japan as a key Asian surrogate in the ongoing battle between the Communists and the Western Bloc. The outbreak of the Cold War in Asia inevitably changed Japan's value to the U.S.

Other considerations, namely, economic imperatives, also played a part in creating such a decisive shift in U.S. policy. An extended American occupation of Japan undoubtedly would be costly because of Japan's devastated economy. For instance, by the end of 1947, Japan's industrial production was still only 45% of its 1930-1934 average. The status of trade was even more forlorn, with exports accounting for only 19% of those pre-war levels. The U.S. supported Japan's shattered economy, but the size of the assistance was simply too large. Therefore, to American policymakers, Japan's rapid economic recovery now became an issue to be addressed.

To assist Japan's quick recovery, the U.S. emphasized focusing on Southeast Asia to keep Japan away from Communist China. These countries were certainly capable of supplying the necessary food and raw materials that Japan required. The resulting increase in productivity from this advantageous trade would make Japan increasingly competitive with other industrialized countries. Thus it was hardly accidental that Japan chose to cultivate links with the Southeast Asian countries, even stretching to Australia, rather than with the Chinese Communists. Japan obediently took the required steps in this direction, by first initiating reparations to these favored Southeast Asian countries.

Conclusion of the Japan-U.S. Security Treaty

The key individual shepherding the vision of a mutually advantageous relationship with the U.S. was Prime Minister Yoshida Shigeru (1946-1947, 1948-1954). The traditional Yoshida line, which is dubbed the "Yoshida Doctrine", dominated Japanese thinking during the post-war period. He stressed a Japan that was fully aligned with the U.S., and a foreign policy that was largely economically determined. Fortunately, Japan could pursue this Yoshida line without difficulty, since Article 9 of Japan's constitution conveniently allowed Japan to avoid rearmament. Although eventually creating the Self-Defense Forces (SDF), Article 9 kept it from being fatally drawn into the U.S. Cold War strategy of containing Communism in Asia (see chapter 8).

Shifting its occupation policy, the American occupiers had anyway pushed Japan in a conservative direction as early as 1948, when the risk of Communist revolution in Japan and China–to say nothing of the Soviet threat–had come to be seen as a greater peril than the revival of militarism. The outbreak of the Korean War reinforced this American perception and made it necessary for the U.S. to secure strategic military bases. This meant that the U.S. wanted to maintain forces on Japanese soil following the official end of the occupation. Both Japan and the U.S. were well aware of America's newly developed strategic interests in Japan. So, as an enticement to encourage an early end to the occupation, Yoshida offered to host American bases in Okinawa, using UN Charter Article 51 as camouflage for this implicit trade-off (see Chapter 8). With its security being assured, Japan could then concentrate on an all-out economic recovery.

In September 1951, the bargaining resulted in the conclusion of the San Francisco

Peace Treaty and the Japan-U.S. Security Treaty. As might be expected, the San Francisco Peace Treaty, initiated under U.S. leadership to meet its Cold War needs, was lenient to Japan, so as not to exacerbate Japan's wartorn economy. It was fortunate for Japan to have concluded such a lenient treaty, but Japan had to pay the price. It failed subsequently to conclude peace treaties with Communist countries such as the Soviet Union. Japan also had to abandon effective control over the Okinawa and the Bonin Islands, and conclude a peace treaty with Taiwan as an authentic government of China. Due to strong animosity towards Japan, South Korea, Japan's former colony, declined to come to a formal peace arrangement. The partial conclusion of the peace treaty, however, divided the nation into two camps: one who supported an alliance with the U.S. and Western countries, and another who supported the idea to become a neutral state. In addition, the subsequent conclusion of the Japan-U.S. Security Treaty caused controversy (see Chapter 8).

Contrary to Japan's wishes and expectations, the terms of the Security Treaty did not leave the two countries on anything like an equal footing. Although the agreement allowed U.S. military forces to be based in Japan, there was no reciprocal obligation for them to defend Japan. Moreover, the treaty provided U.S. forces with the right to suppress domestic disturbances in Japan, an option normally deemed to be unacceptable in an independent state. Revision of the unequal security treaty therefore became an unfinished task for Japan.

Prime Minister Kishi Nobusuke (1957-1960), a former Class-A war criminal, poured his energy to revise the Security Treaty on more equal terms. Kishi focused on getting a commitment from America to defend Japan against aggression, mainly from the Soviet Union and deleting the clause allowing U.S. forces to suppress Japanese

Popular protests around the Japanese Diet buildings in may 1960.
Source: http://ja.wikipedia.org/wiki/%E5%AE%
 89% E4%BF%9D%E9%97%98%E4%
 BA%89

domestic disorder. However, left-wing parties launched a campaign to completely abandon the Security Treaty in any form. Support for this movement was dispersed widely throughout the Japanese public. University students in particular became vocal opponents of these treaty negotiations. Ignoring the potential for unrest, however, the Kishi administration adopted the renegotiated treaty in May 1960, which was more equal. As anticipated, its passage was met with violence and recurrent demonstrations, not only outside the Diet building, but also throughout Japan. However, the anti-Japan-U.S. Security Treaty movement soon disappeared after its adoption.

The Vietnam War and its implications

1965 marked the start of another Cold War division in Asia. The U.S. started air bombing against North Vietnam in 1965 in an effort to support South Vietnam. As part of its Asia-Pacific strategy, the U.S. persuaded South Korea, the Philippines, Australia, New Zealand and Thailand to provide at least a token contingent of military forces to support the war effort in Vietnam. Japan was not an exception. The U.S. put pressure on a newly wealthy Japan to assume a more significant role in financing the anti-communist struggle in Asia. Contrary to U.S. prospects for a quick operation, however, the U.S. was drawn into a stalemate. With increasingly bitter domestic opposition demanding the withdrawal of U.S. troops due to mounting death tolls, economic cost and the continued Vietnamese impasse, America became hard pressed. Desperately hoping to exit from the conflict, the U.S. shifted its strategy, which unexpectedly yielded two substantial results for Japan: reversion of Okinawa to Japanese sovereignty and normalization of diplomatic relations with China.

Not surprisingly, Prime Minister Sato Eisaku (1964-72) had a motive that guided his decision to provide support for U.S. efforts in Vietnam. In exchange for Japan's support, Sato hoped for early reversion of Okinawa. By assuring U.S. President Richard Nixon of America's ability to continue using its existing military bases on the island, he obtained U.S. agreement for reversion of Okinawa, scheduled in 1972. Such reassurance was vital, since Okinawa had played a key strategic role as America's vital Asian military base, especially during the Vietnam War. The reversion provided Japan with a sense that it was now competent to exercise a large degree of influence, as a member of international society.

The second was American normalization of its relationship with Communist China. Japan had long hoped to normalize relations with China, but its ties with the U.S. constrained Japan's hand. As an exit strategy from Vietnam, however, anti-communist Nixon suddenly turned around by visiting China, which supported North Vietnam's war, and normalized the relationship in 1972. Although Japan was taken by surprise, Prime Minister Tanaka Kakuei (1972-74) visited China soon after, and concluded a peace treaty in 1978.

Due to the improvement of Sino-American relations, Japan obtained room to initiate an increasingly autonomous Asian policy, without offending the ideological strictures formerly dictated by the U.S.. Regardless of differences in social, political or economic systems, Japan pursued its diplomatic advantage by improving relationships with all neighbouring countries, edging more toward the middle ground between East and West. It came as no surprise when the Japanese recognized North Vietnam in September 1973, with an embassy opening in Hanoi after the U.S. withdrawal from South Vietnam. Japan's attempt to conduct more autonomous policy was, however, soon frustrated due to the outbreak of the "new" Cold War.

Towards a more substantial alliance in the 1980s

Renewed Cold War tensions caused by the Soviet military build-up in the Far East and aggression against Afghanistan in 1979 encouraged Japan to focus more intently on its national security. Quickly realizing the rising tension, Prime Minister Ohira Masayoshi (1978-80) formulated a concept of "comprehensive security", which marked a watershed in Japanese foreign policy. The new concept illustrated Japan's determination to employ all means possible, such as a combination of diplomacy, national defence, economic and other policy measures, to protect its security that encompassed from national security to natural disasters. For the first time, the Japanese expressed their intention to take full responsibility for their own security, although the means were limited to economic and diplomatic aspects. A sense of responsibility as a major industrialized country and the changed strategic thinking resulted in Japan's readiness to take up more of a security role, in the face of U.S. demands.

Faced with a Soviet military build-up, the U.S. felt obliged to repeatedly pressure the Japanese government into increasing its defence budget and expanding its military role, to counter Soviet threats. An expansion of Japan's security role would allow the U.S. to shift its forces and more of its attention to the Indian Ocean and the Middle East. Japan's rapid economic growth also made Americans think that Japan seemed to be a "free rider", enjoying peace and stability without sharing the burden. In response to the revived Cold War tensions and U.S. pressure, Prime Minister Suzuki Zenko (1980-82) demonstrated Japan's willingness to ensure the safety of sea lanes for up to 1,000 miles in either direction of its home ports, at the 1981 summit meeting with the U.S.. Suzuki went further, by describing the long standing Japan-U.S. relationship as an "alliance" for the first time in the post-war era in the Japan-U.S. Joint Communiqué. But a Japanese military role extending outside the promised 1,000 miles seemed neither constitutionally nor politically realizable. Besides, not only the public, but also most politicians and bureaucrats were still unwilling to embrace an expanded security role. Accordingly, Suzuki's careless statements inevitably provoked domestic controversy.

The subsequent Prime Minister, Nakasone Yasuhiro (1982-87), hoped to elevate Japan's position by taking up a more activist stance. Nakasone limited his grand security strategy for the most part to repairing and improving Japan's relationship with the U.S.. His goal was to have the Americans come to regard the Japanese as an equal partner in containing the Soviet threat, and to expand Japan's security reach to increase Japan's visibility in the world. Fortunately, the Nakasone and Reagan administrations largely saw eye to eye on key diplomatic issues. Frequent meetings between them highlighted the developing close relationship between the two leaders, and demonstrated Japan's focus on strengthening its relationship with the U.S.. Nakasone expanded Suzuki's initiatives, by continuing to strengthen the Japan-U.S. alliance, and bulking up the defence budget. Following this approach, Nakasone in 1987 managed to remove the long-standing 1% of Gross National Product (GNP) cap on defence spending, which was instituted by the Miki administration in 1976. The budget has not largely increased however, fluctuating at around 1% of GNP (for instance, 1.004% of GNP in 1987 and 1.006% in 1989). He also partially lifted the previously imposed export ban on defence-related technology, to strengthen ties with the U.S.. Largely due to his efforts, the Japan-U.S. alliance became more substantial and equal in the 1980s, as he hoped.

Japan's Economic Diplomacy during the Cold War Period

Japan's economic advance in Asia

As mentioned, the San Francisco Peace Treaty tailored by the U.S. aimed to promote Japan's economic recovery as a strong ally. Because of Japan's critical shortage of American dollars, the U.S.-crafted treaty strictly limited Japan's reparations to provision of services. After having tough negotrations, Japan was able to reach agreements with Asian countries such as Thailand, Malaysia, Singapore, the Philippines and Indonesia in the 1950s and 1960s. As hoped, reparations paid by services and goods to the Southeast Asian countries greatly contributed to the rehabilitation of the war-damaged Japanese economy. They became new outlets for Japan's developing heavy industry and suppliers of natural resources. In line with American expectations, the Asian markets offset the loss of Japan's more traditional export destinations, namely, mainland China and Korea. Moreover, the adroit use of war reparations proved to be a convenient tool for reestablishing relationships with the Asian countries. For more than 20 years (ending with the Philippines in July 1976), reparations to these countries continued to act as an underwriter of Japan's economic security by enabling Japan to secure not only natural resources but also export markets. In addition to the governmental reparations, the private sector was also strongly encouraged to seek closer economic links with Southeast Asia, leading to Japan's bourgeoning economic growth.

In addition to the positive effect of the reparations, an "income doubling plan", introduced by Prime Minister Ikeda Hayato (1960-1964) to raise living standards and improve social infrastructure, quickly brought results. To accomplish this proposed growth, the government not only promoted exports and severely restricted imports, but also restrained most forms of investment abroad, to boost competitiveness of domestic industries in export markets. As a result of such protection of its domestic industries, Japan was able to become competitive in a short period, with its average economic growth rate reaching 10.9% during the boom years. In 1964, Japan earned admittance to the Organization of Economic Cooperation and Development (OECD), which meant that Japan obtained a position as a developed country internationally. The Tokyo Olympics held in the same year also boosted Japan's confidence. As an offshoot of this "miracle" growth, Japan considerably expanded its foreign aid program to Asia, which eventually completely replaced the reparations.

Moreover, the outbreak of the Vietnam War further accelerated Japan's economic growth. Ironically, post-war conflicts such as the Korean and the Vietnam Wars proved to be advantageous for rebuilding Japan's economy. The Vietnam War also provided the Japanese with new opportunities to conduct "economic diplomacy", although within a boundary limited by U.S. strategy.

America's rising demands on Japan to support U.S. efforts in Vietnam paralleled Japan's own rising economic strength. Due to deepening U.S. involvement in the Vietnam War, America turned to Japan to bear more of the burden in advancing western interests in Asia. Faced with such overarching demands, Prime Minister Sato put in an effort to establish the Asian Development Bank (ADB), with both the U.S. and Japan contributing 20% of the funds. Japan also began to provide direct aid to South Vietnam, to support the U.S. war in Vietnam. The U.S. demanded additional Japanese aid to Indonesia, where the anti-communist Suharto government was struggling to solidify a new regime. Consequently, Japanese economic assistance to the region from 1967 onwards increased considerably. The U.S. now expected Japan to share responsibility for future Asian development, since economic growth was thought to keep the Asian countries from any Communist infection. In American eyes, this was largely an attempt to reprise the "Marshall Plan", with the U.S. and Japan closely cooperating to achieve a common objective. Employing the pretext of aid, Japan ended up shouldering some of the burden of the Vietnam War without raising public controversy.

Japan's looming economic presence

Up until the late 1960s, the Japanese government had actively discouraged direct foreign investment into Japan to provide Japanese firms with space to grow. Japanese overseas investment was strictly limited as well. This strategy contradicted the policies adopted by other western industrialized countries that were reducing barriers for such economic activities. Despite western expectations to open its markets and lift restrictions, Japan's move towards liberalization was far from satisfactory.

In 1971, suffering from a worsening economy, Nixon suddenly decided to allow the dollar to float, scuttling the post-war financial architecture. This meant the end of the favorable fixed exchange rate ($1=360 yen) that had assisted Japan's post-war miraculous growth by spurring exports. While the floating dollar and corresponding appreciating yen shocked the Japanese, they helped Japan's economic advance into Asia by accelerating its investment. Accordingly, Japan's economic presence in Asia loomed, which made a clear contrast to the dwindling American presence due to the prolonged Vietnam War.

Reacting to the disastrous Vietnam War, the U.S. began to cut aid packages such as military assistance to Thailand, Indonesia and the Philippines. Following the fall of Saigon, the percentage of American aid (including military and economic) to Asia plummeted from 67% in 1973 to a mere 14% in 1976. The power vacuum arising from a diminishing U.S. presence provided corresponding scope for Japan to flex its economic muscle, resulting in the increase of Japan's regional aid, which surpassed that of the U.S. by 1975. By this time, partly because of the Oil Shock of 1973, America's focus was directed increasingly towards the Middle Eastern countries, such as Israel and Egypt. In contrast, Japan's assistance was mostly directed towards Asia.

However, Japan's ever-looming economic presence in Asia made the Asian countries anxious whether Japan was again trying to dominate the region, this time by economic means. Their fear of Japan's economic dominance was illustrated by anti-Japanese protests in Thailand and Indonesia, when Prime Minister Tanaka paid visits in 1974. By then, Japan came to regard the Association of Southeast Asian Nations (ASEAN) as the most reasonable regional option. But these protests made Japan reappraise its Asia policy, which was essentially dominated by economic transactions. With a hope to improve relationships, Prime Minister Fukuda Takeo (1976-77) announced the doctrine in 1977 which emphasized: (1) mutual confidence and trust between Japan and ASEAN, (2) its wish to play a bridging role between Indochina and ASEAN for peace and stability in the region, and (3) its promise not to become a military power. The key was Japan's willingness to regard ASEAN as an equal partner. In contrast to Tanaka's visit, Fukuda was warmly welcomed. Since Japan's economic inflows towards the Asian countries plunged after the 1973 Oil Shock, they looked to Japan's economic assistance as an effective tool to spur their economic growth. Expectations of economic assistance proved the driving force behind Fukuda's warm welcome. Thus, Japan's economic ascendance provided a mixture of both fear and expectation to the Asian countries, but it only alarmed the U.S.

Declining U.S. presence and rise of Japan

As Japan's trade surplus grew, trade frictions between the U.S. and Japan became intense. America's growing trade deficits seemed to symbolize the ascendancy of Japan as an economic power, and the decline of the U.S. economic presence. By 1980, Japan's economy had come to represent 10% of the world's GDP. In contrast, the out of control deficit of the U.S. ballooned. Faced with punitive tariffs from the U.S., Japan had no choice other than accepting a system of supposedly voluntary restraints on their exports. Among exports, the symbol for the trade frictions between the two was Japanese cars.

During the 1980s, America found itself entrapped by historically high twin deficits, encompassing both trade and federal budgets. It was largely a result of Reagan's arms race with the Soviet Union and tax cuts. With trade imbalances in 1985 appearing to threaten its economic viability, the U.S. attempted to rebalance trade patterns by skilfully influencing foreign exchange rates. The G5 countries (the U.S., Japan, France, the UK and West Germany) hoped to lessen America's out of control trade imbalances, and agreed to the terms of the 1985 Plaza Accord, which aimed to reconfigure the foreign exchange rates. However, the result proved otherwise. Even after the 1985 Plaza Accord, the U.S. trade deficit still stood high. Not only did the Accord fail to achieve the desired outcomes that had driven the meetings, but also ironically served mainly to increase Japan's economic influence. U.S. frustration at the failure of the agreement goaded the U.S. into escalating its demands on Japan to open its home market to U.S. products.

To help salvage an increasingly tense confrontation between Japan and the U.S., Japan committed itself to a foreign aid program which would alleviate some of America's financial burden within Asia. Japan tackled the foreign aid issue rather systematically, by setting out a series of targets. Compared to a total of $105 million provided in 1960, its aid increased by a factor of 50 times ($5.634 billion) by

1986. Even when adjusted for worldwide inflation, the increase in Japan's Official Development Assistance (ODA) over the period was impressive. Thus, the boost in overseas assistance was not only an attempt by Japan to seize leadership in Asia, given the vacuum created by U.S. disengagement after the Vietnam War. The expanded initiative was also an attempt to placate the growing wrath of the U.S., as well as the world.

As expected, Japan's dramatic increase in aid was mirrored by its regional recipients. ASEAN countries became major beneficiaries, with Japan solidly in place as each country's largest donor. For instance, Japan's assistance in 1987 accounted for 63.1% of total aid received by Indonesia, 78.5% by Malaysia, 53.7% by the Philippines, 69.4% by Thailand, 50.6% by Singapore and 88.6% by Brunei. It also accounted for 55.7% of total aid received by China in 1989. By 1991, Japan had overtaken the U.S. as the world's largest donor. Such massive inflows of Japanese money into the region through governmental aid programs and the influx of Japanese private capital resulted in regional economic expansion and deeper interdependence.

The strong yen also contributed to the sizable increase of Japan's foreign direct investment (FDI). During this period, Japanese investment in the Asian region, to maintain competitiveness, grew to outstrip that of the U.S., due to an appreciating yen, a growing scarcity of blue-collar workers and an increase in wages. The surge in Japan's FDI did successfully create a division of labor, first producing a number of regional "sub-contractors" for production at the lower value-added end, and then promoting intra-industry trade. As a consequence, Japan's trade with Asia doubled in the 1980s, but Japan's growing dominance did not translate into greater regional imports to Japan. To the rest of the world, Japanese trade policy, which closed its home market without absorbing imports, seemed badly unfair.

As Cold War tensions eased, the Japanese government, encouraged by its unparalleled economic strength, became even more assertive. It believed that by effectively employing its economic muscle, it could target and increase Japan's political clout. However, this assumption unfortunately proved to be valid for only a brief period. The forthcoming Gulf War, together with the inevitable collapse of the bubble economy, would soon expose the limits of an economic-contribution-only approach.

Japan's Security Policy in the post-Cold War Era

Japan's international contribution in the framework of the UN

The 1990s opened with a dramatic and largely unanticipated change, namely the end of the Cold War. Japan assumed that the end of the Cold War potentially opened up some space for Japan to maneuver and establish a new international order which was not dominated by military strength. Japan expected that it could now play a more positive international role, one that might be more commensurate with its growing economic power (now accounting for 14% of Gross World Product).

However, the Gulf War of 1991 came as a shock for the Japanese, by revealing their chronic inability to respond quickly to a pressing issue (see Chapter 8). Depending on the U.S. for its national security, Japan had avoided getting involved in security issues during the Cold War period and exclusively focused on economic affairs. Yet, the Gulf War gave rise to debates as to how to contribute to the peace and stability of the world as a member of international society.

To enable a humanitarian contribution, the Miyazawa government (1991-1993) adopted the Act on Cooperation for United Nations Peacekeeping Operations and Other Operations (hereafter, the PKO law) in 1992. Although the Five Principles adopted simultaneously constrained Japan's participation to a large degree, the law enabled the SDF to participate in peacekeeping operations conducted under the auspices of the UN. Soon after the adoption, Japan for the first time dispatched 600 SDF personnel to the UN Transitional Authority in Cambodia (UNTAC), where they engaged in repairing roads and constructing bridges in "safe" areas. Since then, Japan has been actively involved in peacekeeping missions, such as in East Timor (2002), Haiti (2010) and South Sudan (2012). It also extended its scope of action in 2009 by adopting the Anti-Piracy Measures Law, to enable Japan's naval vessels to protect any ship from pirates off the coast of Somalia, to cooperate with other countries in the framework of the UN.

Japan's pursuit for a larger security role is also illustrated by the decision in 2006 to upgrade peacekeeping missions conducted by the SDF, from incidental to core SDF activities. This meant that international duties gained roughly equal significance to territorial defense. Furthermore, in 2007, the government established Central Readiness Forces[2], with a view to educating and training personnel for international peacekeeping missions, and swiftly dispatching SDF personnel to peacekeeping operations. Although still constrained on its roles and actions, Japan's contribution by military means has been broadening.

Expanding Japan's role in the framework of the alliance

The end of the Cold War and the following demise of the Soviet Union not only changed the international order, but also had an impact on the Japan-U.S. alliance. It seemed that the Japan-U.S. alliance lost the original purpose of its establishment—containment of the Soviet Union—and therefore was drifting apart (Funabashi, 1997). The unstable regional security situation exemplified by the 1993 North Korean missile launch, and its alleged nuclear weapons development program brought security issues to the fore (see Chapter 9), but a "drifting alliance" made the Japanese uneasy that the U.S. might not defend Japan in every contingency. Ongoing trade frictions also added bitterness to the already soured relationships between the two countries.

In addition to the North Korean security threat, China's missile launch towards Taiwan in 1996 further confirmed Asia was not stable. Faced with regional instabilities, Japan saw no other viable option than to broaden its role in cooperation with the U.S.. Japan's renewed perception resulted in a review of the alliance, transforming the alliance whose nature was simply "bilateral", to a more regional alliance for peace and stability in the region. The review of the alliance then led to adoption of the 1997 New Guideline, enlarging Japan's security role under the framework of the alliance (see Chapters 8 and 9). A driving force for the integration of Japan into the U.S. alliance system was a shared sense of crisis that was induced by the regional crises among Japanese policy makers. A changed domestic political landscape also facilitated the process.

Due to the inauguration of the Hosokawa coalition government in 1993, the "55 system" that had long dominated Japan's domestic political scene since the formation of the Liberal Democratic Party (LDP) in 1955, came to an end. Following this domestic turmoil, a new political alignment, the Murayama coalition government (including the Japan Socialist Party (JSP), the LDP, and the *Sakigake* Party) was formed in June 1994, which had an enormous impact on Japan's security and foreign policy. Murayama Tomiichi was the head of the JSP, which had long opposed the SDF and the alliance with the U.S. as unconstitutional. But as Prime Minister, Murayama abandoned the party's long standing tenet, and announced that he would support the SDF and the Japan-U.S. security treaty. Given the reality that Japan has totally depended on the U.S. for its national security, Murayama did not have a choice. Hence, political obstacles which had extensively constrained Japan's security policy disappeared. The abandonment of its principles was, however, a serious blow for the JSP, resulting in the loss of its traditional public support. The waning influence of the JSP meant the revival of the LDP, with Hashimoto Ryutaro as Prime Minister forming government in 1996. This resulted in the redefinition of the alliance and the adoption of the Guidelines in 1997.

Japan's move towards a more proactive role in security issues culminated in its support for the U.S.-led "War on Terrorism", when Koizumi Junichiro, an unequivocal nationalist, took power in 2001. Soon after the September 11 attacks, Koizumi showed his willingness to side with the U.S. by swiftly passing special legislation to enable military cooperation with the U.S. (see Chapters 8 and 9). Next, when the U.S. attacked Iraq by invoking the rationale of the "War on Terrorism" in 2003, Koizumi soon responded to U.S. demands by sending the Ground Self Defense Force (GSDF) to Iraq. As Chapter 8 shows, the decision to support the war was controversial because of the lack of an appropriate UN resolution, but in addition to Koizumi's strong leadership, a rough consensus among political parties on Japan's broader international contribution in the security field, allowing for some minor disagreements, enabled the government to smoothly expand its security role.

In 2004, partly responding to new perceived security threats such as terrorism, the government adopted a National Defense Program Guideline (NDPG)[3] to develop "effective" forces. What was remarkable was that the 2004 NDPG firstly and explicitly identified China and North Korea as "threats". This 2004 NDPG was replaced in 2010 by a new NDPG, which features a "Dynamic Defense Force", by substituting the "Basic Defense Force" concept of the former NDPG, to effectively respond to emerging security challenges. The central idea is to respond seamlessly to situations categorized as "grey zones", namely, in-between situations in peace time and other contingencies. At the backdrop, there were increasing China's research activities in Japan's Exclusive Economic Zones, and intensified tensions between Japan and China near the territorial waters of the *Senkaku* Islands.

Partly responding to the increasingly unstable regional circumstance, the second Abe coalition government (2013~present), which advocates Japan being a "proactive contributor to peace", implemented a series of institutional changes. To begin with, it set up the National Security Council (NSC) in 2013. The aim of the NSC was to formulate a more effective and consistent national security policy. It then adopted the National Security Strategy, a guiding principle of Japan's security and its national interests and objectives. The government also abandoned the arms trade ban policy announced in 1967 (Three Principles on Arms Exports), and installed a new policy in 2014, so that Japan can export or provide defense equipment to other countries, when such provision contributes to peace and stability. It also adopted the Development Cooperation Charter in 2015, to enable provision of assistance to a military arena for peaceful purposes. Japan's quest for a substantial military role culminated in reform of the Guidelines for Japan-U.S. cooperation in April 2015, after 18 years (see, chapter 9). Subsequently, the Abe government adopted the Legislation for Peace and Security in September 2015 (which came into effect in March 2016), to broaden the SDF's role in a security field. The adoption of the new legislation was divisive, since it enables Japan to exercise the right of collective self-defense, if limitedly, without geographical restriction. Although not only opposition parties but also the public made demonstrations against it throughout Japan, the Abe coalition government pushed through the bill.

Japan's Economic Diplomacy in the post-Cold War Era

The Asian economic crisis

During the Cold War period, a combination of Japanese overseas assistance, trade and investment contributed significantly to economic development throughout Asia. In addition to massive capital inflows, a relocation of Japanese manufacturing companies to Asia resulted in a new division of labor, with Asia producing low end products. Japan took its place, if not explicitly, as an innovative leader of new products and technologies. It seemed Japanese subcontractors brought to these Asian countries a Japanese model of economic development, which is characterized by a close coordination between the government and the business sectors and governmental interventions that serve to protect targeted infant industries. The World Bank's 1993 report, *The East Asian Miracle: Economic Growth and Public Policy*, acknowledged the dramatic economic growth of the region and the East Asian strategy of economic development, which differed from the Western approach focusing on the free-market economy.

While Asia enjoyed miraculous economic growth, a collapse of the Thai baht pegged to the U.S. dollar in July 1997 heralded the start of the Asian economic crisis. The rapidly depreciating Thai baht enlarged not only the trade deficit, but also generated a large outflow of short-term capital, making a bad situation much worse. Investors became fearful that Thailand would be unable to sustain its growing current account deficit. In a domino like effect, foreign investors began to view other Asian countries, such as Indonesia and South Korea, with pessimism. Responding to the deteriorating situation, the International Monetary Fund (IMF) intervened to bail out the Thai economy, but its conditionality imposed on Thailand as a requirement for any loan granted, was drastic.

Japan thought the "one-size-fits-all" IMF conditionality (liberalizing FDI, breaking up conglomerates and dismantling close relationships between the Thai government and the private sector) was harsh. It considered the IMF's prescription to open financial markets to foreigners and to restructure their economic systems ignored the pragmatic economic development of Asian countries, which Japan had long supported through its sizeable ODA program. With ASEAN's agreement, the Hashimoto government therefore proposed a concrete plan in September 1997 to establish an Asian Monetary Fund (AMF), a regional institution with Japan at its center, but which excluded the U.S. The proposal implied a clash of economic norms between the Japanese government, whose hallmark was a close relationship between the government and the private sector, and the IMF, which pursued an American style market model. This attempt was, however, frustrated by explicit U.S. rejection.

Unfortunately, the IMF's intervention did not work. Perceiving the IMF's failure to bail out the Asian economies such as Indonesia, South Korea and Thailand, Japan proposed the Miyazawa Initiative in 1998. Its aim was to bilaterally provide funds to the Asian countries in trouble, without imposing strict prior conditions like the IMF required. The proposal was of course hailed by Asian countries which were hit by this economic turmoil.

By shifting its strategy from a multilateral to a bilateral emphasis, the Ministry of Finance (MOF) successfully implemented the Miyazawa Initiative without drawing U.S. opposition. Poll results conducted by the Japanese government in the Philippines, Thailand, and Indonesia measured the success of this alternative strategy. As mentioned, economic interdependence between Japan and the region grew deeper because Japanese manufacturers heavily invested in Asia. Even after the collapse of the bubble economy in 1990-1991, they continued to invest as a way of offsetting the domestic downturn. Given the deepening interdependence of the region, the Miyazawa Initiative was a plan to benefit not only the Asian countries, but also Japan. By supplementing the role of the IMF, the Initiative successfully bailed out the Asian countries. Despite the failed project of the AMF, Japan's economic assistance greatly contributed to the recovery of the region. Yet, its waning economy increasingly made it difficult for Japan to exercise its economic muscle as it did in the past.

Japan's ailing economy and decline of ODA

During the earlier post-war decades, Japan's provision of aid to Southeast Asia had been largely motivated by economic considerations. Through provision of economic assistance, Japan sought to re-establish good relationships with the Asian countries that were supposedly capable of not only absorbing Japan's exports, but also supplying natural resources to Japan. Its economic assistance during the early development stages was essentially tied, which meant contracts for large scale infrastructure projects would be awarded to Japanese firms. Although this mechanism was abandoned in the early 1970s, it undoubtedly served as a booster for Japan's rapid economic recovery and subsequent growth. Asia was also a beneficiary of Japan's economic assistance and enjoyed rapid economic development. Coupled with outpouring trade and investment to the region, the importance of foreign assistance as a tool for Japan's economic diplomacy gained political weight even more.

However, the collapse of the bubble economy and the concomitant staggering economy forced the Japanese government to cut the ODA budget. Dealing with such domestic economic problems became a priority. 1997 was the beginning of two consecutive years of negative growth for the Japanese economy, the first time ever in the post-war era. The collapse of financial institutions (Hokkaido Takushoku Bank and Yamaichi Securities) in the same year seemed to symbolize Japan's waning economic power. More concretely, the banking system was in disarray, with "non-performing loans" (unofficially estimated to be as high as 100 trillion yen) stifling Japanese credit status both domestically and internationally. As a result, for the first time in the post-war era, the government was compelled to decrease the ODA budget by 10.4% in 1998, compared with the previous year. Since 2001, this trend became even more marked. In 2001, Japan slipped from the position of the largest donor, dropping to 5th in the world as of 2011. Lacking enough budgets, it belatedly embarked on improvement of ODA that essentially focused on quantity, rather than quality.

It was the concept of "human security"—a human-centered approach to provide protection to vulnerable people and communities threatened in their survival, livelihood and dignity—that emerged as one of the pillars of Japan's ODA policy. Emphasis on the concept that principally focuses on the security of individuals

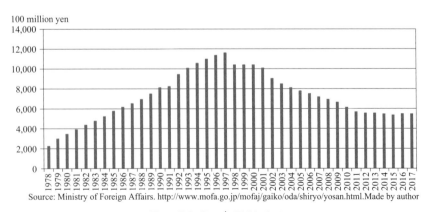

Source: Ministry of Foreign Affairs. http://www.mofa.go.jp/mofaj/gaiko/oda/shiryo/yosan.html.Made by author

Figure 7-1　Japan's ODA budget

facilitated to raise the quality and shift the direction of ODA, which had been essentially directed towards improvement of infrastructure. While supporting elimination of landmines and prevention of conflicts as part of its efforts to enhance human security, Japan began to buttress the concept by linking it to its ODA policy. For instance, when Asia was hit hard by the Asian economic crisis, Prime Minister Obuchi Keizo (1998-2000) expressed Japan's intention to aid the weak, to meet food and medical needs, in line with the concept of human security at the Japan-ASEAN Summit in 1998. Furthermore, aiming to promote human security through protection and empowerment of people, Japan and the UN launched the UN Trust Fund for Human Security in 1999, with Japan's financial contribution. Thus, the nature of Japan's ODA, which had exclusively been fixated on project-based assistance in Asia, has gradually changed. Likewise, its geographical orientation which had underlined Asia became more diverse, spreading to Africa. Such a shift is well illustrated by continuous support for the Tokyo International Conference on African Development (TICAD) with the UN Development Programme and the African Union Commission (the 6th meeting was held in 2016).

One may think why Japan provides economic assistance when its economy is staggering with unparalleled fiscal deficits. Undeniably, there are voices demanding further reduction of ODA. As a trading nation without military power, however, Japan depends on the peace and stability of the world, not only for its economic prosperity, but also its survival. Under volatile circumstances, it would not be able to either export or import various products. Without such resources, Japan would soon stumble. It is, therefore, in Japan's interests to provide economic assistance to help economies of other countries grow to ensure stability of the world.

Regional cooperation in the Asia-Pacific region

In Europe in the latter 1980s, the European Community agreed to accelerate the move for regional economic integration, by removing trade barriers. In the Americas, the formation of the North American Free Trade Agreement (NAFTA) as a regional institution was under way. In Asia, Japan enjoyed overwhelming economic strength, but its trade frictions, in particular with the U.S. intensified even more. Under these circumstances, the Ministry of International Trade and Industry (MITI), concerned with the emergence of exclusive trade blocs in Europe and North America, sought to establish a regional framework in the Asia-Pacific region. The aim was to set up a framework to promote free trade and "open regionalism". In 1989, with an Australian and Japanese initiative, Asia-Pacific Economic Cooperation (APEC) was established to reduce tariffs and other trade barriers across the region.

At an early stage, APEC served as an effective vehicle, somewhat achieving its original purposes. However, due to a consensus-based approach and the lack of a strong binding force, trade liberalization did not proceed smoothly as expected. Not only did it fail to reach agreement on trade liberalization (for instance, Early Voluntary Sectoral Liberalization), but it was also unable to play any role at the time of the Asian economic crisis. As a result, it gradually lost its momentum in the late 1990s. In contrast to the waning presence of APEC as a platform for liberalization and regional cooperation, ASEAN+3 (Japan, China and South Korea), which was first held in the middle of the Asian economic crisis, materialized as an effective framework for regional cooperation and confidence building. In 2005, the East Asian Summit, which embraces the members of the ASEAN+3, India, Australia and New Zealand, was also launched as a regional cooperation framework. Disappointment with APEC as a locomotive for liberalization and regional cooperation provided many countries incentives to seek for conclusion of Free Trade Agreements (FTA).

As a trading nation, the maintenance of an open trading system is indispensable for Japan's survival and economic prosperity. The Ministry of Economy, Trade and Industry[4] had previously depended on multilateral negotiations through APEC and the World Trade Organization as a vehicle to promote liberalization. However, due to the internationally rising trend for free trade agreements, and the inability of these institutions to forward the issue, Japan has come to look towards both bilateral and multilateral mechanisms. As a start, Japan concluded a free trade agreement with Singapore in 2002 (see Chapter 5) and as a main pillar, has pursued the conclusion of Economic Partnership Agreements (EPAs) that broadly include FDI, financial services, industrial harmonization, telecommunications and human resources.

Although APEC has still been an important forum for trade liberalization and regional cooperation, a move to cultivate free trade agreements became increasingly more popular and central internationally. A prospect of the Trans-Pacific Partnership (TPP, see Chapter 5), which once gained momentum, is unclear due to US withdrawal from the negotiations. However, open trade mechanisms may function as a booster to revive Japan's economy. It may also function as a framework for further regional integration.

Issues Ahead

Japan had been the second largest economy after the U.S. in the world since 1972. Its outstripping economic strength was once considered by other countries even as a threat. However, its inability to get out of the "lost decade" after the collapse of the bubble economy, and China's dramatic ascendance as an economic power pushed Japan down to the third largest, next to the U.S. and China in 2010. In addition, the unprecedented appreciation of the yen after the outbreak of the 2010 European sovereign debt crisis, the catastrophe caused by the 2011 earthquake and the ensuing meltdown of the Fukushima nuclear power plant, all of which added tremendous strain on Japan's staggering economy. Faced with ever increasing fiscal deficits and a waning economy, the Abe government implemented "Abenomics", which is supported by aggressive monetary policy, flexible fiscal policy, and a growth strategy including structural reform. As a result, it seems the Japanese economy is slowly recovering.

In the security field, Japan faces serious challenges. Even after the disappearance of the animosity between the US and the Soviet Union, Asia has not been stable at all. China's defense expenditure, underpinned by its growing economy, has been dramatically growing. Its claims of territorial sovereignty over uninhabited islands in the South and East China Seas have caused disputes and tensions with neighboring countries. North Korea's possession of nuclear weapons and its repeated missile launches have also posed a grave security concern, not only to Japan but also to the world. Under the unstable security situation in Asia, the Abe government has sought to strengthen the alliance with the US. However, Article 9 of the Constitution limits the scope of Japan's military action. Should Japan revise the Constitution to become a "normal country" by either removing or revising the famous Article 9, and then expand its scope of action in the military field? What ramifications would this have? Chapter 8 will answer these questions.

Endnotes

1) This chapter is largely drawn from: Hatakeyama and Freedman (2010) *Snow on the Pine: Japan's quest for a leadership in the Asia-Pacific region*, Singapore: World Scientific.
2) The Central Readiness Forces were abolished and reorganized in 2018.
3) The first National Defense Program Outline, which set out the principles of Japan's defence policy, was adopted in 1976.
4) Ministry of International Trade and Industry (MITI) was renamed Ministry of Economy, Trade and Industry (METI) in 2001.

References

1) Borden, William S. (1984), *The Pacific Alliance: United States Foreign Economic Policy and Japanese Trade Recovery, 1947-1955*. Wisconsin: The University of Wisconsin press.
2) Funabashi, Yoichi (1997), *Domei Hyoryu*, Iwanami Shoten.

Recommended Works

1) Hook, Glenn D., Julie Gilson, Christopher W. Hughes and Hugo Dobson (2012), *Japan's International Relations: Politics, Economics and Security*, (third ed.) N.Y.:Routledge.

   This book covers a wide range of issues from security to economic issues. It is a great textbook to comprehensively understand Japan's diplomacy.

2) Pyle, Kenneth B. (1996), *The Japanese Question: Power and Purpose in a New Era*, Washington DC.: The AEI Press.

   A foremost historian on Japan, Pyle explains Japan's power and purpose in the post-war period, by presenting a rich and compatible portrait of Japan's history.

3) Katzenstein, Peter J., and Okawara Nobuo (1993), "Japan's National Security: Structures, Norms, Policies", *International Security* 17 (4): 84-118.

   The article explains Japan's security policy by employing a constructivist perspective, by paying attention to domestic norms, culture and identity.

CHAPTER 8

Japan's Constitution and Changing Interpretations

Japan's current constitution, drafted by the U.S., came into effect in May 1947. It features pacifism, particularly in Article 9. Under the Constitution, the capability of the Self Defense Forces (SDF) is limited to the minimum necessary for self-defense. However, Japan has been expanding its contribution to the peace and stability of the world by interpreting the Constitution flexibly since the end of the Cold War. As Japan's security role has expanded, questions about to what extent and by what means Japan should be involved in such military operations have attracted attention. This chapter examines the constraints of the Constitution and their implications for Japan's contributions to international security.

Enactment of the Constitution

After the Second World War, Japan adopted the Constitution, which includes the famous Article 9. This section briefly explains the content and the American motivations for the Constitution, which has extensively and significantly affected Japan's post-war direction and security policy.

The American occupation of Japan until 1952 clearly shaped Japan's post-war fate. The U.S. occupation forces were led by the overbearing General Douglas MacArthur, who acted as the Supreme Commander for the Allied Powers (SCAP). MacArthur's reign in Japan resembled that of a latter-day emperor, and he had a profound effect on Japan's post-war development. As MacArthur envisioned, the major goals of the U.S. occupation were to demilitarize and democratize Japan. To achieve these goals, the U.S. embarked on a drastic structural reform of Japanese society, which was implemented in five primary areas. First, land reforms effectively removed exploitative landlords and rural tenants, by redistributing land confiscated from Japanese landlords. Gigantic financial and industrial oligopolies that had dominated Japan's wartime economy, known as the *zaibatsu*, were dismantled. Second, voting rights were extended to all citizens, including women. Third, regulations on political expression and the Peace Preservation Law of 1925, which provided the government a legal basis to arrest its opponents, were abrogated. The Special Higher Police were also disbanded. Fourth, the education system took its current form, promoting coeducational egalitarianism. Fifth, labor unions were created to protect the rights of workers. These reforms greatly contributed to the democratization of Japanese society. However, the most essential task to achieve democratization was to revise the Meiji Constitution, a symbol of militarist Japan in the pre-war period.

Early in the U.S. occupation period, MacArthur demanded that the Japanese government led by Shidehara Kijuro (1945-1946) revise the existing constitution. Dissatisfied with a Japanese draft that only minimally revised the Meiji Constitution, MacArthur ordered the General Headquarters government section to draft a constitution based on the following three principles. First, the Emperor is the head of state, and his succession is dynastic. Although Washington and other Allied powers had negative attitudes towards Japan's imperial system, MacArthur preferred to preserve the Emperor, to smoothly govern Japan. Second, Japan denounces war as a sovereign right of the nation for settling its disputes, even if still preserving its own security. The Japanese Army, Navy or Air Force would never be authorized. Third, Japan must abolish its feudal "family" system. Denouncing war even for preserving its national security greatly worried the Japanese side if it was possible to maintain interdependence as a sovereign nation.

However, the constitution drafted by the General Headquarters was softer than MacArthur's injunction. The preamble of the Constitution reflected his spirit, emphasizing the importance of peaceful cooperation with other nations for prosperity. It also proclaims that sovereign power resides with the people. The draft rehabilitated the Emperor as a symbol of the state (Article 1). The essential equality of the sexes (Article 14) and a broad range of civil liberties and human rights were guaranteed. MacArthur's second principle was embodied as Article 9, which stipulates the denouncement of war. One of his original principles, which denied war as a sovereign right of the nation, even for preserving its own security, was intentionally omitted.

The Japanese government eventually accepted the American draft after making a minor revision, which opened a way for the creation of a military force for self-defense (the revision was initiated by Ashida Hitoshi, who later became Prime Minister in 1948). To warrant civilian control and block any reemergence of militarism, Article 66 of the Constitution forbids military personnel from holding cabinet posts. However, the ambiguous wording of Article 9 "planted the seed of decades of controversy", leading to continuous arguments by left wingers that the SDF and the Security Treaty with the US were unconstitutional (Dower, 1999: 369). Although causing controversies, the U.S.-drafted "peaceful" and "democratic" constitution effectively shaped the direction of post-war Japan.

Ramifications of the Constitution: the Japan-U.S. Alliance and the SDF

We have roughly summarized the historical background and content of the Constitution. In this section, we will describe the political background in which the Japanese government negotiated the Japan-U.S. alliance and instituted the SDF, both of which led to lengthy disputes about the legality of the Constitution.

After its defeat in the Second World War, Japan adopted the U.S.-drafted constitution, including Article 9. By disarming and weakening Japan, the Constitution precisely reflected the U.S. aim to ensure Japan would not wage war again. However, due to the outbreak of the Cold War in Asia, the U.S. quickly shifted its position, seeking to revive Japan as a strong ally to contain Communism and stabilize the region. Because the Cold War suggested the need for a more aggressive stance, the U.S. demanded that the Japanese jettison their newly acquired pacifism, and rearm. As a first step, MacArthur ordered creation of a newly constituted National Police Reserve of 75,000 men, only a month after the outbreak of the Korean War in June 1950.

In 1951, with American forces rapidly retreating in Korea, U.S. Secretary of State John Foster Dulles urgently implored Japan to rearm. Given heightened tensions in Asia, rearming Japan as an ally would serve U.S. interests. Ironically, the Japanese government was reluctant to rearm, fully aware of the potential risk of pushing ahead with rearmament, given public sensitivity. Forestalling the Americans, Prime Minister Yoshida Shigeru skillfully argued that the strongly pacifist Japanese public would recoil at any attempt to re-institute a formal military structure. Moreover, because Japan had a weak and barely recovering economy, rearmament would entail levels of expenditure that would impoverish the Japanese. Yoshida concluded that combined with Japan's new-found repugnance towards anything military, rearmament would only generate the sort of domestic unrest that the Communists could exploit. Despite this assumption, he promised a limited level of rearmament to appease the U.S., creating the Security Forces by transforming the National Police Reserve. He hoped that this gesture would be sufficient to accelerate the signing of an acceptable agreement to end the occupation.

In September 1951, Japan and the U.S. signed the San Francisco Peace Treaty that formally ended the occupation. The Peace Treaty states:

> Japan as a sovereign nation possesses the inherent right of individual or collective self-defense referred to in Article 51 of the Charter of the United Nations (UN) and that Japan may voluntarily enter into collective security arrangements.

Notably, the treaty confirmed Japan's right of collective self-defense internationally. Simultaneously, the Japan-U.S. Security Treaty was signed, which has been a cornerstone of Japan's security policy, but also was a source of dispute. As previously mentioned (see Chapter 7), Yoshida desperately hoped to conclude the security treaty, which obliges the U.S. to defend Japan in the name of collective self-defense. He clearly perceived Japan's rising strategic value to the U.S. as a front-line state, and was ready to take advantage of it. In contrast, due to escalating Cold War confrontations, the U.S. desperately wanted to retain military bases in Japan, particularly in Okinawa, to contain Communism. However, the U.S. refused to enter into such a relationship on the grounds that Japan lacked the force even to defend itself, let alone defend the U.S. Therefore, the negotiated security treaty allowed the U.S. to retain military bases in Japan, although the U.S. had no obligations to defend Japan. Nevertheless, having American military bases on Japan's soil was undeniably beneficial for Japan's national security.

The conclusion of the Security Treaty, however, did not mark a termination of U.S. pressure for Japan to rearm. Though Yoshida made a concession by establishing the Security Forces in 1952, more was expected. Succumbing to the U.S. pressure to rearm, Japan established the SDF in 1954 by modifying the Security Forces. One may think that establishment of the SDF was unconstitutional, given Article 9. However, the government argued that the Constitution did not deny the right of self-defense as a sovereign nation (see above) and was thereby constitutional.

Although Yoshida opted to align with the U.S. to achieve the national goals of peace and prosperity, the conclusion of the security treaty with the U.S. and the subsequent creation of the SDF divided the country into two camps. Leftists, such as the Japan Socialist Party (JSP), self-appointed guardians of the Constitution, the Communist Party, and intellectuals were opposed to the treaty and the creation of the SDF, fiercely criticizing both as unconstitutional. Because these opposition parties had maintained reasonable popular support during the Cold War period, Japan's security policy had been significantly constrained, particularly in terms of cooperation with the U.S.

The ideological confrontation over Article 9 also affected the revision of the unequal security treaty. As a result of efforts by the Japanese government, the unequal security treaty concluded in 1951 was successfully revised in 1960 into a more equal one, obliging the U.S. to defend Japan. The opposition parties, however, sternly resisted the revised treaty, on the grounds that the content of the treaty implicitly accepted Japan's right of collective self-defense, thereby potentially drawing Japan into any new war initiated by the U.S. The Kishi administration responded by interpreting Article 9 as follows: the Constitution neither allowed Japan to send troops, nor to use force to defend other countries such as the U.S., in the name of collective self-defense. However, it is legal to contribute to the national security of other countries by lending military bases and providing economic assistance. His statement implied that the government perceived Japan held a limited right of collective self-defense.

Despite Kishi's statement, the government's interpretation of Article 9 was not necessarily consistent. However, approximately ten years later, the government issued an interpretation that Japan had the right of collective self-defense but was not constitutionally allowed to exercise it, and had maintained this interpretation until Shinzo Abe government re-interpreted Article 9. The next section will explain the long-held interpretation of Article 9.

Government Interpretation of the Ambiguous Article 9

How does the Japanese government currently construe the ambiguous Article 9 to rationalize the maintenance of the alliance with the U.S. and the SDF? Article 9 reads as follows:

> Aspiring sincerely to an international peace based on justice and order, the Japanese people forever renounce war as a sovereign right of the nation and the threat or use of force as means of settling international disputes.
>
> In order to accomplish the aim of the preceding paragraph, land, sea, and air forces, as well as other war potential, will never be maintained. The right of belligerency of the state will not be recognized.

Article 9 of the Constitution renounces war and prohibits the maintenance of war potential. However, interpretations of Article 9 vary due to its equivocal wording, leading to a serious political division even after the Constitution came into effect. It still causes debate among politicians and the public. The contentious issues are as follows:

• Does Japan possess the right of self-defense?

The Constitution renounces war as a "means to settle disputes", but whether Japan possesses the right of self-defense as a sovereign nation has been debated. Successive Japanese governments have interpreted that the Constitution does not deny the inherent right of self-defense as a sovereign nation. Therefore Japan is allowed to possess the minimum level of defense-oriented capability, namely, the SDF, to ensure Japan's independence and defend its territory in case of foreign aggression. In line with such interpretations, Japanese governments have adopted exclusively defense-orientated policies and forces to defend the nation. However, Japan does not possess what are referred to as offensive weapons, because this is unconstitutional. For instance, the SDF is not allowed to possess intercontinental ballistic missiles, long-range bombers or offensive aircraft carriers. Left-wing parties claim that Japan lacks the right to wage any wars, whether for self-defense or not. Thus, they argue that the existence of the SDF and Japan's alliance with the U.S. are unconstitutional.

According to the government, use of armed force for the exercise of the right of self-defense is confined to these cases: (1) there is an imminent and illegitimate act of aggression against Japan, or (2) there are no appropriate means to repel this aggression other than the use of force. The geographical scope of the use of force required to defend Japan is not necessarily confined to Japanese territorial land, sea and airspace. It may stretch to areas surrounding Japan, such as the high seas, but the areas to be covered will be assessed case by case. Japan is not, however, allowed to dispatch armed troops to foreign lands, sea or airspace for the purpose of using military power, because that action generally would exceed the minimum level of force required for self-defense.

• Does Japan possess the right of collective self-defense?

The definition of the right of collective self-defense is: the use of armed force by a state to repel foreign aggression against a country with which it has close relations. Using military force to defend other countries is allowed, although the state is not under direct attack. The North Atlantic Treaty Organization (NATO) was formed based on such a concept. For instance, when a NATO member comes under armed attack, other member states are allowed to counterattack the foreign aggressor to defend the state under attack, by invoking the right of collective self-defense. The UN Charter Article 51 clearly articulated the inherent right of collective self-defense. It reads:

> Nothing in the present Charter shall impair the inherent right of individual or collective self-defense if an armed attack occurs against a Member of the United Nations, until the Security Council has taken measures necessary to maintain international peace and security.

The Japanese government interprets that Japan, as a sovereign nation, has the right of collective self-defense but is not allowed to exercise that right due to constitutional restriction, because doing so would exceed the use of armed force permitted under Article 9 of the Constitution.

Expanding roles: in the framework of the U.N.

The changing security environment after the end of the Cold War posed a serious challenge for Japan, as to how to contribute to the peace and stability of the world as a member of the international community. Though largely constrained by Article 9, successive governments have changed their interpretations slightly, as necessary to meet international expectations. In the following sections, we will explore how governments altered their interpretation of Article 9, employing "international contribution" as a pretext with a view toward expanding Japan's security role in the post-Cold War period.

Adoption of the PKO Law

Japan shunned security issues during the Cold War, largely because of anti-militarist domestic norms. In addition, the JSP, the largest opposition party, had insisted that both the SDF and the alliance with the U.S. were unconstitutional. Nobody had openly discussed security issues or Japan's role in the security field, due to public sensitivity. Given that even the status of the SDF and the alliance with the U.S. had been controversial, Japan's low profile in the security field was a natural consequence. The alliance also allowed successive Liberal Democratic Party (LDP) governments to depend completely on the U.S. for national security without seriously considering Japan's national security or its role in the world.

Although successive Japanese governments had consistently avoided assuming any security role overseas, few recognized that the Constitution does not prohibit the dispatch of the SDF overseas to participate in operations conducted under the auspices of the UN, unless the operation aims to settle disputes by force. However, the plenary session of the House of Councillors adopted a resolution to ban the dispatch of the SDF abroad in 1954, the year in which the SDF was organized. When UN Secretary General Dag Hammarskjöld requested Japan to dispatch ten SDF officers in 1958 to serve as military observers in Lebanon, the Japanese government refused, on the grounds that restrictions placed on the SDF explicitly forbade participation in such a role. However, at least constitutionally, Japan was able to participate legitimately in such peacekeeping activities, as long as the UN endorsed them. The decision not to participate in these missions was strictly political in nature.

The 1961 statement by the head of the Cabinet Legislation Bureau sufficiently clarified that participating in a peacekeeping operation endorsed by the UN did not violate the Constitution. However, the government was unwilling to participate in such operations or revise the basic law under which the SDF operated (Tanaka, 1997: 213-214). In effect, there was ample legal room for Japan to participate in a variety of United Nations peacekeeping initiatives, if the Japanese government chose to revise the law imposed upon the SDF. However, doing so would require greater domestic consensus. Creating anything like a widespread agreement on Japan's security policy in those early post-war years appeared difficult. Moreover, during that period, no urgent need or desire to initiate such a drastic change existed. Although Japan's economy accounted for more than 10% of Gross World Product in the 1980s, the public thought that Japan should limit its international role to the provision of economic assistance. For Japan, extending this obligation to humanitarian efforts, especially to military ones, seemed unnecessary.

The Gulf War of 1991 acted as a catalyst for a reprisal of Japan's low-profile attitudes towards international affairs. The UN adopted a resolution and endorsed the creation of U.S.-led multinational forces to remove Iraqi forces from Kuwait. Soon after Iraq's invasion, the Kaifu government (1989-1991) proposed a bill to enable the dispatch of the SDF overseas. The bill was, however, soon abandoned due to lack of support even from within the LDP, the dominant ruling party. As a pacifist nation, the Japanese people had long believed that providing financial assistance should be sufficient. It was unthinkable for the public to dispatch the SDF overseas, even under the auspices of the UN. "One-country pacifism" or an ingrained belief in anti-militarism had been deeply embedded into the minds of the Japanese. An opinion poll conducted during the debate over the bill found that 67% of Japanese people opposed the dispatch of the SDF[1]. More than half of the Diet members also opposed the dispatch at that time[2].

The Gulf War gave rise to an extensive argument among the public over whether Japan should make a humanitarian contribution by sending the SDF overseas. However, the belated result was a huge economic assistance package of $13 billion. Unfortunately, the slow economic contribution elicited a diatribe of "too little, too late" from some in international society, leading to a reappraisal of Japan's foreign policy regarding its security role, and how to relate to the world. The Kuwaiti government even excluded Japan from a list of countries thanked in the *New York Times*. Debates over the "normalization of Japan" presented by politician Ozawa Ichiro also inspired and helped persuade the public, who had been trapped by narrow and traditional anti-militarist norms.

After the Gulf War, the Miyazawa government (1991-1993) submitted another bill to enable the SDF's dispatch overseas. However, the introduction of the bill generated disputes about whether Japan's participation in PKO might lead to violation of the Constitution. The most controversial point in the debates was over the use of force, which is prohibited by Article 9. Dissenting voices argued that participation in such operations would inevitably involve the use of force. The government therefore had to attach constraints to eliminate any possibility of the use of force to assure opposing voices. Although the government successfully passed the Act on Cooperation for United Nations Peacekeeping Operations and Other Operations (hereafter the PKO bill) in 1992, the Five Principles attached considerably limited the SDF's participation in operations and activities to conform to the Constitution, and more importantly, reassure the sensitive public and politicians. Even with these constraints, opposition parties such as the JSP sternly dismissed the bill as unconstitutional. The Five Principles are:

(1) Agreement on a ceasefire by warring parties;
(2) Consent from warring parties for conduct of UN peacekeeping operations, as well as Japan's participation in such operations;
(3) The operations shall strictly maintain impartiality;
(4) Should any of the requirements in the above-mentioned guideline cease to be satisfied, Japan may remove its forces;
(5) The use of weapons shall be limited to self-defense.

The Five Principles essentially prohibited the SDF's participation in peacekeeping forces (PKF) and the primary missions of PKO (monitoring ceasefires, withdrawal or demobilization of armed forces, dismantling, inspection or identification of weapons, patrolling in buffer zones, collection, storage or disposal of abandoned weapons, and so on). As a result, the SDF's main mission at this stage was limited to tasks that did not require the use of force, such as building bridges and repairing roads. Use of weapons was only allowed for self-protection.

Although introduction of the PKO bill was significant, the SDF's subsequent participation in PKO was quite limited due to the constraints. In addition, after the end of the Cold War, the violent nature of conflicts resulted in increases in PKO that required the use of force. This made it more difficult for Japan to participate in peacekeeping missions. To ease the restrictions, the PKO bill was revised in 1998 and 2001, albeit within the limits of Article 9. The revisions enabled the SDF to participate in PKF (however, Japan has not participated in PKF as of 2017) and mitigated restrictions on the use of weapons, allowing the SDF to use weapons to protect others who are under SDF care. The revision also enabled SDF personnel to use weapons to protect munitions depots, vehicles and other equipment. Although the revisions broadened the SDF's activities, the rigid Five Principles still constrains Japan's participation.

Expanding roles: in the framework of the Japan-US alliance

The 1997 New Guidelines

Under unstable circumstances in the Asia-Pacific region exemplified by North Korean nuclear development program and China's missile launch towards Taiwan, the Hashimoto government and the Clinton administration announced the "Japan-U.S. Joint Declaration on Security: Alliance for the 21st Century" in 1996, which expanded the scope of the bilateral alliance, from the security of Japan to that of the Asia-Pacific region. The next year, the New Guidelines for Japan-U.S. Security Cooperation (hereafter, the New Guidelines) were negotiated, establishing a solid basis for more effective and credible Japan-U.S. cooperation under the following circumstances: (1) normal circumstances; (2) an armed attack against Japan; and (3) contingencies in the areas surrounding Japan, that would have a significant influence on Japan's peace and security. Although the New Guidelines stated that "Japan will conduct all its actions within the limitations of its Constitution…", it clearly expanded Japan's military

Column: Japan's Contribution to Peacekeeping Operations in East Timor

In East Timor, forcefully annexed by Indonesia in 1976, confrontations between pro-independence and pro-integration groups escalated and reached a critical stage by 1999. A newly elected president, B. J. Habibie, shifted Indonesia's official policy, by agreeing to hold a direct referendum on independence in August 1999. One result of this change was the creation of the United  Nations Mission in East Timor (UNAMET) in June, which would monitor the coming vote. Initially, the Japanese sent only three officials (including civilian police) due to the unstable stuation.

Subsequently in the referendum, pro-independence groups won a landslide victory, with 78.5% of the vote. Although the Indonesian government promised to both honor and accept the result, the East Timor situation deteriorated rapidly. Pro-integration militias, allegedly backed by the Indonesian military, staged a fierce resistance. The UN responded by adopting Security Council Resolution 1264, which endorsed the dispatch of multinational forces to East Timor. There was no question of Japan participating as part of the proposed multinational force, because it inevitably involved use of force. Instead, Japan offered its traditional alternative, a financial contribution (more than $200 million).

Soon after the deployment of the Australian-led multinational forces, the situation on the ground improved. This change allowed UN peacekeepers to replace the multinational force in February 2000, leading to the establishment of the United Nations Transitional Administration in East Timor (UNATET). But Japan claimed the fragile situation there meant that the circumstances failed to comply with its required Five Principles of commitment.

By February 2002, three months prior to East Timor's official independence, Japan had altered its position by dispatching a SDF Engineering Unit, the largest ever to participate in East Timorese reconstruction because of the improvement in the security situation. Although the SDF's mission was to build bridges and roads, remove rubble and so on, Japan's contribution to the reconstruction and nation building of East Timor was widely hailed.

cooperation with the U.S., in contingencies in the areas surrounding Japan. It states that:

> The primary aim of this rear area support is to enable U.S. Forces to use facilities and conduct operations in an effective manner. By its very nature, Japan's rear area support will be provided primarily in Japanese territory. It may also be provided on the high seas and international airspace around Japan which are distinguished from areas where combat operations are being conducted.[3]

That suggests Japan's actions may be extended to areas surrounding Japan. The 1978 guidelines aimed mainly to articulate how Japan, in cooperation with the U.S., would respond to or deter foreign aggression against Japan. Although the 1978 guidelines referred to the importance of the stability of the Far East, details about to what extent Japan would cooperate with U.S. military action in case of a contingency were not specified. The guidelines essentially focused on arrangements for Japan's defense; the exercise of the right of collective self-defense was intentionally omitted. The New Guidelines, however, made a clear contrast to the former guidelines by clearly specifying Japan's extended military support in cooperation with the U.S., in areas adjacent to Japan.

Furthermore, to ensure the effectiveness of the New Guidelines, three laws (hereafter, the 1999 Laws) were adopted in 1999[4]. These were substantial and significant because they clarified Japan's active support—mainly logistical—in cooperation with U.S. military action in the case of certain contingencies. However, this expansion of Japan's role in the security field led to public disputes about constitutionality.

The New Guidelines and the 1999 Laws were controversial, because they enabled the SDF to provide support to U.S. forces beyond self-defense in certain contingencies, by introducing two new concepts: "rear area support" and "areas surrounding Japan". "Rear area support" to U.S. troops embraces logistical assistance, such as transportation, medical services, surveillance, minesweeping, offering Japanese facilities to U.S. forces, and supply of materials other than weapons and ammunition. "Areas surrounding Japan" indicates areas beyond Japan's territorial seas, land and airspace, such as the high seas and international airspace around Japan, but the term does not specify a geographic boundary for Japan's military support. The government employed these new ambiguous concepts to enable the SDF to offer U.S. forces non-military support, even beyond Japan's territory, in a required contingency. To conform to the Constitution, transport of weapons and ammunition to the U.S. forces in a combat zone, and fueling U.S. aircraft engaging in combat operations are forbidden because those activities are categorized as the exercise of the right of collective defense. However, the government argued that providing "rear area support" is constitutional, because it does not directly aid U.S. military action.

Thus, the 1999 Laws enabled the SDF to provide support to U.S. military action, even when Japan is not under direct attack. The government argued this activity was constitutional and did not correspond to the exercise of the right of collective self-defense, because the support the SDF provides would merely be rear area support, conducted in an area without combat operations. Given that Japan's military support had been confined to the defense of Japan from foreign aggressors during the Cold War period, the adoption of the New Guidelines and the subsequent laws were a watershed and laid the groundwork for Japan's greater military support beyond its territory.

War on Terror: The Afghan War

The September 11 attacks in 2001 came as a shock. The terrorist attacks changed the picture of international security, bringing terrorism to the fore as a common threat to be addressed. Soon after the September 11 attacks, the U.S. retaliated in Afghanistan to oust the Taliban regime which harbored Al-Qaeda by invoking the right of self-defense. NATO countries followed suit by invoking the right of collective self-defense. To support the U.S.-initiated "War on Terrorism", the Koizumi government (2001-2006) soon adopted the Anti-Terrorism Special Measures Law with a time limit of two years. The law enabled the SDF to provide logistical support, through activities such as provision of supplies, medical assistance, and repair and maintenance of U.S. equipment. It also allowed the SDF to use their weapons to protect not only themselves, but also persons "who have come under their control", such as refugees and injured soldiers of other countries.

With the passage of the legislation, the Koizumi government sent a number of SDF maritime vessels to the Indian Ocean to offer logistical support such as refueling and water supply to the U.S. and allied countries. Some in Japan condemned the support as equivalent to the exercise of the right of collective self-defense, but the government emphasized the constitutionality of the mission on the grounds that the SDF would make an international contribution in a non-combat zone. The government argued further that even transportation of weapons and ammunition was not equivalent to use of force, as long as the mission was conducted in a non-combat zone. It employed the term "non-combat zone" to vindicate its decision and dismiss criticism. By renewing the legislation, Japan's support lasted until January 2010, when the Democratic Party of Japan's Hatoyama government (2009) terminated the mission.

War on Terror: The Iraq War

Convinced that Saddam Hussein had been secretly developing weapons of mass destruction and posed a security threat to the world, the U.S. sought a UN resolution to endorse its attack on Iraq. However, unable to obtain support from France, Russia and China, the U.S. formed a coalition of forces with the U.K., Australia and other countries to overthrow the Iraqi government. Following its quick support of the U.S. "War on Terror", Koizumi was determined to again support the U.S. military action as an ally. The Japanese government adopted the Law Concerning Special Measures on Humanitarian and Reconstruction Assistance in Iraq (hereafter, the special legislation) in July 2003, sending 6,000 SDF troops to the southern Iraqi city of Samawah.

The special legislation enabled assistance in two areas: humanitarian relief for the Iraqi people such as water purification, and logistical support to coalition forces such as supply of gasoline and other materials. Japan's participation without an appropriate UN resolution, however, unsurprisingly resulted in a debate over compatibility with the Constitution and the security of the personnel. Koizumi skillfully defended his decision by emphasizing the potential effectiveness of the alliance as deterrence to the North Korean threat. He also played down the dispatch on the grounds that the Ground Self Defense Force was dispatched to "areas without conflicts", where the chance to use weapons was scarce. The government's logic to avoid the appearance of violating the Constitution was simple: the SDF would be dispatched to a safe area for the reconstruction of Iraq, not for combat operations. However, it was reported that the Air SDF unit had to cancel C-130 flights approximately 30 times, because it received information on threats, including advance notice of missile attacks[5]. In this unpredictable situation, foreign troops, mostly Australian, had to ensure the SDF's safety, even in Samawah, where the security situation was relatively calm, because the SDF had rigid constraints in using force. By emphasizing that the SDF would not use force, and thereby was constitutional, the government justified its decision to support the US military action.

The New Legislation for Peace and Security and Revision of the Constitution

The Cabinet Legislation Bureau has maintained the consistent interpretation of Article 9 since the 1970s. Acknowledging that Japan possesses the right of self-defense and collective self-defense, it maintained the position that Japan cannot exercise the right of collective self-defense due to Article 9. Use of weapons beyond self-defense is also prohibited. Although it upheld such interpretations, successive Japanese governments adopted special laws whenever necessary to expand the sphere of the SDF's international contributions. The strategies taken by government were to re-interpret the meaning of the Constitution, and create a new concept such as "areas without conflicts".

However, a move to revise the Constitution, rather than re-interpreting, gained political visibility in 2000s. Because of the lack of a permanent law, the government had to draw up a new legislation and pass it whenever there emerged a need to conduct military cooperation. The previous bills passed relatively smoothly. However, it would not be always the case. To ensure smooth and timely international contributions, the government sought to adopt a permanent legislation.

Such a quest resulted in the adoption of the security bill in 2015 under the Abe coalition government with the Komei Party. The bill was controversial, because it partially allowed the exercise of the right of collective self-defense if it meets certain criteria. This contradicts with the interpretation made by previous governments. Abe has a grand goal of revising the controversial Article 9. However, the requirements imposed by Article 96 for constitutional revision are not easy to meet. Article 96 obliges the government to conduct a referendum, which, according to Article 96, must first be supported by two thirds of the members of both Diet Houses, and must subsequently be supported by at least half the public in the referendum. Given this hurdle, the Abe government chose to re-interpret the Constitution. Politicians have still not reached consensus over the revision.

The bill allowed use of force even if Japan is not attacked when "Three New Conditions" are met:

1. When a foreign country that is in a close relationship with Japan is attacked, and as a result, threatens Japan's survival and poses a clear danger to fundamentally overturn people's right to life, liberty and pursuit of happiness,
2. When there are no appropriate measures available,
3. Use of force should be limited to the minimum extent necessary.

It also enables the SDF to participate in internationally coordinated operations for peace and security (outside UNPKO frameworks) and conduct *"kaketsuke keigo* (rescue missions)" to protect civilians, which had been prohibited on the grounds that such missions fell into the category of an exercise of collective self-defense. Supporters of the bill claim that Japan must enlarge the scope of its contribution to global security as a member of the international community. Given the volatile regional situation exemplified by the North Korean nuclear threat and China's military rise, it would be in Japan's interests to cement its relationship with the U.S. by allowing exercise of the collective self-defense. Conversely, opponents argue that as a peaceful nation, Japan's current contribution via the UN framework is sufficient; enabling the exercise of the right of collective self-defense would inevitably draw Japan into any war the U.S. initiates.

A next step for the Abe government is to revise the constitution to, at least, legitimize the existence of the SDF. However, a revision opening the door for a militarily strong Japan would cause tension between Japan and neighboring countries, particularly South Korea and China. The Japanese must seriously consider the ramifications the revision would generate, and seek national consensus by having extensive debates on the future of Japan.

Endnotes

1) Asahi Shimbun, October 1, 1990.
2) Asahi Shimbun, November 1, 1990.
3) Ministry of Foreign Affairs, "The Guidelines of Japan-U.S. defense Cooperation".
4) These laws are: 1. The Law Relating to Measures for Preserving the Peace and Security of Japan in the Event of a Situation in the Areas Surrounding Japan, 2. A Bill to amend the Self-Defense Forces Law, 3. An Agreement amending the Agreement between the Government of Japan and the Government of the United States of America concerning Reciprocal Provision of Logistic Support, Supplies and Services between the Self-Defense Forces of Japan and the Armed Forces of the United States of America, the so-called amended ACSA (Acquisition and Cross-Servicing Agreement).
5) The Japan Times Weekly Online, December 27, 2008. "Japan must scrutinize ASDF mission in Iraq on constitutional matter". http://weekly.japantimes.co.jp/ed/japan-must-scrutinize-asdf-mission-in-iraq-on-Constitutional-matter [Accessed on April 2012].

References

1) Dower, John W. (1999), *Embracing Defeat: Japan in the Wake of World War II*, NY: W.W. Norton and Company.
2) Tanaka Akihiko (1997), *Anzenhosho: Sengo 50 nen no mosaku*, (*National Security: 50 Years' Search after WWII*) Tokyo: Yomiuri Shimbunsha, 1997.

Recommended Works

1) Dower, John W. (1999), *Embracing Defeat: Japan in the Wake of World War II*, NY: W.W. Norton and Company.
    This is a profound and moving book that beautifully describes how Japan was reborn as a democratic country by transforming its society. It is the winner of the Pulitzer Prize, the National Book Award, and the Bancroft Prize.
2) Sase Masamori (2012), *Shudanteki Jieiken: Aratana Ronso no Tameni (Right of Collective Self-Defense: for New Discussion)*, Tokyo Ichigeisha.
    This book clearly explains the history and interpretations of successive governments on the right of collective defense. The author's argument is clear and easy to understand.
3) Asai Motofumi (2002), *Shudanteki Jieiken to Nihonkoku Kenpo (Right of Collective Self-Defense and Japan's Constitution)*, Tokyo: Shueisha Shinsho.
    This book tries to answer various questions over the right of collective defense and the Constitution, covering a wide range of issues, including the "War on Terrorism".

CHAPTER 9

The Japan-U.S. Alliance

This chapter illuminates the evolution of the Japan-U.S. alliance after World War II. The first part depicts the changing and unchanging nature of Japan-U.S. relations from geopolitical and historical perspectives. In the second section, the formation of the Japan-U.S. alliance in the late 1940s and the early 1950s is to be explicated, following the brief introduction of major theories of alliance formation. The third section addresses how Japan and the U.S. have managed alliance dilemmas since the late 1950s, highlighting the institutionalization of burden-sharing. The final part explores future challenges.

Geopolitical and Historical Backgrounds

Since Japan engaged in modern diplomacy at the end of the Edo Period, relations with the U.S. have been of critical importance to Japan. One reason is concerned with geography. Japan is located at the western end of the Pacific Ocean, flanked by great powers like China and Russia. Without adequate natural resources, Japan has been dependent on foreign trade, making the best use of the sea routes of the Pacific Ocean. Meanwhile, the U.S., situated at the other side of the ocean, started to be a Pacific nation after cultivating its western frontier on the mainland in the late 19th century. It employed open door diplomacy, telling Asia-Pacific countries to open their markets to the world. In 1853, Commodore Matthew C. Perry visited Japan with his "Black Ships" and asked to open some of its ports so that the U.S. could use them as a logistical platform from which to embark on foreign trade with China or other Asian countries.

As maritime powers located at the opposite ends of the Pacific Ocean, Japan and the U.S. share a general interest in preserving a stable regional environment for foreign trade. However, the specific interests of both countries were not always in agreement; rather, Japan and the U.S. often had serious conflicts over what kind of international order they should bring to the Asia-Pacific region. Despite the establishment of the multilateral framework for policy coordination among great powers in the Asia-Pacific region based on the Washington Naval Treaty in 1922, it was not long before its cooperative spirit weakened because of the friction concerning China's markets. In the 1930s, Japan attempted to build an exclusive economic zone, the Greater East Asia Co-Prosperity Sphere, under its own leadership and integrate Manchuria (the north-eastern part of China) and mainland China into the zone in opposition to the demands of the U.S. to open the Chinese market. Following Japan's occupation of Vietnam, then under French rule, the Franklin D. Roosevelt administration (1933-1945) decided in August 1941 to impose economic sanctions on Japan, including an embargo on petroleum. In the end, both countries entered into the Pacific War on December 8 of that year with the Japanese attack on Pearl Harbor in Hawaii.

In the wake of Japan's capitulation in August 1945, the Allied forces, led by General Douglas MacArthur as the Supreme Commander for the Allied Powers (SCAP), occupied Japan and assumed responsibilities to direct Japanese policymakers. As Chapter 7 of this book puts it, the occupation forces initially intended to weaken Japan's industrial economy and to demilitarize and democratize Japan's political system. However, in the late 1940s, the U.S. changed such a harsh policy toward Japan; the Harry S. Truman administration (1945-1953) began to reinvigorate Japanese industry and enhance its defense capability. Furthermore, it signed a security treaty, as well as a peace treaty, with defeated Japan in September 1951. This Japan-U.S. security relationship has formed the basis of Japan's foreign policy to date, as Prime Minister Suzuki Zenko (1980-82) and President Ronald W. Reagan (1981-1989) described it as an "alliance" in a joint communiqué in May 1981.

Formation of the Japan-U.S. Alliance

What Is an Alliance?

One of the basic functions of states is to secure their people and territory from outside threats and assure their own survival in a principally self-help international system. They have two national security options: allying with other states and/or reinforcing their own armaments. While international relations theorists provide slightly different definitions of alliance, with regard to its formality in particular, an alliance is generally conceptualized as a cooperative arrangement between states that aims to address common military threats (Walt, 1987; Snyder, 1997). In brief, an alliance is an interstate cooperation on the use of armed forces for deterrence, defense, and/or offense.

In this respect, an alliance should be distinguished from the concept of collective security; a kind of security system where almost all the states in an international system, not just particular allied states, are included and committed to the principle of non-use of force, and impose sanctions for violations of the rule. In other words, military threats are expected to come from inside the system (member states) in the case of collective security, as opposed to outside (non-members) in the case of alliances. The United Nations is ideally an embodiment of the collective security system; according to its Charter, resorting to armed force to solve international conflict is generally prohibited, and an infringement of this rule must be sanctioned economically and/or militarily by a majority of member states that follow resolutions by the Security Council.

Why Are Alliances Formed?

The most fundamental theoretical argument on alliance formation is based on the logic of balance of power in the international system. As shown in Chapter 2 of this book, states have a tendency to maintain equilibrium of military capabilities and halt an emergence of a hegemon. Therefore, they aggregate their own capabilities by forming alliances and meet threats coming from more powerful states. Great powers generally support weaker powers in military conflicts (Waltz, 1979).

According to the balance of threat theory, however, what is more decisive in choosing an alliance partner is subjective perceptions on a gap in material resources. Although objective military capability itself may be an important factor when states decide with whom to form alliance, intentions of other countries will also affect threat perceptions; states tend to stand by less threatening ones (Walt, 1987).

While both balance of power and balance of threat theories expect states to employ balancing behavior against a certain threat (whether conceived as proportional to military capability per se or not), different patterns of forming an alliance are predicted by other theories. One such state behavior is bandwagoning with greater powers; states with smaller capability are likely to bandwagon with, not balance against, powerful, threatening states (Rothstein, 1968). "Bandwagon for profit" can be also observed in that even great powers sometimes collaborate with stronger belligerents when they anticipate economic gains (Schweller, 1994).

Moreover, alliances may be formed not just to affect the power relations between allies and non-allies through balancing or bandwagoning, but also to regulate the relationship between allies themselves. Since allies are more or less interdependent with each other in accomplishing common goals, they are constrained by mutual behavior. Greater allies in particular are likely to have much more influence on their smaller partners because the latter's survival is contingent on the former's capability and intentions. This aspect of alliance formation is called "tools of management" (Schroeder, 1976).

Why Was the Japan-U.S. Alliance Formed?

The Japan-U.S. security treaty was signed in September 1951 in the context of the Cold War between the capitalist and communist blocs. While the confrontation had intensified in Europe since the late 1940s, the threats from communist countries began to surge in the Asia-Pacific as well, represented by the conclusion of an alliance treaty between the Soviet Union and the People's Republic of China in February 1950. Also, a war broke out on the Korean Peninsula in June 1950, a proxy war between the Soviet Union and China on the one hand and the U.S. on the other.

As the Japan-U.S. alliance was formed in the midst of the Korean War, it was aimed at defending Japanese territory from military invasion by the communist countries, mainly the Soviet Union. At the time, Japan was still economically and militarily weakened and in a politically unstable condition in the aftermath of World War II, so it did not have sufficient capability to defend itself against aggressive action from its neighboring states. Also, due to domestic legal and political constraints, including the non-armed force clause of the Constitution (Article 9), Japan could not build up powerful forces at that moment (see Chapter 8 of this book). Therefore, it was reasonable for the Japanese government under Prime Minister Yoshida Shigeru

(1946-1947, 1948-1954) to seek others' help in assuring its security, and the only available option for Japan was to receive assistance from the U.S., whose military forces had been stationed in Japan since 1945.

However, in terms of military capability, the Soviet Union, the main source of threat to Japan, was less powerful than the U.S., Japan's ally; the GDP of the former represented one-third of the latter's in 1950. In other words, Japan's alignment with the U.S. did not follow the prediction of balance of power theory (though it might accord with the logic of balance of threat theory as long as the Japanese people and their leaders increasingly felt threatened by aggressive intentions of the Soviet Union and its allies). Rather, Japan's decision seems better explained as bandwagoning with the U.S., the stronger party of the two superpowers.

In contrast to Japan, which was still in economic difficulty and had no option but to follow U.S. leadership due to the lack of intimate friends in the world, the U.S., as one of the two superpowers, might have been able to address the threat from the other even without Japan's help. However, there were benefits to the U.S. in cooperating with Japan. The most critical, among others, was the virtually free use of its military bases in Japan, from which the U.S. Forces could project its troops to Asian countries. Moreover, Japan had an economic, as well as military, potential to affect U.S. behavior in the Asia-Pacific region once it was incorporated into the rival camp. Therefore, security cooperation with Japan was a rational decision for the U.S. in containing Soviet threats.

As a consequence, the disparity in material capabilities between the allies was substantial; the Japan-U.S. alliance was an alliance between a global superpower and a far more vulnerable junior partner in both economic and military terms. Japan depended more heavily on the U.S. for its security against neighboring communist countries than vice versa. This asymmetric relationship of the two allies allowed the U.S. to take advantage of the alliance as the "cap in the bottle": a leverage to restrain Japan's diplomatic behavior. This constraint was also helpful in reassuring other U.S. allies in the Asia-Pacific, such as Australia and the Philippines, which were damaged by the battles with Japan during World War II and were concerned about the resurgence of Japan's military power under the patronage of the U.S. Accordingly, the Japan-U.S. alliance was successfully installed as the pivot of U.S.-led hub-and-spoke security system in the Asia-Pacific region, which consists of bilateral and trilateral alliances involving the U.S.

Evolution of the Japan-U.S. Alliance

How Is the Alliance Relationship Managed?

A well-known dynamic that may operate between allies is the "alliance dilemma" over fear of entrapment and fear of abandonment. If states make a clear commitment to assisting their allies, this will make the alliance ties stronger and reduce the possibility of being deserted by the allies when they are really in need of help; however, the allies can be involved in matters without much self-interest. If states offer an ambiguous commitment to their allies, this may lower the chance of being embroiled in others' business, but instead weaken the ties between the allies and increase the likelihood of being abandoned when they are in trouble (Snyder, 1997). Such a dilemma takes place because allies often have different views on how to realize shared objectives and because their interests in other issues may not be the same.

While some alliances disintegrate in a relatively short term due to the alliance dilemma, others will persist for some time despite such a dilemma. In the latter case, reiterated interactions between allies may create a patterned and institutionalized relationship. Practices on burden-sharing, both in daily activities and in emergencies, are likely to be formulated between allies as norms and guidelines, and the terms and conditions of the alliance commitment to providing mutual military support will be specified in detail. In short, successful management of the alliance dilemma will enhance credibility of the alliance and make the alliance ties firmer and more stable.

How Was the Japan-U.S. Alliance Managed during the Cold War?

As the alliance has two objectives, securing Japan's defense and constraining Japan's external behavior, the dilemma of security and autonomy has been a recurring theme in Japan's relations with the U.S. In the Cold War era, while Japan could be secured from increasingly threatening communist countries by being integrated into the U.S.-centered alliance system in the Asia-Pacific region, this integration deprived Japan of its diplomatic autonomy and forced it to follow U.S. strategy in dealing with neighboring countries. In other words, Japan's security policy during the Cold War was driven by and swung between two contradicting fears of abandonment and entrapment.

Revision of the Security Treaty

As discussed in Chapter 7, the Japan-U.S. Security Treaty was revised in January 1960. While the earlier version of the treaty allowed the U.S. to station its forces in Japan and use those military bases for its operations in the Far East, the U.S. did not make a firm commitment to the defense of Japan's territory. In the meantime, the treaty lacked provisions by which Japan could restrain U.S. operations initiated from Japan; U.S. Forces could make use of their bases irrespective of Japan's interests. In a word, Japanese administrations feared both abandonment and entrapment under the earlier treaty.

Thus, one of the major objectives for the Kishi Nobusuke administration (1957-1960) in revising the treaty was to clarify the obligation of U.S. Forces to provide military support to the defense of Japan by writing it down in the provisions of the treaty in exchange for admitting the U.S. rights to retain bases in Japan. From Japan's point of view, U.S. Forces in Japan were a "trip wire," a guarantee which urged the U.S. to defend the Japanese people, along with U.S. soldiers, if Japanese territory was under military attack. This revision would mitigate the fear of abandonment on the Japanese side.

However, the Japanese people were concerned that the revised treaty would help perpetuate U.S. military bases in Japan, and that the continued use of these bases by the U.S. would entrap Japan in armed conflict between the U.S. and communist countries. In order to ease such fear of entrapment, a prior consultation system between the two governments was conceived in the Exchanged Notes between Prime Minister Kishi and U.S. Secretary of State Christian A. Herter: "Major changes in the deployment into Japan of United States armed forces, major changes in their equipment, and the use of facilities and areas in Japan as bases for military combat operations to be undertaken from Japan other than those conducted under Article V of the said [revised Security] Treaty, shall be the subjects of prior consultation with the Government of Japan." [1]

Extended Nuclear Deterrence

Following the use of atomic bombs in 1945 by the U.S., the Soviet Union made strenuous efforts to build its own nuclear forces and succeeded in developing thermonuclear bombs in 1953 and then their delivery means (intercontinental ballistic missiles) in 1957. China also engaged in nuclear development and carried out a nuclear explosion in 1964. Faced with these hostile nuclear powers, Japan was forced to decide how to deter nuclear attacks.

One option for Japan was to develop its own nuclear weapons. In the 1960s, the Japanese government secretly investigated the plausibility of nuclear development. However, the Sato Eisaku administration (1964-1972) finally renounced the option of possessing nuclear weapons because of the unavailability of testing sites and safe storage of nuclear bombs and because of expected negative implications for relations with the U.S. and neighboring countries. Nuclear development by Japan would instigate a security dilemma (arms races) between Japan and its neighboring countries and facilitate nuclear proliferation against the spirit of the 1968 Non-Proliferation Treaty (NPT).

Deciding not to develop nuclear weapons of its own, Japan chose to be under the umbrella of extended nuclear deterrence provided by the U.S. In other words, the U.S. would fight back against any adversaries attacking Japan with nuclear weapons, so that those adversaries would hesitate to attack Japan in the first place. Deterrence depends on the credibility of the U.S. commitment to fulfilling nuclear retaliation. To enhance the credibility of nuclear commitment by the U.S., Japan may be asked to cooperate with U.S. nuclear strategy, including a temporary installation of nuclear weapons at U.S. bases in Japan and transit of nuclear-armed naval vessels like those in the U.S. Seventh Fleet.

While such a firm commitment to appreciating U.S. nuclear strategy will lower the possibility of being abandoned by the U.S. in the face of nuclear crises, Japan might be entrapped in those crises and suffer nuclear attack. Then, Prime Minister Sato declared in 1967 the Three Non-Nuclear Principles of not possessing, not producing and not permitting the introduction of nuclear weapons. Japan became an NPT member in 1970 and committed to non-proliferation, devoting itself to the peaceful use of nuclear energy.[2]

Reversion of Okinawa

Although the San Francisco Peace Treaty in September 1951 marked the end of the U.S. occupation for the Japanese mainland and affirmed the residual sovereignty of Japan in Okinawa (Ryukyu), the U.S. was mandated to administer Okinawa for two more decades. Backed by the demands of the Okinawan people who hoped to be reintegrated into Japan, the Sato administration negotiated for the reversion with the Lyndon B. Johnson administration (1963-1969) in the late 1960s. The dispute between Tokyo and Washington was mainly concerned with whether and how the U.S. could use its military bases in Okinawa after the return of administrative rights to Japan, including the deployment of nuclear weapons; up to 1,300 tactical nuclear weapons were estimated to have been stored on Okinawa by 1967. Since the U.S. was involved in the Vietnam War at the time and its bases in Okinawa performed a critical role in its operations against North Vietnam as strategic and logistic bases from which to dispatch contingent troops, the Johnson administration hoped to use its military bases in returned Okinawa as it did under U.S. rule.

Japan, on the other hand, had to allow the U.S. to continue using its bases in Okinawa in order to assure the commitment of the U.S. with adequate capabilities to defending Japan and to avert being abandoned. However, it did not want Okinawa to be entangled in any U.S.-led conflict. In addition, the Sato administration had already manifested the anti-nuclear principles, so it expected the same rules to be applied to returned Okinawa. In 1971, the Richard M. Nixon administration (1969-1974) finally agreed to return Okinawa without storage of nuclear weapons in 1972.

The Nixon Doctrine and Sino-U.S. Rapprochement

In the mid-1960s, the U.S. under the Johnson administration intervened in Vietnam on a large scale, but the U.S. Forces bogged down in a quagmire. While the Nixon administration reinforced U.S. operations in Indochina in order to complete a supposedly honorable withdrawal, the U.S. economy was exhausted and could not afford Cold War expenses as it used to. Then, President Nixon declared in the Nixon Doctrine (or Guam Doctrine) in September 1969 that the U.S. would reduce its commitment to the defense of its allies in the Asia-Pacific region, including South Vietnam. In place of reduced U.S. troops, he demanded that allies share more burdens, particularly in terms of ground forces.

Another repercussion of the U.S. morass in Vietnam was the rapprochement between the U.S. and China. In addition to the geostrategic considerations of tipping the balance among the great powers (the U.S., the Soviet Union, and China) to the advantage of the U.S., the Nixon administration expected China under Mao Zedong to exert its influence on North Vietnam, for China had been providing economic and military assistance to its communist ally in the south; if China ameliorated its relationship with the U.S. and stopped assisting North Vietnam altogether, the latter would be pressed to halt hostilities and make a truce with the U.S.

The sudden amelioration between the U.S. and China had significant implications for Japanese foreign policy. China was no longer an adversary; rather, it was a quasi-ally of the U.S. in countering the Soviet threat. With a new China card in hand, the U.S. might neglect Japan as an ally. Together with the reduced U.S. commitment announced in the Nixon Doctrine, the reconciliation of China and the U.S. heightened Japan's fear of possible abandonment.

In this context, Prime Minister Tanaka Kakuei (1972-1974) rushed to restore its diplomatic relationship with Communist China in 1972 so that Japan would obtain a China card of its own. Also, successive administrations in Japan intended to tighten security cooperation with U.S. Forces to tie them down for Japan's defense. In 1978, Japan and the U.S. finalized the Guidelines for U.S.-Japan Defense Cooperation, which formulated for the first time the burden-sharing in joint action between Japan's Self Defense Forces (SDF) and U.S. Forces in the event of an armed attack on Japanese territory. Furthermore, the annual host nation support, or sympathy budget, was first provided to the U.S. Forces in Japan in 1978 in order to share the financial burden of stationing the troops, although the Status of Forces Agreement in 1960 only requires Japan to provide facilities and areas for use. The budget has been regularly raised for three decades and culminated at 257.3 billion yen in 2001, which accounted for approximately three-fourths of the expenditure for U.S. Forces in Japan.

The New Cold War

In the 1980s, the alliance was reinforced against the background of the reinvigorated standoff between the Soviet Union and the U.S., while the quasi-alliance relationship between China and the U.S. born in the previous decade still continued. Prime Minister Suzuki used the term "alliance" for the first time to depict the security cooperation between Japan and the U.S. The alliance was further strengthened under the leadership of Prime Minister Nakasone Yasuhiro (1982-1987) and President Reagan in the mid-1980s. According to remarks by Nakasone to *The Washington Post*, the Japanese Archipelago should be an "unsinkable aircraft carrier" of the U.S. One of the focused issues was Japan's contribution to sea lane defense between Japan and the oil-rich Middle East. Also, the Nakasone administration loosened restrictions on Japan's defense policy, increasing the defense budget over the one percent ceiling of Japan's GNP, which was set by the Miki Takeo administration (1974-1976) in 1976, and transferring defense-related technology to the U.S. against the Three Principles on Arms Exports, which were declared in a Diet session in 1967 and complied with by successive administrations in Japan.[3]

How Has the Japan-U.S. Alliance Been Managed since the End of the Cold War?

Although some international relations scholars predicted the collapse of the Japan-U.S. alliance due to the lack of a common adversary, the alliance has endured for more than twenty years after the end of the Cold War (Mearsheimer, 1990; Waltz, 1993). Coping with the alliance dilemma, Japan and the U.S. have been deepening their security cooperation and are embarking on new roles in the globalized world.

From Alliance Adrift to Redefinition of the Alliance

As a result of the disintegration of the Soviet Union in December 1991, the U.S. became the sole superpower for the moment. As the Soviet threat disappeared, it seemed that Japan lost its objective to maintain close security ties with the U.S. As a unipolar superpower in the post-Cold War international system without comparable rivals, the U.S. for its part did not have to maintain costly alliance relationships with a junior partner like Japan. Rather, it criticized Japan as a free-rider on the U.S.

security system without paying appropriate costs. During the Persian Gulf Crisis in 1990 and the following Gulf War in 1991, the George H. W. Bush administration (1989-1993) bluntly asked Japan to offer personnel assistance, in addition to financial support, to the U.S.-led multi-national forces, though the Kaifu Toshiki administration (1989-1991) hesitated at first to send SDF troops to the conflict areas. In the meantime, the U.S. criticized Japan's foreign trade practices as unfair; as trade friction heightened to the level of "Japan bashing," the general climate between the two countries was aggravated. Without common adversaries, both Japan and the U.S. did not have to fear abandonment by the ally; rather, each feared entrapment by the other's minor conflicts. The alliance seemed unnecessary and could drift apart in the near future.

However, in the mid-1990s, both countries confronted serious regional conflicts in the Asia-Pacific and came to recognize the importance of maintaining the alliance relationship even after the Cold War. One such incident was the nuclear missile crisis on the Korean Peninsula in 1993-1994. When the U.S. was informed of North Korea's nuclear development program, it assumed to take military measures against North Korea and asked the SDF to provide assistance to U.S. operations. However, Japan was not ready to overcome its political and legal constraints and offer military support to its ally, except in the case where Japan's own territory was directly attacked by foreign powers. Japan's inability to cooperate with its ally in contingencies where Japan might be heavily affected, if not directly invaded, would hurt the credibility of the alliance relationship. In addition, Japan might be directly attacked by North Korea with sophisticated unconventional weapons.

The other incident that had critical implications for the alliance relationship was the Taiwan Strait Crisis in 1995-1996. At the presidential election in Taiwan, China launched missiles off the Taiwan coast in order to put pressure on democratic Taiwan not to reelect the anti-mainland incumbent, President Lee Teng-hui. The U.S. expedited two aircraft carriers to the Taiwan Strait. This was the first conflict that might have led to military confrontation between Communist China and the U.S. after the end of the Cold War.

These two regional crises led the U.S. and Japan to recognize the need to revitalize alliance cooperation and prepare for similar contingencies in the future. Japan feared abandonment by the U.S., and the U.S. reaffirmed the importance of Japan's help, including the use of military bases in Okinawa. The East Asia Strategy Report, published in February 1995 under the leadership of Assistant Secretary of Defense Joseph S. Nye, Jr., and often called the Nye Report, valued the alliance and the continued U.S. military presence of 100,000 personnel in the post-Cold War Asia-Pacific region as an international public good, like oxygen, from which all countries benefit, but whose importance would not be noticed before people lose it. For the U.S., the alliance would work as a cornerstone of its forward deployment strategy in the region by making it possible to dispatch its troops throughout the Pacific. Based on this report, Prime Minister Hashimoto Ryutaro (1996-1998) and President Bill Clinton (1993-2001) issued the Japan-U.S. Joint Declaration in April 1996, which redefined the alliance as a stabilizer of the Asia-Pacific region that would contribute to the reduction of security uncertainties in the post-Cold War era.

Following the Joint Declaration, the Guideline was revised in 1997. While the earlier version in 1978 was largely concerned with cooperation in the case of a direct territorial invasion against Japan, both governments this time established the division of labor between the SDF and U.S. Forces for situations in areas surrounding Japan, even without a direct military attack against Japan's territory. In this context, the Acquisition and Cross-Servicing Agreement (ACSA), signed first in 1996 by Japan and the U.S., has been expanded to include provision of munitions by the SDF to U.S. Forces for situations in areas surrounding Japan.

The Rise of China

Though not mentioned in the Joint Declaration of 1996, part of the *raison d'être* of the alliance after the Cold War is to hedge against a rising China. In the 1970s and 1980s, the U.S. and Japan kept on relatively good terms with Communist China as a quasi-ally against a common threat, the Soviet Union. This close security relationship between the three countries was premised on the ideological and military split between China and the Soviet Union. However, after General Secretary Mikhail Gorbachev of the Soviet Communist Party visited China in May 1989, relations between the two ommunist countries were ameliorated, and one of them, the USSR, finally dissolved in December 1991. Without that common threat, the triangular relations between China, Japan, and the U.S. saw the end of this amicable relationship; China is now emerging as a regional power with the potential to threaten the preeminence of the U.S. in the Asia-Pacific.

The problem is that China has been growing its military capability, including nuclear weapons, strategic and ballistic missiles, and naval power projection capabilities, while its intentions are unclear. In this respect, the Taiwan Strait Crisis in 1996 warned Japan and the U.S. of the potential risk of a rising China and its reckless behavior with an adequate capability. This concern was one of the driving forces that prompted Japan and the U.S. to reformulate their alliance relationship as a hedge against uncertain Chinese behavior, though the Joint Declaration welcomed the engagement of China in the existing U.S.-centered Asia-Pacific order.

Taking into account the closer economic interdependence between China and Japan and between China and the U.S., it is inevitable for Japan and the U.S. to engage China. The Clinton administration agreed with China to build a strategic partnership, and the George W. Bush administration (2001-2009) encouraged China to behave as a stakeholder in the region. Japan followed suit; Prime Minister Abe Shinzo (2006-2007, 2012-) visited China in 2006 and reached an agreement with the Chinese leadership to construct a Mutually Beneficial Relationship Based on Common Strategic Interests. China in the late 1990s and 2000s continuously emphasized its peaceful emergence as a regional power and the establishment of cooperative security in the region, publicly pledging not to impose a hegemonic order on neighboring countries.

However, there is no denying that China may employ a bolder external policy as its economic might grows. While it exceeded Japan in terms of GDP in 2010 and is the second largest economy in the world, China has also seen rapid growth in military expenditure, reinforcing naval power projection capabilities, including an increase in submarines and the deployment of aircraft carriers; its first domestically built aircraft carrier was launched in April 2017, following the Liaoning, a refitted Soviet carrier that went into commission in September 2012. In addition to the lack of transparency of its intentions, China has recently taken offensive measures in the East and South China Seas, exacerbating decades-long territorial disputes with Japan over the Senkaku Islands (claimed as the Diaoyus by China) and with Southeast Asian countries over the Spratly Islands. This could also threaten the sea lanes from the

Middle East through the Indian Ocean to East Asia.

In this context, the alliance's role as a hedge toward China's aggressive behavior has been underscored. Prime Minister Abe in his second term from the end of 2012 reiterated the intention to strengthen the alliance relationship with the U.S., emphasizing the need of U.S. help in defending Japan's maritime territories in the East China Sea, including the Senkaku Islands. The Barack H. Obama administration (2009-2017) in turn adopted a new grand strategy of "rebalancing" that stressed the importance of the Asia-Pacific region for the U.S., while predicting that the U.S. will not be the only superpower in the world of 2030 (NIC 2012). In the face of declining U.S. hegemony along with a rising China as a potential naval power, Japan and the U.S. updated the Guidelines in April 2015.

The War on Terror

After being attacked by the terrorist group Al Qaeda on September 11, 2001, the U.S. embarked on the War on Terror, retaliating against Afghanistan, ruled by the radical Islamic regime of the Taliban, which provided refuge to the members of Al Qaeda. In 2003, the Bush administration led a "coalition of the willing" and attacked Iraq under President Saddam Hussein; President Bush and other U.S. officials at the time suspected that Iraq was developing nuclear weapons and assisting Al Qaeda. Strictly speaking, the wars in Afghanistan and Iraq were armed conflicts between sovereign states, not ones between states and terrorist groups. However, these wars were fought by the U.S. with a view to defeating terrorists. According to the Bush Doctrine, issued in January 2003, the U.S. and its allies need to attack terrorist groups and their sovereign friends in a preventative manner, for it is difficult to deter groups that do not care about their own survival. Also, the global deployment of U.S. Forces needs to be transformed so as to react to terrorist movements more swiftly with small contingents.

Although Japanese people might not feel an imminent threat from terrorist groups like Al Qaeda or rogue states like Iraq, the Koizumi Junichiro administration (2001-2006) strongly supported U.S. operations in Afghanistan and Iraq by passing special measures laws to dispatch SDF troops to non-combat areas in the Indian Ocean and in Iraq, expecting a U.S. commitment to supporting Japan in any future conflicts arising in areas surrounding Japan. Also, confronting new types of global threats like terrorist attacks and the proliferation of weapons of mass destruction, along with traditional concerns over rising powers like China, Prime Minister Koizumi and his successors deepened cooperation with the U.S.; in 2005, the Japan-United States Security Consultative Committee (SCC, or 2+2, established in 1994) set up common strategic goals and launched the transformation of the alliance by reviewing the role, mission, and capability of the SDF and U.S. Forces. Moreover, Japan and the U.S. have been engaging in the joint development of missile defense systems since 2006 and seeking to improve the interoperability between the SDF and U.S. Forces in Japan. Prime Minister Koizumi and President Bush declared the "U.S.-Japan global alliance" in June 2006.

Envisioning a more global role for the alliance, the new Guidelines in 2015 eliminated geographical restrictions on bilateral defense cooperation, including a greater coordination to secure freedom of navigation and unimpeded commerce in the South China Sea. They also expanded the scope for Japan's roles and missions in a more global alliance, such as mine-sweeping oprations during hostilities in the Hormuz Strait and logistical support for U.S. Forces in areas beyond Japan's immediate neighborhood. The revision followed a cabinet resolution in the previous year that reinterpreted Japan's pacifist constitutional provision and allowed the exercise of the right to collective self-defense.

U.S. Bases in Japan

One of the aims for the U.S. to keep its alliance relationship with Japan has been the forward deployment of its military forces in Japan. According to the revised Security Treaty in 1960, Japan offers the U.S. the right to hold its bases in Japan to maintain peace in the Far East in exchange for the U.S. pledge to provide security for Japan. As of June 2017, approximately 39,600 U.S. military personnel are working at the bases and facilities in Japan, from Hokkaido to Okinawa.

Although the U.S. Forces in Japan contribute to the defense of Japan and the maintenance of regional order, they may also incur an alliance dilemma. For one thing, their military operations outside Japan may raise the fear of entrapment among Japanese people. Though the U.S. is obligated to offer prior consultation to Japan, strict application of the provisions may bother U.S. operations. The U.S. may keep its distance from Japan, and this will in turn stir the fear of abandonment on Japan's side.

In addition, local civilians living in the vicinity of the U.S. bases have suffered from problems involving U.S. Forces, including criminal offenses perpetrated by U.S. personnel, noise pollution owing to military exercises, and destruction of the natural environment in the neighborhood. While U.S. bases in Japan have contributed to the national security of Japan and the U.S., they have sometimes hurt the human security of local residents. This is especially true for Okinawa, where approximately 75 percent of the bases and facilities for the exclusive use of U.S. Forces in Japan are located.

For the U.S. as a global power, Okinawa gives a strategically, as well as logistically, important foothold, not only to defend Japan's territory, but also to project U.S. Forces as far as the Middle East, beyond the Asia-Pacific. During the Cold War years, U.S. bases in Okinawa underpinned containment policy in the Asia-Pacific as evidenced in the Vietnam War, where military personnel and equipment were sent into the field from Okinawa. From the geostrategic view point, U.S. bases need to be located in Okinawa even after the end of the Cold War to cope with regional crises and the shifting balance of power, providing maritime defense against a potentially belligerent China over the Senkaku Islands.

In 1995, an unfortunate incident occurred in Okinawa; a 12-year-old girl was abducted and raped by U.S. marines and a sailor, while local authorities could not arrest these suspects due to the provisions of the Status of Forces Agreement, according to which U.S. authorities hold jurisdiction over off-base crimes committed by its military personnel until the suspects are indicted by Japanese authorities. This tragic case incited many Okinawans to demand the removal of military bases. The Japanese and U.S. governments reacted to the indignation by endorsing flexible implementation of the provisions and struggling for the reduction of military bases and facilities in Okinawa, including the reversion of Marine Corps Air Station Futenma within five to seven years. However, the agreement in 1996 on the reversion of Futenma required finding a substitute, and the SCC finally decided in 2006 to relocate the personnel and facilities of Futenma airbase to newly reclaimed land off the coast of Henoko as well as to Guam. While this relocation was conceived as part of a global transformation of U.S. Forces to adapt to a new security environment after the terrorist attacks of 2001, successive administrations in Japan have been facing fierce protests from residents in Henoko.

Toward a Multifaceted Alliance

As a corollary of the theories on alliance formation, alliances are likely to collapse once the original threats disappear (Walt, 1997). However, the Japan-U.S. alliance has survived the end of the Cold War, the most sweeping change in the international structure in the last few decades, and its functions have since diversified. During the Cold War, cooperation between the allies was limited to deterrence and defense. Yet, in the 1990s, it began to address uncertain risks of regional conflicts in the Asia-Pacific, and in the 21st century, the allies are tackling non-traditional security issues of terrorism, piracy, and cyber attacks on a global scale. Furthermore, in the process of assuming new roles, the mechanism of cooperation by the allies has been detailed and institutionalized.

In the wake of the Great East Japan Earthquake in March 2011, the SDF and U.S. Forces launched a joint relief effort called Operation Tomodachi. Non-military issues like natural disasters and humanitarian relief will be promising areas for alliance cooperation. Also, security cooperation may not be limited to bilateral terms. In the past decade, trilateral security policy coordination has been more or less developed in the Asia-Pacific, including the cooperation between Japan, the U.S., and a third party like Australia, India, or South Korea. The Japan-U.S. alliance and other bilateral alliances in the region, moreover, need to coexist with the burgeoning multilateral frameworks for security cooperation, such as the ASEAN Regional Forum (ARF), the East Asian Summit (EAS), and the Six Party Talks.

Endnotes

1) Exchanged Notes, Regarding the Implementation of Article VI of Treaty of Mutual Cooperation and Security between Japan and the United States of America, http://www.ioc.u-tokyo.ac.jp/~worldjpn/documents/texts/docs/19600119.T2E.html [Accessed February 28, 2013]. In March 2010, a panel of experts appointed by the Ministry of Foreign Affairs confirmed the existence of a "narrowly defined secret pact"

between the Japanese and the U.S. governments at the time of the 1960 treaty revision, which permitted the U.S. military to use its bases in Japan without prior consultation in the event of a contingency on the Korean Peninsula.

2) During the Cold War, the U.S. Navy routinely transited Pacific waters with nuclear weapons onboard. This gave rise to a friction between the Japanese and the U.S. governments with regard to the interpretation of "transit": while the latter found a difference between the transit and introduction of nuclear weapons, the former officially stated that the transit of nuclear weapons through Japanese territory and waters should be regarded as an introduction of nuclear weapons, and that allowing their transit would violate one of the Three Non-Nuclear Principles. However, the panel of experts at Japan's Foreign Ministry reported in 2010 on the presence of a tacit agreement by the two governments in the 1960s, which confirmed that the transit by U.S. vessels carrying nuclear arms did not constitute the introduction of weapons into Japan and did not require prior consultation.

3) Under the Three Principles in 1967, arms exports to the communist bloc countries, countries subject to arms exports embargo under the United Nations Security Council's resolutions, and countries involved in or likely to be involved in international conflicts were not permitted. These principles were replaced by the Three Principles of Transfer of Defense Equipment and Technology in April 2014.

References

1) Mearsheimer, John J. (1990), "Back to the Future: Instability in Europe after the Cold War," *International Security*, vol. 15, no. 1, pp. 5-56.
2) Rothstein, Robert L. (1968), *Alliances and Small Powers*, New York: Columbia University Press.
3) Schroeder, Paul W. (1976), "Alliances, 1815-1945: Weapons of Power and Tools of Management," in Knorr, Klaus (ed.), *Historical Dimensions of National Security Problems,* Lawrence: University of Kansas Press, pp. 247-286.
4) Schweller, Randall L. (1994), "Bandwagoning for Profit: Bringing the Revisionist State Back In," *International Security*, vol. 19, no. 1, pp. 72-107.
5) Snyder, Glenn. H (1997), *Alliance Politics*, Ithaca: Cornell University Press.
6) Walt, Stephen M. (1987), *Origins of Alliances*, Ithaca: Cornell University Press.
7) Walt, Stephen M. (1997), "Why Alliances Endure or Collapse," *Survival*, vol. 39, no. 1, pp. 156-179.
8) Waltz, Kenneth N. (1979), *Theory of International Politics*, New York: McGraw-Hill.
9) Waltz, Kenneth N. (1993), "The Emerging Structure of International Politics," *International Security*, vol. 18, no. 2, pp. 44-79.
10) National Intelligence Council [NIC] (2012), *Global Trends 2030: Alternative Worlds*, http://www.dni.gov/index.php/about/organization/national-intelligence-council-global-trends [Accessed January 26, 2013].

Recommended Works

1) Calder, Kent E. (2009), *Pacific Alliance: Reviving U.S.-Japan Alliance*, New Haven: Yale University Press.
   This comprehensive analysis of the political, economic, and social foundations of the Japan-U.S. alliance asserts the quiet erosion of multidimensional ties between the two countries in the 2000s.
2) Funabashi Yoichi (1999), *Alliance Adrift*, New York: Council on Foreign Relations Press.
   Written by a leading journalist, this work provides a detailed description of the process of redefining the Japan-U.S. alliance in the 1990s with four specific case studies.
3) LaFeber, Walter (1997), *The Clash: U.S.-Japanese Relations throughout History*, New York: W. W. Norton.
   A distinguished historian tells the entire story behind the disagreements, tensions, and skirmishes between Japan and the U.S. from the time of Commodore Perry's arrival to the 1990s.

CHAPTER 10

Japan's Diplomacy and East Asia

This chapter examines Japan's diplomacy and East Asia. First, it will briefly summarize Japan's historical background from the Meiji Restoration to the end of World War II. Second, it will examine Japan's diplomacy in East Asia in the Cold War period. Third, it will explore some linkages of domestic politics and international relations in East Asia in the Post Cold War period. Fourth, it will analyze changes and continuities in Japan's diplomacy and East Asia in the 21st Century.

History of Imperial Japan and World War II

After the Meiji Restoration in 1868, Japan aimed to build a rich nation with a strong military. Japan defeated China in the Sino-Japanese War of 1894-1895, and ruled Taiwan until 1945. After the Russo-Japanese War of 1904-1905, Tsarist Russia, the United States and Japan all acknowledged that the Korean Peninsula was Japan's critical interest. In 1910, Japan annexed Korea. After Japan's annexation of Korea, the Japanese Army continued to advance its territorial ambitions in Manchuria, the northeast part of China. In particular, as China carried out a series of revolutionary diplomatic and commercial policies in the 1920s, the Japanese Army considered that China threatened Japan's vital interests. In 1931, Japan's Kwantung Army planned a conspiracy and destroyed the South Manchurian railway, as if China had done it. Then the Kwantung Army and the Japanese Army that was stationed in Korea engaged in military action without any authorization from Tokyo. It was the breakout of the Manchurian Incident. As China adopted a non-fighting principle, the Japanese Army occupied cities in Manchuria, and designed to build the puppet state of Manchukuo. It was established in 1932.

Furthermore, from 1937 to 1945, Japan and China engaged in prolonged military battles. Initially, the Japanese Army conducted serious offenses. But during these battles, Japan neither controlled China, nor got any positive diplomatic outcomes. The military battles were deadlocked. As for alliance strategy, Japan made an alliance with Germany and Italy. Then, Japan gradually advanced into the northern part of French-ruled Indochina.

In 1941, Japan and the United States negotiated over Japan's withdrawal from China. Soon after these negotiations, Japan sent troops to the southern part of French-ruled Indochina. Responding to such action, the United States banned oil exports to Japan. Judging that the situation was seriously deteriorating, Japan decided to go to war against the United States. It declared the Greater East Asian War, attacking Pearl Harbor in Hawaii in December, 1941.

In the military battles from 1937 to 1945, Japanese military campaigns devastated Chinese and Asian cities and rural areas, and killed citizens as well as soldiers. Japanese were victims as well. For example, the American firebombing seriously damaged Tokyo and killed a large number of civilians in the spring of 1945. Okinawa became a brutal battleground. In August, 1945, the United States used atomic bombs, and destroyed Hiroshima and Nagasaki. Furthermore, as the Soviet Union declared war against Japan, the Soviet military advanced into Manchuria, and captured Japanese citizens and soldiers. The Soviet Union sent them to forced labor camps in Siberia. In the end, Japan lost its sovereignty in 1945.

Japan and East Asia in the Cold War Perid

The SCAP and the Tokyo Trials

After Japan's surrender, it was the Supreme Commander for the Allied Powers in Japan (SCAP) that initiated all the procedures for the occupation and war crimes prosecutions. In practice, the United States and General Douglas MacArthur--an American commander in the Pacific Theater of World War II and the head of SCAP-- did have a significant impact on the International Military Tribunal for the Far East (IMTFE, known as the Tokyo Trials), as well as the whole occupation policy.

SCAP arrested war crime suspects. There were three categories in war crimes-- Class A, Class B and Class C. By the end of the year of 1945, more than 100 former government and military officials were held in custody as suspected Class A war criminals who committed crimes against peace and humanity. In addition to the Tokyo Trials, the United States, Great Britain, Australia, France, the Netherlands, the Philippines, China and the Soviet Union conducted trials for so-called Class B and C war crimes. At the Class B and C war crimes trials, soldiers as well as officers in the field were sentenced based on their own laws and jurisdiction.

The Tokyo Trials opened in 1946, and ended in 1948. The Tokyo Trials implied that the war criminals were responsible for the war, whereas the Japanese people were the victims. As for the emperor, the United States considered that prosecuting the emperor as a war criminal would promote anti-American feeling in Japan. In order to carry out occupation policies effectively, MacArthur decided not to prosecute Emperor Hirohito, although Australia firmly maintained that the emperor must be put on trial. Furthermore, some atrocities and brutal acts in China, such as medical experiments and research by Unit 731 of the Japanese Army, and the issue of comfort women in Asia were not fully investigated at the Tokyo Trials.

At the Tokyo Trials, for Class A war crimes, seven defendants were sentenced to death; 16 defendants were sentenced to life imprisonment; one defendant was sentenced to 20 years' imprisonment; and one defendant was sentenced to seven years' imprisonment. The Japanese government accepted the judgments through the Treaty of Peace with Japan (the San Francisco Peace Treaty). Indeed, it was this treaty that officially ended the state of war between Japan and the United States and its Allies. In the postwar period, the Tokyo Trials influenced Japan's official view of war history in the past.

Japan and China in the Cold War Period

In China, after World War II, civil war between the Chinese Communist Party (CCP) and the Kuomintang (KMT) party escalated in 1946. In 1949, after achieving military victory, the CCP controlled the entire mainland of China. Mao Zedong declared the foundation of the People's Republic of China (PRC or China). In contrast, Chiang Kai-shek's KMT was forced to move to Taiwan. Under Chiang Kai-shek's leadership, the Republic of China (ROC) was based in Taiwan.

Due to the foundation of the PRC and the displacement of the ROC, neither the Beijing government (PRC) nor the Taipei government (ROC) signed the San Francisco

Peace Treaty. In fact, from 1950, Great Britain recognized the Beijing government as the representative of China, whereas the United States established an official relationship with the Taipei government. With American pressure, Japan recognized the Taipei government as the representative of China. In 1952, Japan and the ROC signed a peace treaty. From 1952 to 1972, Japan recognized the Taipei government as the only legitimate representative of China.

As for the PRC, Japan and the PRC maintained an unofficial diplomatic relationship through economic and cultural exchanges via private channels. In the late 1960s, China's alliance strategy changed, as it came to consider the Soviet Union not as an ally, but a threat. China perceived that the Soviet Union acted like an imperial state, and aimed to maintain a hegemonic position in the region. Therefore, China assessed that restoring the relationship with the United States would be beneficial for its national security.

As for the United States, in 1969, in the Guam Doctrine, President Richard Nixon implied that the United States would reassess its commitment and assistance for the defense of its allies, including military withdrawal from Vietnam. In fact, the United States reconsidered its alliance strategy in Asia. In 1971, President Nixon surprised the world, announcing that he planned to visit Beijing. Then, in 1972, the United States and the PRC restored their relationship.

Soon after the United States and the PRC restored their relations, Japan steadily and speedily prepared for normalizing its relations with China in 1972. Prior to official normalization, the PRC claimed that Japan should recognize that: the PRC is the only legitimate representative of China; Taiwan is an inalienable part of the PRC; the question of Taiwan is an internal matter; and that the peace treaty between Japan and Taiwan is illegal, and thus must be terminated.

In September 1972, Prime Minister Tanaka Kakuei and Foreign Minister Ohira Masayoshi visited China. They negotiated with Premier Zhou Enlai. After the summit talks, Japan and China issued the joint communiqué for the diplomatic normalization. It stated that "the Japanese side is keenly conscious of the responsibility for the serious damage that Japan caused in the past to the Chinese people through war, and deeply reproaches itself". In it, China declared that it renounced its demands for war reparations from Japan in the interest of the friendship between the Chinese and the

Japanese peoples. After normalization with the PRC, Japan recognized Taiwan as a territory of the PRC, so that no official diplomatic relationship existed in principle. However, in reality, a stable economic and cultural partnership has continued between Japan and Taiwan.

As for China, after Zhou Enlai and Mao Zedong passed away in 1976, Deng Xiaoping assumed power in China. Under Deng Xiaoping's leadership, China conducted the Four Modernizations programs—agriculture, industry, national defense and science and technology. With these programs, China aimed to grow its economy. Deng Xiaoping visited Japan, and the Treaty of Peace and Friendship between Japan and China was signed in 1978. In return, in 1979, visiting China, Prime Minister Ohira announced that Japan would provide 50 billion yen for six infrastructure construction projects in the fiscal year of 1979. Later, as the second stage of these loans, Japan further promised 470 billion yen. For the third stage of the loans, Japan offered 810 billion yen in total. Japan's Official Development Assistance (ODA) significantly helped strengthen the Chinese economy.

Japan, ROK, and North Korea in the Cold War Period

After Japan's colonial rule and its surrender, the United States and the Soviet Union occupied and divided the Korean Peninsula into two parts at the 38th parallel. In 1948, whereas Rhee Syngman became the head of the Republic of Korea (ROK, South Korea, or Korea) in the south, Kim Il-sung founded the Democratic People's Republic of Korea (DPRK or North Korea) in the north. In June, 1950, the Korean War broke out, as Kim Il-sung mobilized troops against the south. Soon after the breakout of the war, the United States led the formation of the United Nations Forces, and countered Kim's troops back into the north. Then, in October, 1950, the Chinese People's Volunteer Army (PVA), which, in fact, was considered the Chinese Army, crossed the border to support North Korea. China's involvement in the Korean War intensified the military situation in the Korean Peninsula. The fighting continued, but in 1953, an armistice agreement was signed between the south and the north. The Korean Demilitarized Zone (DMZ) was created near the 38th parallel. The two divided Korean nations have existed since then.

Neither Korea nor North Korea signed the San Francisco Peace Treaty. In fact, during the Korean War, the United States coordinated for Japan and Korea to prepare for official negotiations. However, the negotiations were unsuccessful, as Korea's anti-Japanese feeling was so strong, and Japan was insensitive about its colonial past. For example, President Rhee stood firmly against Japan, demanding a sincere apology for Japan's colonial rule. In contrast, Japan did not understand such Korean national sentiment well. Some Japanese government officials even commented that Korea had benefitted from Japan's colonial rule. The negotiations between Japan and Korea were far from being developed.

In Korean politics, President Rhee stepped down in 1960. After his resignation, Japan and Korea started negotiating. In 1961, Major General Park Chung-hee launched a coup and took power. Park fully recognized the Korean people's strong voice for demanding an apology from Japan. However, he considered that cooperation with Japan would be essential for developing the Korean economy and strengthening the nation. Finally, under American pressure, Japan and Korea established a diplomatic relationship in 1965. Through the negotiations, they agreed that Japan would provide US$300 million in economic aid, and loan US$200 million. Japan would relinquish all claims against Korea. They also decided that Korea would relinquish any further reparation claims against Japan. When Japanese Foreign Minister Shiina Etsusaburo visited Korea, he stated that "the Japanese people have felt remorse and deeply reflected upon the fact that there was an unfortunate time in the past in the long history."

While Japan and Korea have become trade partners since the normalization, Japan and North Korea have not established a diplomatic relationship. In the late 1970s and 1980s, North Korean state agents kidnapped some Japanese in Japan and Europe. But at that time, there were no official discussions on the disappearance of these Japanese.

When Japan established formal relationships with China and Korea respectively, Japanese government officials expressed feelings of remorse about what Japan had done in the past. But at the negotiation meetings, the leaders in East Asia paid more attention to building a positive relationship based on economic cooperation than to sincerely discussing Japan's past aggression and reconciliation. Indeed, in the Cold war period, as an economic giant in Asia, Japan was a driving force to lead significant economic growth in the region. Economic partnership with Japan was crucial for both China and Korea to develop their own economies.

Historical issues in East Asia

Despite economic cooperation, historical issues such as the textbook controversy, and Prime Minister Nakasone Yasuhiro's official visit to the Yasukuni Shrine had negative impacts on Japan's diplomacy in East Asia, temporarily, in the 1980s. As for the Japanese textbook issue, in 1982, the Japanese media reported that textbook screeners of the Ministry of Education guided that the term of "advance", not "invasion" should be used regarding Japan's action aginst China in high school textbooks. Later, it turned out that it was a misinformed report. Such a word was not in the textbook. However, China and Korea protested, claiming that Japan distorted its history of aggression. Facing criticism from China and Korea, Japan recognized that sufficient attention must be paid to calm anti-Japanese feeling abroad. In fact, after this textbook controversy, the "Asian Neighbor's Clause" was included in the Ministry of Education's textbook guidelines. This clause states that, through history education, mutual understanding and international cooperation were to be promoted with sincere consideration.

In 1986, another textbook controversy erupted, as the National Congress for the Defense of Japan, a conservative group, published a textbook named 'New Edition of Japanese History'. The textbook described that Japanese aggression, in fact, helped liberate Asian countries from European colonial rule. It also mentioned that Japan protected Korea, and provided Korean people with good education and economic development. To make matters worse, the Education Minister Fujio Masayuki commented that Japan's annexation of Korea was the result of mutual agreement between the two, so that Korea was partly responsible for it. The 'New Edition of Japanese History' and the Education Minister's statement angered Korea and China. Once again, the textbook controversy became a sensitive diplomatic issue. Prime Minister Nakasone dismissed the Education Minister, and thus diplomatic tensions were not escalated.

As for the Yasukuni Shrine, it enshrines and honors Japanese who fought and died for Japan in the wars in which Japan was engaged. After World War II, Emperor Hirohito, Prime Ministers Yoshida Shigeru, Miki Takeo, and Fukuda Takeo visited the Yasukuni Shrine for war commemoration, although they were not official visits.

At that time, there was little protest from foreign countries. However, in 1979, it turned out that the Yasukuni Shrine enshrined the spirits of Class A war criminals who were executed following the Tokyo Trials. These war criminals were the military and political leaders who led Japan's aggressive war. Considering such a situation, Emperor Hirohito stopped visiting the Yasukuni Shrine.

In 1980, Prime Minister Suzuki Zenko and 18 other government officials visited the Yasukuni Shrine in a private capacity. The Chinese media warned Japan not to visit the Yasukuni Shrine in an official capacity. Back in 1972, when China negotiated with Japan for normalization of relations, China considered that it was Japanese leaders, not ordinary Japanese citizens, who started the military offenses in China. Therefore, China decided not to demand war reparations, as Japanese people were not responsible for the aggression. From this point of view, for China, the Japanese government officials' visit was unacceptable.

After Prime Minister Suzuki, it was Prime Minister Nakasone who made an official visit to the Yasukuni Shrine on August 15, 1985, at the 40th anniversary of the end of the war. For Nakasone, the official visit was to mourn for and honor the Japanese war dead. However, China strongly protested it. From China's point of view, it implied that the Japanese government honored those who were responsible for the war. A month after Nakasone's visit, a large scale student protest erupted in Beijing on September 18, the anniversary day of the Manchurian Incident. The students demonstrated their anger. They even condemned the Chinese government for not confronting Japan with a hard line. Considering such a deteriorating situation, Prime Minister Nakasone no longer visited the Yasukuni Shrine during his administration.

Despite the historical issues, Japan and China generally maintained a positive relationship in the 1980s. For instance, late in the 1980s, as the Soviet leader Mikhail Gorbachev initiated political reforms in the Soviet Union, political demands for reform, liberalization and democracy spread in other Communist countries. In China, when a large scale student demonstration was organized at Tiananmen Square in Beijing in June, 1989, the Chinese government used force to suppress such student movements. The foreign media reported on the demonstration for democracy and the government's violent crack-down, later known as the June 4 Tiananmen Incident. The United States and other Western European countries strongly criticized China from the viewpoint of human rights, imposing economic sanctions against China. As an ally with the United States and Western European countries, Japan froze the disbursement of loans. However, as a neighbor, Japan cautiously acted not to let China remain isolated from the world. Japan helped ease China's relationship with the Western countries.

Japan and East Asia in the Post Cold War Period

Japan and China in the Post-Cold War Period

As ideological tensions between the United States and the Soviet Union had ended by the late 1980s, domestic political situations in East Asian countries had changed. As for China, in addition to Communist ideology, China felt it necessary to emphasize patriotism to the Chinese people. After the June 4 Tiananmen Incident, Chinese govenment considered "patriotism and the self-reliant spirit" as the fundamental source of strength for the nation, as Chinese leader Jiang Zemin stated that "patriotism and socialism are essentially united". In 1990, he urged "extensive and deep-going patriotic education", including the teaching of Chinese traditional culture, as well as the "history of patriotic struggle" against foreign imperialism since the Opium War. Indeed, from 1990, the State Education Commission instructed educational institutions to conduct patriotism education. In 1993, the State Education Commission officially set patriotism as a guiding principle for China's educational reform. The patriotic education effectively started the next year. As China emphasized patriotic education persistently, more war museums and memorials were constructed or renovated as well. A series of national museums, such as the September 18 History Museum, the Memorial of the Nanjing Massacre, and the War of Resistance Museum. were constructed.

China's patriotic education did not aim to promote anti-Japanese feeling among Chinese. However, emphasizing Japan's aggressive past in China may not be always positive for both countries. In fact, the Sino-Japanese relationship faced diplomatic challenges. For instance, in 1998, at the 20th anniversary of the Treaty of Peace and Friendship between Japan and the PRC, when Jiang Zemin visited Japan, he demanded an official written apology. When his demand was declined, Jiang Zemin publicly criticized Japan's past aggression, even at the dinner held at the Imperial Palace. Unfriendly sentiments existed between the two countries.

The Japan-China relationship deteriorated in the early 2000s, as Prime Minister Koizumi Junichiro visited the Yasukuni Shrine every year during his premiership. He did so because the Bereaved Families' Association was one of the important supporters for his political base. On his visits to the Yasukuni Shrine, Koizumi expressed sincere remorse about Japan's aggression, and proposed to engage in continuing dialogues with China and Korea. However, China and Korea criticized Koizumi's visits repeatedly.

In addition to such historical issues, the Japan-China relationship has not been positive for years. On the one hand, China has achieved economic growth, and thus its presence has been quite significant not only in East Asia but also in the world. On the other hand, China seems to act unilaterally and is often considered the challenger to the status quo. For example, beyond the existing order of international law of the sea, China has conducted unilateral attempts to change the status quo in waters and airspace. In the East China Sea, Chinese vessels have intruded into Japan's territorial water for several years. In the South China Sea, China has engaged in land reclamation and various infrastructure development. It has damaged China's relationship with neighboring countries such as the Philippines and Vietnam. As for the Japan-China relationship, in the principle of the "Mutually Beneficial Relationship Based on Common Strategic Interests," Japan continues to engage in dialogue and cooperation with China for security and prosperity in East Asia. But in reality, dialogue between the two does not guarantee a cooperative relationship.

Japan and Korea in the Post-Cold War Period

As for Korea, in the late 1980s and early 1990s, Korea's political and economic situation changed dramatically. In domestic politics, since Park's military coup in 1961, the nature of Korean domestic politics was characterized as the politics of an authoritarian regime. In 1979, Park was assassinated, and in 1980, General Chung Doo-hwan took power and continued to govern the society in an authoritarian way. When people organized political demonstrations for democratization, President

Chung suppressed them with the military forces.

In 1987, President Chung Doo-hwan named his military colleague Roh Tea-woo as the Presidential candidate for the ruling Democratic Justice Party. Rallies and demonstrations for demanding democracy spread nationwide again. Responding to the people's strong demands, Roh made a speech on political reforms and democracy, including amendment of the Constitution, the Presidential election law, and political freedom. Roh's speech was known as the June 29 Declaration.

Thereafter, Korea experienced its democratic transition, and then consolidated democracy. As for the Korean economy, with export-oriented industrialization and an economic development strategy, Korea strengthened its economy significantly. Then, the Seoul Olympics were held in 1988. As for Korea's diplomacy, as the Cold War ended, Korea established diplomatic relations with the Soviet Union in 1990, and with China in 1992. Korea and North Korea both became members of the United Nations (UN) in 1991. Korea's democratization and its membership of the UN helped promote the movement of Korean women's human rights on an international scale. Then, the issue of comfort women became a diplomatic issue between Japan and Korea early in the 1990s.

During Japan's aggression in Asia, some girls and women in Japanese-controlled territory, including Korea and Taiwan, and women in Asia of various ethnicities and nationalities provided sexual services to Japanese soldiers. The Korean Council for Women Drafted for Sexual Slavery by Japan organized a demonstration every Wednesday in front of the Japanese Embassy in Seoul. Its activities expanded, and it appealed to the UN Commission on Human Rights (UNCHR).

Initially, the Japanese government viewed that these women were prostitutes, as no documentary evidence confirmed government involvement. However, in 1992, just before Prime Minister Miyazawa Kiichi's visit to Korea, based on several official documents, the Japanese media reported on the Japanese Army's involvement in establishing and operating "comfort stations". Later, after two official investigations, the Japanese government apologized for such involvement. Then, the Asian Women's Fund was founded with support from Japanese government officials, including Prime Minister Murayama Tomiichi. The Asian Women's Fund started the atonement projects to former comfort women in the Philippines, Korea, Taiwan, Indonesia, and the Netherlands. In

1996, most junior high school history books described about comfort women during the war. Japanese conservatives criticized such Japanese attitudes as too apologetic and too negative about Japan's own history. Some scholars did not feel right about the fact that history education was influenced by the government's political concerns towards neighboring countries. These conservatives and historians formed the Japanese Society for History Textbook Reform, Tsukuru-kai, in 1996. The goal of Tsukuru-kai was to write Japanese history from more nationalistic and patriotic viewpoints.

Despite such issues, in 1998 when Korean President Kim Dae-jung visited Japan, Japan and Korea reconfirmed their future-oriented partnership in the 21st century. In the Japan-Republic of Korea Joint Declaration: A New Japan-Republic of Korea Partnership towards the Twenty-first Century, it stated that "the present calls upon both countries to overcome their unfortunate history and to build a future-oriented relationship based on reconciliation as well as good-neighborly and friendly cooperation". Then, a Korean ban on Japanese cultural products was lifted so that Korean people openly started to enjoy Japanese culture. In the same way, in the 2000s, Japanese people enjoyed watching Korean TV programs and listening to Korean pop music. In 2002, the two countries jointly hosted the FIFA World Cup with great success.

Regarding the rise of the conservative view of history in Japan, in 2002, history scholars from China, Japan, and Korea started a joint project on textbooks. In this project, textbooks on the contemporary history of the three countries were published. Such a joint project and dialogues among historians have continued between Japan and China, as well as Japan and Korea at various levels. These projects, academic exchange programs, and cultural events aimed to help mitigate historical animosities and build trust in the future.

However, in reality, Japan and Korea's relationship has been far from positive. In particular, Japan and Korea have intensively discussed the issue of comfort women. At the governmental level, both agreed in 2015 that Korea would establish a foundation for supporting the former comfort women, and Japan would finance the foundation. Both understand that they would refrain from accusing or criticizing each other on this issue. However, at the societal level, Korean NGOs have continued to build statues of a young girl as a symbol of honoring the victims in public spaces. The

NGOs have criticized not only Japan's wrongdoing in the past, but also Japan's attitude toward its historical understanding/interpretation. The Korean government has understood such societal sentiment. It seems that the 2015 agreement is now under question. Historical reconciliation between the two countries is very difficult.

Japan and North Korea in the Post-Cold War Period

As for the Japan-North Korea relationship, in 1990, a bipartisan delegation traveled to North Korea. At that time, North Korea proposed an official negotiation for normalization, but it refused to discuss the abduction issue. Therefore, no bilateral negotiations were substantially engaged in. In 1994, after Kim Il-sung died, Kim Jong-il continued to rule North Korea in a dictatorial manner. In 1998, North Korea launched a missile without prior notice over Japanese territory. North Korea's pursuit of developing nuclear weapons, and this missle launch seriously threatened Japan's security and destabilized East Asia.

Dramatic change took place in 2002, when Prime Minister Koizumi and North Korean leader Kim Jong-il met in Pyongyang, the capital of North Korea. At the summit talks, North Korea admitted that it was responsible for abducting Japanese citizens. At the end of the talks, the Pyongyang Declaration was delivered. In it, concerning issues between Japan and North Korea were pointed out. A month after the summit talks, five Japanese who were abducted by North Korea returned to Japan. Koizumi's diplomacy was major progress, but the abduction issue has made little progress since then.

As for North Korea's nuclear weapon program, it has been a major concern for peace and stability in East Asia. In 1993, North Korea declared its withdrawal from membership of the Treaty on the Non-Proliferation of Nuclear Weapons (NPT). A year later, the United States and North Korea agreed on a framework for denuclearization. However, as North Korea's missile launch of 1998 exemplifies, North Korea has acted in a threatening manner in East Asia. In 2003, the United States, China, Russia, North Korea, South Korea, and Japan formed the Six Party Talks, and started to discuss North Korea's nuclear weapon programs, as well as abduction and other issues. In 2005, the Six Party Talks made a statement, including that North Korea committed to abandoning all nuclear weapons and existing nuclear programs, and returning to the NPT. However, North Korea never complied with the way the statement laid out. Instead, it conducted nuclear tests repeatedly.

After the death of Kim Jong-il in 2011, Kim Jong-un became the head of North Korea. Under his leadership, North Korea has actively engaged in nuclear and missile development. It not only poses a direct threat to Japan, but also seriously undermines the peace and security of East Asia. Facing such a critical situation, Japan and the United States have cooperated closely to deter North Korea's reckless action and maintain peace in East Asia.

Japan's Diplomacy and East Asia in the 21st Century

Japan's Domestic Politics and its Diplomacy Discourse

Early in the 1990s, Japanese domestic politics experienced unprecedented change. Such change influenced Japan's diplomatic discourse. As the dominance of the Liberal Domestic Party (LDP) ended in 1993, Prime Ministers from non-LDP parties such as Prime Ministers Hosokawa Morihiro and Murayama acknowledged Japan's aggressive nature during the past war in more direct ways. Indeed, they admitted Japan's wrongdoing in the past, and expressed a sincere apology to Asian countries. For instance, in 1993, Prime Minister Hosokawa, the leader of non-LDP coalition government, characterized Japan's war in the past as an aggressive war. He stated that "during Japan's colonial rule over the Korean Peninsula, the Korean people were forced to suffer unbearable pain and sorrow in various ways". At the National Memorial Service for the War Dead, in addition to honoring the Japanese war dead, Prime Minister Hosokawa invited war victims from Asia, and tried to reconcile with Asian countries.

The Hosokawa cabinet was short lived, and the LDP was back in power again, forming a coalition with the Social Democratic Party of Japan and New Party Sakigake. In forming the coalition government in 1994, these political parties agreed that the government would pass the resolution for the commemoration of the 50th anniversary of the war's end. Such a resolution was to reflect Japan's wrongdoing on the past and contribute to peace and prosperity in Asia. They decided to carry out commemorative projects as well. Prime Minister Murayama from the Social Democratic Party of Japan succeeded Hosokawa's position. In 1995, on the 50th anniversary of the war's end, after the Murayama cabinet officially approved the Prime Minister's talk, Prime Minister Murayama said that "Japan must eliminate self-righteous nationalism, promote international coordination as a responsible member of the international community and, thereby, advance the principles of peace and democracy". He expressed his deep remorse and a heartfelt apology. As for the 1995 Diet resolution, it stated that on "the occasion of the 50th anniversary of the end of World War II, this House offers its sincere condolences to those who fell in action and victims of wars and similar actions all over the world". It also stated that "we must transcend the differences over historical views of the past war and learn humbly the lessons of history so as to build a peaceful international society".

Following Prime Ministers have continued to maintain the same position as Murayama did. For instance, Prime Minister Koizumi repeatedly stated his remorse in a straightforward tone. In 2005, on the 60th anniversary of the end of the war, Koizumi mentioned Japan's sincere attitude for manifesting its remorse. Then he emphasized that Japan has contributed to peace and prosperity in Asia through ODA, and Japan's participation in United Nations peace keeping operations. In this way, while expressing remorse and an apology, Japanese Prime Ministers hoped to build a future-oriented cooperative relationship, based on mutual understanding and trust with Asian countries.

In 2015, Prime Minister Abe once again emphasized deep remorse and heartfelt apology for Japan's actions during the war. He also made sure that Japan can contribute to the peace and prosperity of the world based on values of freedom, democracy, and human rights. In addition, he led legislation for peace and security so that the Self-Defense Forces could play a proactive role in international cooperation, and engage in security cooperation more closely with the US military. The US-Japan alliance is the centerpiece for Japan's security and peace in East Asia.

Territorial Disputes: Takeshima/Dokdo and the Senkaku/Diaoyu Islands

Besides historical issues, territorial disputes exist in East Asia. Japan has a territorial dispute with Korea over the Takeshima/Dokdo Islands. With China, the issue of the Senkaku/Diaoyu Islands has been one of the crucial agendas. As for Takeshima/Dokdo, it is a group of islands in the Sea of Japan. In 1905, the Japanese government confirmed that Takeshima was under the jurisdiction of the Oki Islands Branch Office, Shimane Prefecture. After the Japanese surrender in 1945, SCAP occupied Takeshima. However, Korea claimed to the United States that Dokdo/Takeshima was a part of Korea, prior to its annexation by Japan. Despite the Korean claim, the United States concluded that Takeshima remained under Japanese sovereignty, and that it was not included among the islands that Japan released from its ownership under the San Francisco Peace Treaty.

The United States hoped to utilize Takeshima as a training area, after the Security Treaty between the United States and Japan was to be signed. Knowing the American position that Takeshima remained under Japanese sovereignty, Korea declared the so-called Rhee Syngman Line, concerning maritime sovereignty in 1952. Since then, Korea has controlled Takeshima/Dokdo. In 1965, when Japan and Korea established official diplomatic relations, they subtly avoided discussing the Takeshima/Dokdo issue.

Although the territorial dispute over Takeshima/Dokdo has existed since, it was not a major diplomatic issue for a long time. However, in the 1990s, Korea built a lighthouse and facilities for stationing ships there. In 2005, Takeshima became a diplomatic issue when the Shimane Prefecture Assembly passed an ordinance establishing "Takeshima Day." In 2012, President Lee Myung-bak made an official visit to Takeshima/Dokdo for the first time. The dispute over Takeshima/Dokdo has remained one of diplomatic issues between Japan and Korea.

As for the Senkaku/Diaoyu Islands, in 1885, Japan conducted surveys on the Senkaku Islands, and confirmed that the Senkaku Islands had not been under the control of China. Then, the Senkaku Islands were incorporated into Okinawa Prefecture. After Japan's surrender, from 1945 to 1972, the United States administered the islands directly. In 1968, the United Nations Economic Commission for Asia and the Far East (ECAFE) conducted an academic survey. The survey report indicated the possibility of the existence of petroleum resources in the East China Sea. Then, in 1971, China began to claim its "territorial sovereignty" over the Senkaku Islands. But, since the Okinawa Reversion Agreement in 1972, the Senkaku Islands have been under the jurisdiction of Japan.

In the course of negotiations for the Japan-China Joint Communiqué in 1972, Zhou Enlai did not claim the Senkaku Islands as Chinese territory. He only mentioned that the Senkaku Islands became an issue because Taiwan claimed its ownership, due to the potential oil resources. In the negotiation of the Treaty of Peace and Friendship between Japan and China, Deng Xiaoping commented that Japan and China did not need to discuss it at the moment, as there would be no solution. But he expressed that, in the future generation, with wisdom, it would be settled.

In 1992, China enacted Law on the Territorial Sea and the Contiguous Zone that stipulates that the Senkaku Islands belong to China. Despite China's unilateral legalization, Japan continues to maintain that no territorial disputes exist between China and Japan, as the Senkaku Islands are clearly under jurisdiction of Japan. Since the 2000s, China has intensified activities in waters surrounding the islands. In 2010, a Chinese fishing vessel rammed a Japanese Coast Guard cutter. After the crew members of the vessel were arrested, anti-Japanese protests were widespread in China. In 2012, as the Japanese government announced the purchase of Senkaku Islands from the private owner of the islands, anti-Japanese protests escalated violently in China again. The territorial dispute caused seriously deteriorating diplomatic relations between Japan and China.

As is discussed in the above sections, historical and territorial disputes between Japan and neighboring countries are far from settled. On the one hand, Japan has developed solid diplomatic relationships with neighboring countries over the years. Japan has expanded dialogues and collaborated projects with Korea and China at various levels. To be sure, these East Asian countries have shared common interests on economic prosperity and peace. On the other hand Japan has faced serious challenges in diplomacy, as chauvinistic nationalism and conflicts of interest occasionally deteriorates diplomatic relationships. Japan and neighboring countries may need to continue economic cooperation, cultural exchanges, and security dialogues in the region.

References

1) Berger, Thomas U. (2012), *War, Guilt, and World Politics after World War II*, Cambridge: Cambridge University Press.

2) Futamura Madoka (2008), *War Crimes Tribunals and Transitional Justice: The Tokyo Trial and the Nuremberg Legacy*, London: Routlege.
3) Hatano Sumio (2011), *Kokka to Rekishi: Sengo Nihon no Rekishi Mondai (State and History: Postwar Japan's History Problems)*, Tokyo: Chuokoron-Shinsha.
4) He Yinan (2009), *The Search for Reconciliation: Sino-Japanese and German-Polish Relations Since World War II*, Cambridge: Cambridge University Press.
5) Iokibe Makoto (ed.), Translated and annotated by Eldridge, Robert D. (2010), *The Diplomatic History of Postwar Japan*, London: Routledge.
6) Kawashima Shin and Hattori Ryuji (eds.) (2007), *Higasi Ajia Kokusai Seiji Shi (History of East Asia's International Politics)*, Nagoya: Nagoya University Press.
7) Lind, Jennifer (2008), *Sorry State: Apologies in International Politics*, Ithaca: Cornell University Press.
8) http://www.mofa.go.jp/ for official statements, speeches, declarations, communiqués and treaties.

Index

A
Able Archer 55
alliance 162
alliance dilemma 167, 177
anarchy 20, 32
Anti-Ballistic Missile (ABM) 65, 79
anti-militarism 152
Arab-Israeli Six-Day War 52
Arab Spring 60
areas surrounding Japan 150, 154, 174, 177
Article 51 147
Article 9 149
ASEAN 130
ASEAN Plus Three (APT) 110, 138
Asia Pacific Economic Cooperation (APEC) 108–109, 141
Asian Monetary Fund 137

B
balance of power 3, 9, 10, 21, 22, 23, 27, 37, 164, 168
balance of power theory 21, 23, 27, 35, 36, 166
balance of threat 21, 23, 24, 37
balance of threat theory 35, 164, 166
balancer 10, 22
balancing 22, 23, 24, 31, 32, 36, 164, 165
Balassa 105
bandwagon 165
Berlin Wall 51
Bretton Woods System 102
BRICS 61
bubble economy 132, 138

C
cap in the bottle 166

Central Union of Agricultural Cooperatives 116
Chapter 6 and a half 89
Chemical Weapons Convention (CWC) 78
Chiang Kai-shek 184
Chicken Game 70
China's missile launch 134, 154
Chinese World Order 16
clash of civilizations 33, 34
Clash of Civilizations 34
classical realism 20, 21, 22, 35
classical realist 22
collective security 164
comfort women 192, 193
communism 120
Comprehensive (Nuclear) Test Ban Treaty (CTBT) 74, 75
Comprehensive Economic Partnership in East Asia (CEPEA) 114
comprehensive security 124
Concert of Europe 10
Congo 94
constructivism 19, 31, 32
constructivist 32
constructivist argument 33, 39
constructivist theories 35
Crimean War 8
Cuban Missile Crisis 51, 72

D
democratic peace 26, 27, 29
democratic peace argument 32
democratic peace theory 27, 31, 32, 38
Deng Xiaoping 186, 198
détente 48
deterrence by denial 65
deterrence by punishment 65

dissolution of Yugoslavia   93
division of labor   131
Douglas Mac Arthur   183, 184

E

East Timor   95, 155
economic interdependence   26, 27, 29, 38
economic interdependence theory   26, 27, 38
European Union (EU)   59

F

Five Principles   153
foreign direct investment (FDI)   130
Free Trade Agreement (FTA)   104, 114, 139
free trade agreements   139
Free Trade Area of the Asia Pacific (FTAAP)   114
Fukuda Takeo   130

G

General Agreement on Tariffs and Trade (GATT)   101
globalization   11, 101
Greater East Asia Co-Prosperity Sphere   163
Gulf War   131

H

Hashimoto Ryutaro   135, 174
hub-and-spoke security system   166
Hugo Grotius   7, 8
human security   139

I

Ikeda Hayato   126
imagined community   1, 6
Inter-Continental Ballistic Missile (ICBM)   65, 79, 80
interdependent   26, 27
Intermediate-Range Nuclear Forces (INF)   80
International Bank for Reconstruction and Development (IBRD)   103
International Court of Justice (ICJ)   7, 77, 87
International Criminal Court (ICC)   88
International Law   3, 6, 7, 8, 9
International Monetary Fund (IMF)   103, 137
intersubjectivity   31
Iraq War   158
Iron Curtain   44

J

Japan-U.S. Security Treaty   123, 145, 165, 168

K

Khmer Rouge   53
Kim Il-sung   182, 186, 194
Kim Jong-il   194
Kishi Nobusuke   124, 168
Koizumi Junichiro   87, 135, 155, 176, 191, 194, 196
Korean War   48, 122, 144, 165, 186

L

League of Nations   81
liberal paradigm   26
liberal perspective   25, 38
liberal schools   31
liberal theory   27, 29
liberalism   19, 25, 26, 32
liberation of Kuwait   57
localization   12

M

MacArthur   144, 163
Mao Zedong   171, 184, 186
Marshall Plan   45
Mikhail Gorbachev   56, 174, 189
Ministry of Agriculture, Forestry and Fisheries (MAFF)   112
Miyazawa Kiichi   133, 138, 151, 192
Murayama Tomiichi   135, 192, 196
Muslim View   13
Mutual Assured Destruction (MAD)   65

N

Nakasone Yasuhiro   81, 127, 172, 188, 189
National Defense Program Guideline   135
national interests   20, 21
nation-state   1
neoliberal institutionalism   26, 29
neorealism   20, 21, 22
neorealist   23, 35
New Guidelines   135, 177
Non-Aligned Movement (NAM)   50
noodle bowl   108
normative   32
norms   31, 32, 34, 40
North American Free Trade Agreement (NAFTA)   110
North Atlantic Treaty Organization (NATO)   46
Nuclear Weapons Free Zone (NWFZ)   76
Nye Report   174

O

Official Development Assistance (ODA)   130, 186, 196
Ohira Masayoshi   126, 185, 186
Oil Shock   130

Okinawa   123, 125, 147, 170, 177, 178
Operation Tomodachi   179

P

P5   86
pacifism   146, 153
Park Chung-hee   187, 191
Partial (Limited) Test Ban Treaty (PTBT or LTBT)   74
PKO   89, 151, 196
PKO law   133
Plaza Accord   129, 131
power transition   21, 24
power transition theory   24, 35, 37
Prisoner's Dilemma   67, 68, 69
principles of non-aggression   82

R

realism   19, 20, 22, 25, 31
realist   20, 21, 31, 35
realist perspective   35
realist theories   21, 31, 35
rear area support   156
regionalism   102
regionalization   102
reparations   122, 128
Responsibility to Protect (R2P)   6, 97
revision of the Constitution   157
rules of origin (ROOs)   108
Rwanda   93

S

San Francisco Peace Treaty   124, 170
Sato Eisaku   125, 169
Security Council   86, 164
security dilemma   69, 70, 169
Self-Defense Forces (SDF)   123, 171, 196
September 11, 2001   60, 176
Sovereignty   4, 5, 6

spaghetti bowl effect 108
Status of Forces Agreement 171, 178
Strategic Arms Limitation Treaty (SALT) 79
Strategic Arms Reduction Treaty (START) 80
structural realism 20
Submarine-Launched Ballistic Missile (SLBM) 65, 79, 80
Supreme Commander for the Allied Powers (SCAP) 163, 183, 197
Suzuki Zenko 125, 163
sympathy budget 171

T

Tanaka Kakuei 171, 185
textbook controversy 186
third wave 100
Thirty Years' War 2
Three Non-Nuclear Principles 169, 180
Three Principles on Arms Exports 172
Tiananmen Square 57, 189
Tokyo Trials 183, 184
trade creation effects 107
trade diversion effects 107
trade frictions 132
Trans-Pacific Partnership Agreement (TPP) 100
Treaty on the Non-Proliferation of Nuclear Weapons (NPT) 75, 76
tribute 15

U

Uniting for Peace Resolution 85
use of force 151

V

Viet Cong 52
Vietnam War 52, 125, 170, 178

W

War on Terror 60, 157-8, 176
War on Terrorism 135, 157
Warsaw Pact 46
Westphalia Treaty 3
World Trade Organization (WTO) 5, 11, 101

Y

Yasukuni Shrine 188, 189, 191
Yoshida Shigeru 123, 145, 165

Z

Zhou Enlai 185, 186, 198

執筆者紹介

竹内　俊隆　（京都外国語大学国際貢献学部長・教授）　Chaps.1 and 4
　TAKEUCHI Toshitaka
　Dean and Professor
　Faculty of Global Engagement
　Kyoto University of Foreign Studies

市原麻衣子　（一橋大学法学研究科准教授）　Chap.2
　ICHIHARA Maiko
　Associate Professor
　Graduate School of Law
　Hitotsubashi University

クレイグ・マーク　（共立女子大学国際学部教授）　Chaps. 3 and 5
　Craig MARK
　Professor
　Faculty of International Studies
　Kyoritsu Women's University

金　ゼンマ　（明治大学国際日本学部准教授）　Chap.6
　KIM Jemma
　Associate Professor
　School of Global Japanese Studies
　Meiji University

畠山　京子　（新潟県立大学国際地域学部教授）　Chaps.7 and 8
　HATAKEYAMA Kyoko
　Professor
　Faculty of International Studies and Regional Development
　University of Niigata Prefecture

小田桐　確　（関西外国語大学外国語学部准教授）　Chap.9
ODAGIRI Tashika
Associate Professor
College of Foreign Studies
Kansai Gaidai University

杉山　知子　（愛知学院大学総合政策学部教授）　Chap.10
SUGIYAMA Tomoko
Professor
Faculty of Policy Studies
Aichi Gakuin University

シリーズ監修者

杉田　米行（すぎた　よねゆき）　大阪大学言語文化研究科教授

編著者紹介

竹内　俊隆（たけうち・としたか）

京都外国語大学国際貢献学部長・教授
（大阪大学名誉教授）

TAKEUCHI Toshitaka
Dean and Professor
Faculty of Global Engagement
Kyoto University of Foreign Studies
（Professor Emeritus, Osaka University）

ASシリーズ第10巻

Understanding International Relations Second Edition
── The World and Japan ──

2013年10月30日　初　版第1刷発行
2018年5月15日　改訂版第1刷発行
2020年4月30日　改訂版第2刷発行

■編 著 者────竹内俊隆
■発 行 者────佐藤　守
■発 行 所────株式会社 大学教育出版
　　　　　　　　〒700-0953　岡山市南区西市855-4
　　　　　　　　電話（086）244-1268　FAX（086）246-0294
■印刷製本────モリモト印刷㈱

© Toshitaka Takeuchi 2013, Printed in Japan
検印省略　　落丁・乱丁本はお取り替えいたします。
本書のコピー・スキャン・デジタル化等の無断複製は著作権法上での例外を除き禁じられています。本書を代行業者等の第三者に依頼してスキャンやデジタル化することは、たとえ個人や家庭内での利用でも著作権法違反です。

ISBN978-4-86429-518-5